DOING WOMEN'S FILM HISTORY

To Adrienne
My dearest friend   ✗
En memory of all our
escapades & more

With love   Cécile

Thurs- 17 Dec . London

WOMEN AND FILM
HISTORY INTERNATIONAL

Series Editors
Kay Armatage, Jane M. Gaines,
and Christine Gledhill

A new generation of motion picture historians is redis-
covering the vital and diverse contributions of women
to world film history, whether as producers, actors,
or spectators. Taking advantage of new print material and moving-picture archival discoveries as well
as the benefits of digital access and storage, this series
investigates the significance of gender in the cinema.

*A list of books in the series appears
at the end of this book.*

DOING WOMEN'S FILM HISTORY

Reframing Cinemas,
Past and Future

Edited by
CHRISTINE GLEDHILL
and JULIA KNIGHT

UNIVERSITY OF ILLINOIS PRESS
Urbana, Chicago, and Springfield

Library of Congress Cataloging-in-Publication Data
Doing women's film history: reframing cinemas, past and
future / edited by Christine Gledhill, Julia Knight.
pages cm. — (Women and film history international)
Includes bibliographical references and index.
ISBN 978-0-252-03968-3 (hardback)
ISBN 978-0-252-08118-7 (paper)
ISBN 978-0-252-09777-5 (e-book)
1. Women in the motion picture industry—History.
2. Motion pictures and women.
3. Women in motion pictures.
I. Gledhill, Christine. II. Knight, Julia.
PN1995.9.W6D615   2015
791.43'652042—dc23   2015017206

To all women film pioneers throughout history and across the world,

especially those we've yet to find.

Contents

Foreword

SALLY POTTER

In 2011 I was invited to a conference called "Doing Women's Film History" but was unable to attend. I liked the title of the conference and the use of the verb "to do"—thinking, watching, writing, speaking, and listening all being seen as actions. In lieu of my presence I decided to send a video message of support. The conference has now become a book, and the organizers suggested that my message could become a foreword. I was intrigued to read the transcript of the message I had sent and realize that its simple intention was increasingly relevant in the battlefield of ideas linked with gender. We all need encouragement—we are often starved of it. Praise is in short supply, even when overdue. Here is what I said in my virtual message:

> Cinema is a medium of transformation. The fact that you are at this conference means that you are interested in transformation: transformation of difficulty into opportunity, the invisible into the visible, the silent into the heard. I want to say bravo to those of you who've been at it for a while. And to those of you who are just starting out, bravo for beginning. I want to offer you encouragement in all your endeavors, and I want to be with you—at least in virtual form—in the demonstration of SP-ARK, my online archive, where you are able to see some of the secrets, if you like, of the process of filmmaking: what goes on in the magical, strange, and alchemical process of making something come into being. Thank you for your efforts: your studies, your thoughts, and all that you are doing which cumulatively become a necessary and undeniable reality.

All I would add to this is a thank you to those who have put together the book and those who are reading it. It is through these conversations, spoken and silent, that our history becomes visible and meaningful.

Acknowledgments

We are grateful to the Centre for Research in Media and Cultural Studies, University of Sunderland, for supporting the first Doing Women's Film History conference, mounted in 2011 by Women's Film and Television History Network—UK/Ireland (see womensfilmandtelevisionhistory.wordpress.com), where most of these chapters were initially presented (for conference papers see www.wfh.wikidot.com). Our thanks go to all the delegates at that conference—from more than fifteen countries—who engaged tirelessly in enthusiastic debate over three days and demonstrated the need for a book such as this. We thank Sally Potter for her words of encouragement at the conference's opening, kindly rewritten as a foreword for this book, and for pioneering the development of online archiving (see www.sp-ark.org). For their inspiration as role models in our pursuit of women's film history, we would like to acknowledge Jane M. Gaines and all those working on the Women Film Pioneers Project and its magnificent database, now made available online by the Center for Digital Research and Scholarship at Columbia University, New York (see wfpp.cdrs.columbia.edu). We thank also Nathalie Morris and Clare Watson, who set up the Women and Silent British Cinema Web site, which demonstrates the diversity of women's contributions to British cinema in its early decades (see womenandsilentbritishcinema.wordpress.com). Finally, we are indebted not only to our contributors for their willingness to revise and frequently re-revise their conference papers but also to Daniel Nasset and his colleagues at the University of Illinois Press for supporting the publication of this project and making it happen.

DOING WOMEN'S
FILM HISTORY

Introduction

CHRISTINE GLEDHILL

and JULIA KNIGHT

The past decade has witnessed a rapid growth in research projects, conferences, film seasons, festivals, DVD series, and publications devoted to women's participation in the history of cinema. Many of these initiatives are international in scope, including the biennial Women and the Silent Screen conference, which, since its inception in 1999, has been staged in the Netherlands, the United States, Canada, Mexico, Italy, Australia, and, in 2015, Pittsburgh; the more recently established biennial Doing Women's Film History conference, due to hold its third edition in Leicester, UK in 2016; the Women Film Pioneers Project online database, based at Columbia University, New York;[1] and the Women and Film History International book series at University of Illinois Press. Other initiatives have taken an explicitly national focus, such as the two Women and Silent Britain events at London's National Film Theatre in 2007 and 2009, the Women and Silent British Cinema Web site, and the Women's Film and Television History Network—UK/Ireland.[2]

Doing Women's Film History contributes to this growing field of activity and has a twofold purpose. First, it brings together a wide range of case studies investigating women's work in and around cinema across its histories as they play out in different parts of the world—including India, Chile, Turkey, Russia, and Australia, as well as the United States and Europe—from the pioneering days of silent cinema through recent developments in live HD transmissions. Second, given the complex conditions of women's work in cinema and frequent scarcity of its records, our contributors confront in diverse ways a range of conceptual and methodological questions about *how* to research women's film history—how, for example, to identify women's often uncredited and undocumented participation in their respective cinema cultures; where, in the absence of formal archives, to locate previously unimagined sources of evidence; and how to reconceptualize film history in order to locate the impact of women in that history. Across this volume's wide-ranging chapters, such restructuring of historiographic focus is brought to bear on mainstream fiction, documentary, and experimental filmmaking practices, as well as on the practices that support and promote the circulation of films—distribution and exhibition, together with journalistic and scholarly critical discourses. Ultimately, in reframing film history to accommodate new approaches to women's filmmaking, this book poses questions relevant to film history tout court.

Historiographic problems are foregrounded in Monica Dall'Asta and Jane Gaines's prologue, which maps overarching issues about women's film history, feminism, and the researching and writing of film history. Thereafter the book comprises three broadly themed sections, pursued across different geopolitical contexts. Part 1, "Searching for Sources, Rewriting Histories," deals with cinema's pioneering days. Here contributors discuss their search for new sources of evidence in the absence of traditional archives and utilize a diversity of innovative methodologies that open new historiographic perspectives or questions. Part 2, "Feminism, Politics, and Aesthetics," raises questions about feminist approaches to and demands of the historical past and future history-making, examining the conditions in which gender becomes operative in the history of filmmaking, whether mainstream fiction, experimental, or documentary. These chapters explore the range of practices adopted by women filmmakers in different national contexts; the debates probing relations among gender, aesthetics, and feminism; and the influence of films by women and about women, not only on film histories but on cinema's role in social history. Part 3, "Women at Work," explores the various spaces of women's work in and around cinema, including distribution, exhibition, and reception. Contributors here examine the impact, in different historical moments and geopolitical contexts, of gendered practices and discourses, suggesting the necessity of expanding the categories by which film history is researched and constructed.

However, the three parts of the volume do not represent discrete compartments of research and conceptualization, operating in isolation from one another. Interweaving across these sections, shared connections emerge, highlighting a number of interrelated themes and issues. These can be grouped into four broad problematics: evidence and interpretation; feminist expectations of both contemporary and past women's filmmaking; the impact of women's film history on existing historical narratives and theories; and factors that determine the visibility of women's films and build audiences for them. In this introduction, therefore, we draw together each of these areas of concern from across the volume's three sections, highlighting the way seemingly separate research avenues intersect with and affect each other.

Questions of Evidence

From the start, we confront the impossibility of "recovering" the past. "Facts" do not tell themselves, do not exist independently of the questions we ask, and would not give us back the past even if we could collect them all. As Dall'Asta and Gaines discuss in their prologue, historical "facts" are deduced from surviving artifacts and documents and are submitted to the conventions of narrative form in the writing of history. In *Dust* (2001), Carolyn Steedman suggests our sources have been produced from someone else's perspective, for their own particular purposes (150–51). They are already part of existing stories—told by studio publicists and social commentators or found in autobiographies, interviews and chance remarks—which we then retell as history (see Sobchack, 2000, 302). Nevertheless, much of our work is spent looking for "facts" as the basis of evidence, which, as Luke McKernan argues, forms the bedrock of history, distinguishing it from works of pure fiction. Interpreted in the light of our questions, "facts" become evidential supports that we, employing deductive logic, link together in narrative threads in order to weave particular histories. But as Steedman writes, unlike many novelists, we can never conclude by printing "The End," because we know that future revelations of as-yet-undiscovered "tellings" will introduce new perspectives to unsettle our existing histories (147–49).

Indeed, getting hold of misleading "facts" or misinterpreting evidence can send our stories in the wrong direction. As McKernan notes, people lie, documents may falsify information, and data can be transcribed incorrectly in the process of digitizing records. Thus he shows how one researcher, believing that Mary Murillo's assumed surname meant she was Latino, came to a dead end, while Kimberly Tomadjoglou notes Alice Guy's misremembering the date of her directorial debut, resulting in fruitless controversies about historical "firsts." Demonstrating how our starting point determines what we find, Dall'Asta and Gaines interrogate the delayed development of Anglo-American women's film history, arguing that feminist theory's commitment to the absence of "woman" from the patriarchal text assumed a matching absence in the film industry's pioneering days—an assumption now proved incontrovertibly wrong.

Enticing leads, as Michele Leigh demonstrates, may prove dangerous unless findings can be verified. The search for corroborating evidence may produce its opposite: conflicting evidence that generates multiple, sometimes contradictory stories. These are not necessarily fabrications: different things can be true of the same event, depending on the perspective from which it is approached. Thus Leigh likens the work of looking for evidence to that of a crime-scene investigator, hunting down clues to unravel a mystery, involving detection and lateral thinking, as well as deductive logic, in order to tease out histories that illuminate our questions. It may also involve "imaginative speculation," as in Eliza Anna Delveroudi's conjectural title, "When Iris Skaravaiou Met Iris Barry," which draws two pioneer film critics into an "imaginary community" between 1920s Athens and London.

What evidence we find, however, depends on the "material remnants" of the past—the physical objects—that have been deliberately saved or have fortuitously survived, and this can be highly variable. Sarah Street's exploration of Natalie Kalmus's role as Technicolor's color consultant during the 1930s and 1940s depends on the preservation of her papers by the Margaret Herrick Library in Los Angeles, while Julia Knight's discussion of the UK feminist film and video distributor Cinema of Women (COW) hinges entirely on the retention of their records by a successor organization. In contrast, some contributors confront the challenges of research in countries, which—as Debashree Mukherjee and Neepa Majumdar note of India—give little priority to archiving cinema, be that its documents or indeed the films; in many countries archival materials have been lost or destroyed—as Michele Leigh observes of early Russian cinema—due to war and revolution. Even where archives do exist, researchers encounter problems through the selective or arbitrary nature of deposits—for example, the scarcity of 1920s/1930s American screenwriters' contracts noted by Giuliana Musico, or the partial recording of information observed by Kay Armatage regarding omission of HD personnel credits for live Metropolitan Opera transmissions. Equally problematic is gaining access to what *does* survive. The advent of online resources benefits some kinds of research, and Luke McKernan highlights the value of online newspaper archives and digitized census, family history, and shipping records. But levels of access remain variable: while Kalmus's papers are cataloged, listed online, and available to any researcher at the Margaret Herrick Library, Knight came across COW's boxed-up and uncataloged records only through personal contacts.

While many of these issues are endemic to all historical research, we confront the particular problem that many women have left few historical traces, their roles in production or film culture obscured by more publicly visible or self-promotional male partners or concealed behind collective or collaborative practices. Thus Michele Leigh seeks to uncover the creative role of Antonina Khanzhonkova hidden, she suggests, behind her husband's fronting their production company as businessman. Delveroudi, researching Iris Skaravaiou, finds few personal references either in her columns or in the form of autobiography, diaries, or letters. In some cases such basics as birth and death records prove elusive. This absence of personal record suggests how many women may have regarded their work in the nascent film world: as secondary to or, as several contributors suggest, co-extensive with domestic and marital partnerships. On the other hand, as Muscio notes, the more aggressively expanding American film industry offered women important new career opportunities, especially at the level of scriptwriting, on the basis of which American women gained more publicity and acted more independently than perhaps did their European sisters.

In the absence of traditional archival documents, several of our contributors have turned to less-conventional sources and approaches. Michele Leigh trawled existing histories and biographies for chance mentions of Antonina Khanzhonkova that provided clues, which, when pieced together, enabled her to speculate on Antonina's hitherto unsuspected creative direction of a studio headed by her husband. In researching the conditions and status of women's work in the early Bombay film industry, Debashree Mukherjee turned to gossip and scandal drawn from film magazines, biographies, fan letters, and interviews, while Neepa Majumdar used similar journalistic sources to explore stardom in the context of labor relations in India's pre-independence cinema. Yet this is only possible for individuals who attract public attention—most notably those who achieve stardom—while other forms of women's labor remain less visible. Taking a different route, Canan Balan examines the work of male novelists and journalists for their representations of female film fans in post–World War I Turkey. As "evidence," these require the analyst to distinguish between women's activity as audiences and male fantasies about female spectatorship, in which women may, Balan suggests, focus anxieties about Westernization of Turkish culture and identity.

Encountering the Past

As a feminist enterprise, women's film history has an investment in the careers, life stories, and assumed struggles of women who, through the decades and across the world, have staked a claim on the making, circulation, and reception of films. We want them, as Tomadjoglou notes of Alison McMahan's search for Alice Guy, to offer us role models, to be our forerunners, our inspirational guides. But frequently we find identification disrupted by awkward findings round which we have to steer our stories: their often seeming indifference to their pioneering roles; the refusal of some—witness Kathryn Bigelow—to recognize the significance of their gender; failures to achieve their goals, as in the case of Elvira Giallanella's never-screened pacifist film *Umanità* (1919); or the seeming racial and class blindness of those filmmakers we seek to celebrate for their subversion of gender roles. Like ourselves, the women we research are formed by their times—while they may push against the grain, they are nevertheless caught within what their times allow to their imaginations and roles.

This fracture, between feminist perspectives now and the perspectives within which our historical subjects worked, creates across these chapters two forms of temporal relation. Drawing on Walter Benjamin, Dall'Asta and Gaines argue that while we can never go back to their times, nevertheless women's surviving films and documents exist as "historical objects" in our present. Our engagement with them creates a "wedge" in time, making the women we research "momentarily coincident" with us and enabling us to "constellate" with them. If to paraphrase Bakhtin (1986, 7), we ask of their work questions they did not think to ask, their works may gesture to future conditions and perspectives different from those that constrained them. Thus in reimagining their careers and recirculating their films, we enable their historical projects to continue in the present through our collaboration with their pasts.

At the same time, the women we research may also alert us to the blind spots lurking in our contemporary imaginaries; and there is the danger that we may simply not find enough of a shared project with which to constellate. The problem of Leni Riefenstahl comes to mind. Thus a significant number of our contributors *do* seek to travel back in time, not to reconstruct lives but to understand the conditions of production and imagination that frame practices, create blind spots, generate resistances, and inspire future projections. Thus Kimberly Tomadjoglou refocuses understanding of Alice Guy's legacy by examining her adaptation of the paternalist practices of Gaumont, where she began, to the matriarchal organization of her own studio in America. Rashmi Sawhney investigates the historical imagination of 1980s Indian women filmmakers seeking "companionship" with generations of women enduring or resisting convention in India's colonial past. Giuliana Muscio contextualizes the work of American women scriptwriters within the gendered liberalization of an emerging consumer capitalism, as does Debashree Mukherjee, examining the ambivalent roles played by female film stars in a modernizing India. Neepa Majumdar analyzes Shanta Apte's tactical use of the hunger strike to break her contract, while Eylem Atakav, focusing on 1980s Turkey, explores the paradoxical space opened up under politically repressive military rule for an emerging women's movement and cinematic representation of women's issues.

Changing the Story

Our contributors have drawn on such different sources, methods, and conceptions of cinema, that not only do stories told by traditional film history need recasting, but the assumptions of film historiography are challenged. Women's film history's unorthodox sources of evidence—gossip, novelistic constructions of cinema-going women, influence of the domestic on the workplace—change what counts in film history. Practices disregarded or marginalized in traditional film history—such as partnerships, co-creation and experimental multimedia work—challenge conventional notions both of authorship and the film object.

These new perspectives not only expand film history, but they also require rethinking deeply entrenched conceptions of cinema itself. As Giuliana Muscio shows, understanding the major role played by women writers in the American film industry of the 1920s throws new light on the emergence of "classical Hollywood narrative," both as a social force and a form of storytelling. Women writers of the fictions adapted and the scripts that shaped the films contributed significantly to the core of what Hollywood cinema was to become—a story-based cinema not only in a formal sense or as a studio mandated category but as a site of cultural imagining and negotiation, where economics and aesthetics ambivalently coincide. Putting women writers back into this development connects their story-making not only to the substance of "classic" Hollywood but to the imagining of the "modern" women who became central to the development of new cultures of consumption. This suggests the ambivalence of the new, potentially liberating spaces generated by the profit-seeking engines of capitalism.

Acknowledging the scriptwriter opens consideration not only of the multiple and neglected departments in which women work in the film industry—design, costume, production management, the cutting room, laboratories, publicity, marketing, distribution, exhibition—but of the essentially collaborative nature of many filmmaking processes and the finished product itself. As already noted, both in mainstream and experimental production we find women working in collaboration with male colleagues or husbands—as Michele Leigh records of Antonina Khanzhonkova, Kim Tomajoglou of Alice Guy Blaché, and Sarah Street of color consultant Natalie Kalmus—or in female partnerships, as Cécile Chich records of Greek avant-garde artists working in France, Maria Klonaris and Katerina Thomadaki. Even history and theory production is, in the end, collective: as Michele Leigh notes, one historian's footnote may be another's starting point, and co-writers Monica Dall'Asta and Jane Gaines come to a moment when neither can remember who thought of what. Identifying individual input in a collaborative practice is complicated still further by women's propensity for multitasking, especially pertinent to the earlier days of film production, when roles were less defined and more fluidly practiced, and latterly by the collective structures of feminist film organizations like COW.

If this makes it difficult to assign creative ownership, the geopolitical range of women's work covered in this volume—and the resulting engagement with specific and very different national contexts—challenges the centrality in received film history of American and English-language cinema. But while many of our contributors explicate the local conditions of women's work in their respective cinemas, they also reveal the impact of the international circulation of films and filmmakers, highlighting the need to both localize film historiography *and* develop intercultural film histories. Thus Eliza Anna Delveroudi records the importance to Iris Skaravaiou of contact—through journals, magazines, and a visit to Paris— with North European critics such as Iris Barry and avant-garde filmmakers such as Germaine Dulac. Kimberly Tomadjoglou argues that Alice Guy's travels between French Gaumont, American studios, and back again is central to understanding the conditions of film practices otherwise difficult to comprehend, while Elizabeth Ramírez Soto analyzes recent Chilean homecoming films as documents informed by experiences of exile. Similarly, Rashmi Sawhney questions regional stratification of Indian film history in order to investigate the emergence in the 1980s of a women's cinema across different states, challenging traditional histories focused largely on Bombay-based Hindi filmmaking.

Just as women's film history challenges film historiography, the recovery of women's films raises equally pertinent questions for film theory. Here, established conceptual frameworks and categories don't always work and aren't always helpful. While the evidence reveals remarkable, even exceptional women, and feminist desire to identify women's agency and autonomy persists, one of the key methods of organizing film texts—namely, individual authorship—is, as we have seen, irrelevant to the ways many women work. Thus Tomadjoglou, in historicizing the practice of Alice Guy, rethinks her creativity in terms not of "auteur" but of *metteur-en-scène*—thereby recognizing her generative role in managing the creative output of her studio. At the other end of the century, Kay Armatage records the complexity of Barbara Willis Sweete's creative orchestration of multiple personnel and technical operations in HD transmissions of live opera, in which the input of composer, stage director, and performers are re-mediated through her technical expertise and cohering cinematic aesthetic. Contrariwise, Cécile Chich suggests that avant-garde practice—where women *can* have more authorial control—has, paradoxically, been marginalized by feminist film theory's focus on mainstream cinema as a site of patriarchal representation and spectatorship. Maria Klonaris and Katerina Thomadaki, on the other hand, by sharing the roles of performer and cinematographer break the dualism of camera and object, changing the nature of the text and spectatorship and intervening not only in feminist film theory but also in the history of feminist filmmaking.

However, although we might wish that women filmmakers would bring a distinctive female viewpoint to their work, generating a feminine sensibility or feminist aesthetic, much of the evidence gathered in this volume raises questions about the relation of women filmmakers to gender. On the one hand, several chapters show that women's contributions to cinema often fall under categories conventionally thought "suitable for a woman"—for example, Natalie Kalmus' work with color; Alice Guy's playful development of domestic comedy; the film choices of the female audience studied by Karina Aveyard. On the other hand—as Tomadjoglou, Muscio, Mukherjee, Majumdar, Sawhney, and Ramírez Soto, writing about different historical periods and national contexts, reveal—it is through their capacity to use gender positioning tactically that women have found a role and space within their respective film industries and film cultures. However, expectations of the difference that women will make snag on the assumption that this must reflect in some way their social gender, as Katarzyna Paszkiewicz shows in analyzing the discursive circulation of Kathryn Bigelow's *The Hurt Locker* (2008) and the debates that broke out about the suppression of gender in her Academy Award acceptance speech. As Paszkiewicz demonstrates, the debates about the relationship between gender, film genre, and sexual politics are convoluted. Thus women's film history has to perform a delicate balancing act between establishing the roles women *did* play in film history and recognition of practices that, arising from women's gender positioning, are outwith both feminist politics and traditional concepts of historical significance. In this respect, Klonaris and Thomadaki's work points beyond gender, fusing the cinematic with the theatrically performative, transsexual, and androgynous body, challenging not only conceptions of cinema but categories of gender and heteronormativity that would confine women's film and media work to conventionally gendered spheres or to essentialist notions of femininity.

Making Women's Filmmaking Visible

Finding the women who worked in and around cinema or identifying the impact of their practices on film histories is not by itself a sufficient goal for women's film history. For crucial to the project is the possibility of *viewing* the products of women's labor or films that were significant to women as audiences. But as McKernan notes, there are no central registers of extant film scripts or films. Moreover, as Dall'Asta and Gaines indicate, even though a 35mm print may survive, unless the film is publicly projected it does not exist as a work of cinema. The desire to ensure the continuing existence of women's cinema underpins the staging of women's film festivals, film seasons, and special screenings. In this sense, as Dall'Asta and Gaines argue, women filmmakers need us in order to exist historically. It is down to us, then, to facilitate opportunities to see their films.

In the era of LoveFilm, Netflix, Mubi, Reframe, Jaman, Hulu, and other online film distributors across the globe, we tend to assume we can have instant access to whatever film we want to watch wherever we may be. But due to complex digital-rights issues and differing distribution and business models, this is not the case. Furthermore, lack of commercial viability may also render many films largely unavailable to contemporary cinema audiences—such as the experimental work of Maria Klonaris and Katerina Thomadaki—or to audiences outside their country of origin—such as the Turkish "women's films" Eylem Atakav discusses or the Chilean homecoming documentaries explored by Elizabeth Ramírez Soto. Such films struggle to find wider distribution, which means many of us can see them only at film festivals or occasional screenings at specialist exhibition venues. As Julia Knight shows, the distributor Cinema of Women (COW) faced recurring challenges in trying to make such films accessible to wider audiences in the United Kingdom via theatrical release.

The public projection of films—ensuring they exist as works of cinema—also depends on the existence (and hence viability) of the exhibition venues themselves. While those of us living in urban centers can usually take for granted access to one or more cinemas, the picture changes dramatically in rural areas. The risk in 2009 that the single cinema of Australian small-town Sawtell would close occasioned Karina Aveyard's study of the efforts of its older female audience to ensure the cinema's long-term sustainability, highlighting in turn the social importance of cinemagoing to those women. Their activism also precisely demonstrates the importance of women as audiences in the history of cinema in terms of keeping women's films—however we delineate that category—in circulation and hence available to women's film history. As Julia Knight shows, building audiences of especially (although not exclusively) women was similarly central to COW's work. However, opportunities to view films must work in conjunction with public discourse, both journalistic and scholarly, in order to make films "visible" and build audiences for them—as Delveroudi shows Iris Skaravaiou doing for film culture in 1920s Greece by tailoring her commentary on international film stars to her readers' interests. Conversely, focusing on film scholarship, Rashmi Sawhney notes how literature on Indian regional cinemas, published in regional languages with little translation, has contributed to the marginalization of such cinemas in the construction of Indian film history. Such public discourses, captured in the historical materials saved in archives, libraries, and other collections, contribute significantly to the narratives through which our histories are formed, transformed, contested—as Katarzyna Paskiewicz demonstrates in her analysis of the discursive reception of *The Hurt Locker* and Bigelow's Oscar win—and even "deformed," as Canan Balan explores through her analysis of Turkish novelists' "imaginary" women audiences.

■ ■ ■

Across the three sections of this volume, we trace the historical and continuing importance to each other of cinema and women, where cinema functions as a cultural "space" for women's creative expression, employment, and consumption, and where women impact on the continuing history of cinema's becoming. Karina Aveyard notes that in 1926 Iris Barry declared, "[Cinema] exists for the purpose of pleasing women." But (to paraphrase Marx) it is clear that women make and respond to cinema in conditions not of their own choosing. Continuing development of women's film history requires, as Michele Leigh suggests, a "constellation" of researchers, pooling new discoveries and creating new fissures in traditional historical thinking that new evidence demands. While recognizing the inevitable incompleteness of the histories we compile, the activity of constellating with the women we research and with each other never stops: history is never "finished," fixed for all time. We may preserve "historical objects," but the process of history-making is ongoing. Film history will inevitably be "recalibrated" as cinema changes under an expanding range of practices, especially as digital technologies open new challenges to filmmakers and film preservationists, necessitate rethinking distribution and business models, and introduce new modes of exhibition, consumption and, indeed, archiving. Sally Potter's construction of SP-ARK, the world's first online interactive multimedia film archive, attempts just such a process of constellation, compiling not only a mass of material associated with the inception, production and distribution of her film, *Orlando* (1992), but developing digital mechanisms to enable students and researchers to create pathways through the archive and communicate with each other: a form of "organic knowledge sharing."[3]

Our enterprise, then, is not merely about putting women back into history alongside men or about creating a separate space called "women's film history" apart from "men's film history." Rather, the questions that asking about women pose to traditional ways of doing film history demand new ways of thinking cinema itself. Insofar as these challenge the dominance of the director, recognize co-creation and collaboration, refuse dominant conceptions of cinematic essence, and reorganize notions of aesthetic value, it is not only women who stand to gain. Asking about women promises new perspectives on film history itself and the many cinemas it generates, both past and future.

Notes

1. See Women Film Pioneers Project at https://wfpp.cdrs.columbia.edu (accessed January 10, 2015).

2. See Women and Silent British Cinema (WSBC) at https://womenandsilentbritish cinema.wordpress.com, and Women's Film and Television History Network (WFTHN) at https://womensfilmandtelevisionhistory.wordpress.com (accessed January 10, 2015).

3. See https://www.sp-ark.org (accessed March 8, 2015).

References

Bakhtin, M. M. [1970] 1986. "Response to a Question from the *Novy Mir* Editorial Staff." In *Speech Genres and Other Late Essays*, edited by Caryl Emerson and Michael Holquist, 1–7. Translated by Vern W. McGee. Austin: University of Texas Press.

Sobchack, Vivian. 2000. "What Is Film History? Or, The Riddle of the Sphinxes." In *Reinventing Film Studies*, edited by Christine Gledhill and Linda Williams, 300–315. London: Arnold.

Steedman, Carolyn. 2001. *Dust*. Manchester: Manchester University Press.

Prologue

Constellations: Past Meets Present in Feminist Film History

MONICA DALL'ASTA

and JANE M. GAINES

The History of the History, or History's History

In English the word "history" is everywhere: it's already in the title of this collection, *Doing Women's Film History*, as well as in the title of our jointly written
article, and we see no way around it. In thinking about the conference at which
we delivered this article as a paper, we predicted that while we might all resort to
unambiguous usage as, for example, in references to "history departments," the
majority of our uses would most likely draw on a certain doubleness, if not ambiguity. This is to be expected. After all, the Latin root *historia*, meaning both an
"account of past events" and "a tale, a story," would appear to license what has become a common practice of confusion (See Gaines 2013, 70–71; Bruno 1984, 54).[1]

This doubleness is there every time we say "moving image history" or even "her
history." As with the Italian *storia*, the vernacular term "history" has come to refer
both to the events of the historical past and to the narrative of those events, or, to
the events of the life "she" lived and the story of that life. Neither have other languages avoided the problem; German and French theorists of history have noted
this ambiguity as well (see Gaines 2013, 71; Rancière, 1994, 1–3). Today we are at
a crucial juncture in the "history" of feminism and film, especially following the
Doing Women's Film History conference, where we set an agenda for researching
and writing about women "in" and "as" "history" in the cinema century. We want

to know whether to think the term "history" as a productive ambiguity (the history of the history) or as a highly ideological conflation, an operation that conceals the fact of the construction of an interpretative narrative.

This is a theoretical question of immense importance to our wonderful field for several reasons. First, our training in critical theory has taught us to grasp how narratives function in support of existing power. Second, we have therefore been cautioned against taking empirical facts as unproblematic evidence, here of the existence or not of women working in the first decades of cinema. This is where the written as well as the lived "history" of our branch of feminism gets especially interesting. Because, third, in no other field has the first academic work been founded on an implicit narrative of absence that was later reversed by such a flood of empirical evidence to the contrary.[2] This is a narrative challenged by new research as well as by newly discovered and restored film prints. Consider, for instance, recent retrospectives of Germaine Dulac, Alice Guy Blaché, Asta Nielsen, and Lois Weber.[3] Further, after the discovery of parts of *The Curse of the Quon Gwon* (1916), we now recognize Chinese American Marion E. Wong as writer, director, and actress in the film that she also produced, and, similarly, that a Mexican American actress gave her name to Beatriz Michelina Features, which produced the extant *Just Squaw* (1919).[4] Later, we examine the case of Italian director-producer Elvira Giallanella's recently discovered *Umanità* (Humankind, 1919).

What was the first feminist narrative of women and silent-era film?[5] Between the mid-1970s and through the 1980s the academic narrative was that in the American silent-film industry "there were, effectively, no women."[6] By extension, there were no women in any other silent-era national film industry. As Alison Butler notes, however, by the 1990s there was new interest in historical research in silent cinema, new discoveries and publications such Anthony Slide's book documenting a surprising number of silent-era women filmmakers (Butler 2008, 398; Slide 1996b). Butler does not, however, refer to Slide's book of nearly twenty years earlier, in which he asserted, "During the silent era, women might be said to have virtually controlled the film industry" (Slide 1977, 9). In other words, in the 1990s it is less a matter of "new discoveries" than of "new interest" in, and of, "new questions" put to Slide's narrative from 1977. The narrative in which women "controlled" the industry begins to be posed against the narrative that "it controlled them."

Why is the difference between these narratives an issue? It is an issue because we are not satisfied with a theory of historical revisionism whereby what we call "history" (meaning the events as well as their narration) is continually being updated and called "history" all over again.[7] Are we attempting to "revise" the events themselves, or are we only adjusting our *versions* of these events? Yet, from today's historiographic perspective, what are the events of the past anyway, other than what

FIGURE P.1. Marion E. Wong, writer-director-producer (private collection)

we think we know of them and how we narrate them? "No women at all" and "more women than at any other time" are two competing versions of historical events. The contradiction between these two versions is too significant to ignore and deserves more study. Do we explain the difference between these narratives through a critical theoretical approach, or do we address this issue by writing yet another narration of empirical findings?

If a historian of ideas were to study the field of feminism and film, he or she might find a source for these competing versions in the 1970s theoretical investment in women's "absence." Looking back, it can be shown that the theorization of "absence" worked to justify the development of methods that explained why, although women might have been represented, there were still no "women" in cinema (Doane, Mellencamp, and Williams, 1983, 7; Johnston 1973, 26). This "absence," the result of a strategic use of psychoanalytic theory, concerned women onscreen, not women filmmakers. Yet in one of the original formulations, Mary Ann Doane, Patricia Mellencamp, and Linda Williams explained that feminist film theory developed out of a theory of absence because there was no tradition of the kind that literary scholars could claim based on great Victorian women writers in English. The feminist film critic, they remark, "has reason to be envious" of that tradition (7). This statement underscores the fact that in 1983 leading scholars had no knowledge of the hundreds of women who had worked as writers, directors, and producers, not only in the U.S. silent-era film industry but in Italy and Germany, in Britain and France, as well as where we least expected to find them—in Mexico, Brazil, Chile, and in Egypt, as we will see.[8]

In 1983, Doane, Mellencamp, and Williams justify the theoretical work on absence, conjecturing that although we might see Lois Weber and Dorothy Arzner as analogous to British novelists Jane Austen and George Eliot, this move alone would still not constitute a tradition. To whom would these women have themselves "traced" a lineage, they wonder (7). Today, while we still hesitate to advocate "lineage tracing," we might speculate that Weber and Arzner were aware of the earlier work of writer/director/producer Alice Guy Blaché, who may have begun making films as early as 1896 (Slide 1996a, 28; McMahan 2009, 49; Simon 2009, 9–10). But the attempt to compare literary fiction writers and silent cinema directors is telling for another reason. In retrospect we now wonder if it was not a good thing that feminist literary history was never a model for feminism and film. If the literary model had been followed, more traditional histories might have been written; statements of apparent fact might have credited an individual woman artist with generic breakthroughs, for example: "Alice Guy made the first fiction film." Today we know that however much feminism and film may want to assert this, the statement about the first fiction film is itself a fiction that fabricates a world by its own narrative means. We access this world by following the story of how young Alice, Leon Gaumont's secretary, made a film she later called *La Fée aux choux* (The Cabbage Fairy), possibly as early as 1896, but more likely between 1900 and 1902, as Kim Tomadjoglou discusses in chapter 6. Since both of us have also researched this fortuitous "making" (as well as the remakings that followed), we know that the historical event still eludes our narratives, just as it eluded Guy's own narrative, which seems to conflate the several versions she made of this film (Dall'Asta 2008; Gaines 2004).[9]

Thus it is that we know the difficulties involved in making a coherent narrative out of historical events such as the making of a film about babies hidden under cabbages, events that are only apparently straightforward. But the issue here is the degree to which we want to adopt a metahistorical approach, the method associated with Hayden White, who has scandalized history departments by arguing that narrative history employs fictional devices.[10] In other words, when we try to understand our present practice by considering it in relation to previous accounts, we take what we are calling a *critical-historical* approach that deals with the problem of "the history of history," the approach we use to expose the never-neutral amnesias of traditional historiography and to counter its claim to objectivity with the inevitability of its "fictions." But we want to know if this challenge does or does not help in devising a methodology for a different historiographical practice, one that would take us beyond the position that history writing is yet another fiction, the approach associated with metahistory. Some critics, for instance, have remarked on the danger of the history-as-fiction position, which could be used to deny such

FIGURE P.2. Alice Guy Blaché ca. 1907 in Gaumont Co. Archive (Credit Belgian Film Archive)

historical atrocities as the genocide of Jews during World War II (See Ginzburg 1991; White 1992). According to these critics, if we think of history writing as an arbitrary operation of "emplotment," we may not be able to distinguish between "false" and "true" discourses, between ideological constructions and reliable accounts. Certainly history-as-fiction runs the risk of implying that all historical discourse is "made up," and the charge of fabrication constitutes a danger since there is so much at stake in the position of women in the world film events that we together research, write, and sometimes make moving images about.[11]

But how do we know what is and is not a reliable account? We certainly do not want to go back to the old historicist belief in faithful representation of the past. Since our critical training has geared us to think of all accounts as "fictions," we are perplexed when we are called upon to signify the existence of past events. Do we defer to the past as autonomous and independent of fictionalization? To continue this line of inquiry, we need to distinguish between "historical facts," the concatenation of which constitutes traditional historiographic writing and unnarrated surviving artifacts or evidentiary pieces. In our field, as in no other, the extant 35mm motion picture print is the historical artifact par excellence, the centerpiece that organizes surviving documents in its orbit: the screenplay, the account book, the poster; a narrative object that encourages historical narratives while it also invites us to find the dreams of its makers and spectators in its "realization."

As distinct from "facts," which are linguistic entities that do not themselves have any actual physical existence and which traditional historiography deduces from documents and re-presents in narrative form, "historical objects" are material remnants of the past that survive in the here and now (see Barthes 1986, 138). As such, they are displaced in time. Of course we can conceive of them as "documents," yet only on the condition that we do not charge them with the ability (so longed for by historicists) to return us to their original place and to show us past events "as they really happened." Events cannot be replayed or accessed by retellings. They can only be evoked; further, the image they create changes with every recollection.

Historical objects are of momentous importance in this search for a critical-historical method. Severed from their original context, removed to another time—the present which is (just one of) their (possible) future(s)—they stand before us like so many unrelated "monads," fragments of a fourth-dimensional picture that, if ever it existed, has for us gone forever. They resist the kind of causal concatenation of traditional historical narration that attempts to provide linkages between them. The historicist faith in filling in by addition, by accumulating documents to burst through the gap, attempting to restore totality in a narrative, is simply wishful thinking. Rather, the gap might better be seen as prompting multiple narratives, no one of which can ever pretend to exhaustiveness.

The problem for a critical-historical approach, then, is how to "constellate" elements separated by an incalculable gap of time (both between them and between them and us) (Benjamin 1970, 262–63, § xvii). The technique or art of reproduction (such as we perform each time we make a citation, reprint a document, or screen a film before a present-day audience) is key to a critical-historical approach based not on an effort to represent but on an effort to evoke by means of historical montage an image of the past (Benjamin 1999, 461n2, 6).

Becoming Elvira

So this is what a critical-historical approach urges us to see: that the motion-picture objects and other physical remnants left by the active presence of women in silent cinema are scattered pieces of a puzzle that we can never hope to complete. What are we going to do with these objects? Interrogate them, right, but looking for what? A first answer is that we are looking for the women behind them. But again, these women do not exist in our time, although we know they *have* existed because they left signs of their work behind them in the form of historical objects. But we cannot really meet them; we cannot touch them or talk to them. They are like phantasms to us, and we cannot simply conjure them up again. So what do we imply when we say that we "find a woman," when in fact what we find is simply a surviving remnant of her work—ideally a motion-picture print? Rather than saying that we "find" *her*, we might better say that we take her signs—signs found in the historical film object. We then use these signs to evoke an image of her today. This image, as any image of memory, is at the same time past and present: we

18

would not have the image if it did not appear here and now. But at the same time it is not present in the way that we are, because it "belongs" to the historical past (Benjamin 1970, 255, § v).

In this collaboration, we have each been influenced by a key idea borrowed from the work of the other. While Jane wanted to return to Monica's provocative idea of the "beautiful failure," Monica wanted to elaborate Jane's question, "Are they Us?" We realize that our thinking for some time had started to crisscross (Dall'Asta 2010; Gaines 2009). In addition, we now know that we have both been using the same metaphor of "constellation" culled from Walter Benjamin (1999, 462–63).[12] This shared thinking brought us to reflect both on how the two of us are "constellated" together as scholars and how we are "constellated" as well with the subjects of our historical research. In a way, the peculiar present-pastness of the historical motion-picture object allows us to create a temporal wedge in our present that makes us momentarily coincident with the historical past. As we are undertaking this research, we come to align ourselves with the women we study. Forming a constellation with them, we locate ourselves historically just at the moment that we "find" them by borrowing their signs. So what we "find" when we locate one of these figures is that, actually, we are discovering and locating ourselves in our own historical moment. Who else *would* we find?

To illustrate this with an example, we turn to the recently excavated figure of Elvira Giallanella, an Italian director and producer never mentioned in previous accounts of Italian silent cinema but who suddenly made her way into feminist historiography after the discovery in 2007 of a 35mm print of her 1919 antiwar film *Umanità* (see Veronesi 2010). We may be glad to have found her, but we also know at the same time that we have not really found her, for what we have now is actually not Giallanella herself but simply a piece of her work. Besides being the only film made by Giallanella, *Umanità* is also a unique example of a pacifist film shot by a woman in the immediate aftermath of World War I, staged on the very geographic terrain over which the war had just been fought. Adding to its uniqueness, *Umanità* does not make use of professional actors and is interpreted by two children who are shown roaming a scene of deserted ruins in the company of a gnome, a fantasy figure conjured out of their imaginations. Truly amazing in its portrait of the trauma of war as experienced by children, the film is especially surprising for another reason: the very existence of *Umanità* exposes our own in-ability *to even imagine the existence of such an object,* to conceive of an antiwar film produced and directed by an Italian woman in 1919. A skeptic might ask: Are you kidding? Aren't you using this woman only to advance the needs of the present? Well yes, but the opposite is also true because today the historical object exists, although the woman does not. Here historical research provokes the imagining of

FIGURE P.3. Frame Enlargement, *Umanità* (d. Elvira Giallanella, 1919)

FIGURE P.4. The "Theater of War" in *Umanità* (d. Elvira Giallanella, 1919)

an image, given that the phantasmatic is the only possible condition of existence for Giallanella today. So we come to the truly paradoxical conclusion that they need us as much as we need them. They need us in order to exist historically, exist, that is, as provocative images in and for the present.[13]

This historiography requires the best of our imaginative capabilities. Like approaches to other forgotten groups, women's film historiography faces the emptiness of the past: an immeasurable void that is all that went unrecorded, an oblivion from which we painstakingly draw every piece of evidence. But unlike more traditional approaches, a critical-historical feminist film historiography is well aware that historical knowledge is built precisely upon this nothingness since we know that the holes and lacunae that we find contain both what did and what *never* did happen.[14] Ours is then the challenge, to quote Giorgio Agamben (2009), of "gaining access to a past that has not been lived through, and therefore that technically cannot be defined as 'past' but that somehow has remained present" (102). In his mix of tenses Agamben helps us to describe the *present* of Elvira Giallanella's work as well as the past and the future of her post–World War I pacifist commitment.

However, as soon as we begin to look for this phantasm of a woman, we encounter dead ends. Only a few scattered pieces of information have been found that imply Giallanella's life: we learn that she started work in the film industry before making *Umanità* and that around 1913, already a leading figure in the Vera Film company, she started her own independent company, Liana Film, in order to make *Umanità*. We discover that she planned *Umanità* as the first of a series of educational features that never materialized after the first title. And finally, we learn that the film was never distributed and therefore most likely was never seen in public before 2007 (Veronesi 2010).[15]

We can then say that although the 35mm film print exists, *Umanità* never existed as a work of cinema because in its time it was never publically projected. Now to constellate Elvira Giallanella with our present, consider how lack of distribution and exhibition has been a challenge to many women film and video makers in the last and present century (see Julia Knight's contribution, chapter 15). This is one way the absence that is Elvira Giallanella resonates with our own lives and the lives of the makers we research. Remembering that the relation of constellation is two way, here is how we think it: On the one hand, we see how Giallanella needs *us* to bring her work into existence, to find a new antiwar audience for a film that never had one and therefore to bring to completion what she could not during her lifetime. But on the other hand *we* need her to make sense of the continued negation of women, of those experiences of loss, failure, and demise that define the lives of so many. We stand also, then, on feminism's founding paradox, what historian Joan W. Scott (1996) has called the "sameness versus difference conundrum," which acknowledges "women" as both singular and plural, that is, continually produced "as women" again and again although diversely situated across cultures and decades (3–4). We are the same as much as we are different. We thus cannot misinterpret the historical significance of *Umanità* because effectively *we are Elvira Giallanella*. Since we are Elvira, we know that all women's apparent failures experienced in our now-constellated lives may at some point (depending on all of us) come to unexpected fruition, a fruition we reconfigure as both passion and struggle. Becoming Elvira, as women makers striving for recognition today, we see moments of women's demise in a different perspective. We learn now to watch all makers *historically*, that is, as powers of the historical present into which we have brought them.

On Becoming Historical Others

And here, picking up the point about how we watch historically, we want to emphasize something that we often forget: the present is itself historical. This is why it no longer makes sense to us to think of the intellectual history of our field— that of feminist academics and their discourse—as separate from the history of women who worked inside as well as outside silent-era national film industries. Another way of putting this would be to say that the reasons Elvira Giallanella and *Umanità* matter are themselves historical; they are, as we make them, part of the narrative of feminism and film, as well as part of historic antiwar protests and struggles on behalf of gender equality. We are constellated with women makers, then and now, in relation to the unfinished business of world feminism. One more example of an early aspiring woman illustrates how their historical constellation with us produces their artistic and political efforts as highly successful, exquisitely beautiful failures. One thinks of the 2010 Women and the Silent Screen conference in Bologna, where Ouissal Mejri screened a streamed clip of the restored version of Bahija Hafez's *Al-Dahaia* (The Victims, 1932). We cannot help but be struck by how the uprising in Cairo in February 2011 brings us into alignment with this Egyptian woman director/writer/actress/composer who was renounced by her family because she chose to make motion pictures (Mejri 2010).

Given then the impossibility of history's history—the perfect correspondence between a history (of) and historical events (themselves)—we strive instead for something predicated on this very ambiguity. We claim our present telling as coexistent with past events. First, we are constellated with them when we do not fear, as Foucault phrased it, to "conceive of the *Other* in the time of our own thought" (Foucault 1972, 12). Monica demonstrates the power of this conceptualization in her theory of the "beautiful failure," exemplified by Elvira Giallanella, the woman whose past "failure" is reconceived as an "achievement" for the present. Now, after several public screenings to enthusiastic audiences, *Umanità* stands to us for the overwhelming triumph of Giallanella's failure! Second, we are constellated with

22

historical others on the premise that the historical past is continuously created, even now, even today as we write. This continuous creation challenges the "time after time" mode of thinking that would see us as successors. Instead, we consider ourselves the contemporaries of historical others with whom we now "share" a history—that of women and film, video, and now digital works. Here is where we are constellated with them: in "doing women's film history" we are all involved in a historical production in which women who dared to make works thought to be "ahead of their time" are confirmed as "in" and "for" our time as well.

Notes

1. Ambiguity is written into the word's etymology, going back to the Indo-European root *weid*, meaning "to know" as well as "to see," through the Greek ἱστορία (historia). Already in Herodotus the term oscillates between the idea of "learning or knowing by inquiry" and that of a "record" or "narrative." See Etymology Dictionary, www.etymoonline.com.

2. The recently published research confirming this has grown too large to list here. For confirmation see Stamp 2013.

3. See *Alice Guy Blaché*, Whitney exhibition catalog (Simon 2009). Major exhibitions in *Il Cinema Ritrovato*. Cineteca del Commune di Bologna, Italy, featured Germaine Dulac (2009), Alice Guy Blaché (2011), Asta Nielsen (2012), and Lois Weber (2013).

4. See Jenny Lau and Mengquin Xie, "Marion E. Wong," and Mary Anne Lyons, "Beatriz Michelina" (Gaines, Vatsal, and Dall'Asta 2013).

5. It was most likely Sharon Smith's article (1973).

6. See Gaines (2012, 160), for the argument that the narrative developed from "There were no women" in the 1970s to there were "no women in 1925," the year no woman directed a U.S. industry motion picture, to the more recent "over by 1925," allowing for a silent era heyday.

7. Ironically Slide seems to be taking back his earlier contention in challenging women film historians as to the "real numbers" (2012, 120).

8. See Joanne Hershfield and Patricia Torres St. Martin, "Writing the History of Latin American Women Working in the Silent Film Industry," and Eliana Jara Donoso, "Women in Chilean Silent Cinema" (Gaines, Vatsal and Dall'Asta 2013).

9. See Kimberly Tomadjoglou's reference in Chapter 6 to the 2012 research by Maurice Gianati, who thinks Guy's first film was not *Le Fée aux* choux, the one-shot extant film now dated 1900, but *Sage-femme de première classe* (1902).

10. According to its major theoretician Hayden White in 1973, metahistory exposes the work of traditional history as a form of narration working to produce a "truth effect" by using ideological rhetorical devices.

11. See the documentary in progress on Alice Guy Blaché, *Be Natural* (2015).

12. Benjamin (1999, 462–463) repeats an almost similar idea twice: "It is not that what is past cast its light on what is present, or what is present its light on what is past; rather, image is that wherein what has been comes together in a flash with the now to form a constellation."

13. White argues in this regard that "events are real because they are remembered, not because they occurred" (1987, 20).

14. Steedman is close to this when she says: "So there is a double nothingness in the writing of history and in the analysis of it: it is about something that never did happen in the way it comes to be represented (the happening exists in the telling of the text); and it is made out of materials that aren't there, in an archive or anywhere else" (2002, 154).

15. *Umanità* was restored by the Cineteca Nazionale in Rome and the restoration premiered at the "Non solo dive: Pioniere del cinema italiano" Conference, in Bologna, Italy, November, 2007.

References

Agamben, Giorgio. 2009. *The Signature of All Things: On Method*. New York: One Books.

Barthes, Roland. 1986. "The Discourse of History." In *The Rustle of Language*, 127–40. Translated by Richard Howard. New York: Hill and Wang.

Benjamin, Walter. 1970. "Theses on the Philosophy of History." In Walter Benjamin, *Illuminations*, edited by Hannah Arendt, 253–64. Translated by Harry Zohn. New York: Fontana/Collins.

———. 1999. *The Arcades Project*. Translated by Howard Eiland and Kefin McLaughlin. Cambridge, Mass.: Harvard University Press.

Bruno, Guiliana. 1984. "Towards a Theorization of Film History." *Iris* 2.2: 41- 55.

Butler, Alison. 2008. "Feminist Perspectives in Film Studies." In *The Sage Handbook of Film Studies*, edited by James Donald and Michael Renov, 391–407. Los Angeles: Sage.

Dall'Asta, Monica. 2008. "Alice al di là dello specchio." In *Alice Guy: Memorie di una pioniera del cinema*, 9–43. Bologna, Italy: Cineteca di Bologna.

———. 2010. "What It Means to Be a Woman: Theorizing Feminist Film History beyond the Essentialism/Constructionism Divide." In *Not So Silent: Women in Cinema before Sound*, edited by A. Söderberg Widdig and Sophia Bull, 39–47. Stockholm: Acta Universitatis Stockholmiensi.

Dall'Asta, Monica, Victoria Duckett, and Lucia Tralli, eds. 2013. *Researching Women in Silent Cinema: New Findings and Perspectives*. Bologna, Italy: DAR, University of Bologna.

Doane, Mary Ann, Patricia Mellencamp, and Linda Williams, eds. 1983. "Feminist Film Criticism: An Introduction." In *Re-Vision: Essays in Feminist Film Criticism*, 1–17. Los Angeles: American Film Institute.

Foucault, Michel. 1972. *The Archaeology of Knowledge*. Translated by A. M. Sheridan. New York: Pantheon.

Gaines, Jane M. 2004. "First Fictions." *Signs* 30 (1): 1293–317.

———. 2009. "Are They Us? Women's Work on Women's Work in the Silent International Film Industries" (in Italian, "Esse sono noi? Il nostro lavoro sulle donne al lavoro nell'industria cinematografica muta"). In *Non solo dive: Pioniere del cinema italiano*, edited by Monica Dall'Asta, 19–30. Bologna, Italy: Cineteca di Bologna.

———. 2012. "Pink-Slipped: What Happened to Women in the Silent Film Industry?" In *Blackwell's History of American Film*, edited by Roy Grundman, Cindy Lucia, and Art Simon, 155–77. New York: Blackwell.

———. 2013."What Happened to the Philosophy of Film History?" *Film History* 25 (1–2): 70–80.

Gaines, Jane M., Radha Vatsal, and Monica Dall'Asta, eds. 2013.*Women Film Pioneers Project*. New York: Columbia University Libraries, Center for Digital Research and Scholarship. Available at http://wfpp.cdrs.columbia.edu (accessed January 10, 2015).

Ginzburg, Carlo. 1991. "Checking the Evidence: The Judge and the Historian." *Critical Inquiry* 18 (1): 79–82.

Johnston, Claire. 1973. "Women's Cinema as Counter-Cinema." In *Notes on Women's Cinema*, edited by Claire Johnston, 24–31. London: Society for Education in Film and Television.

McMahan, Allison. 2009. "Madame Blaché in America: Director, Producer, Studio Owner." In *Alice Guy Blaché: Cinema Pioneer*, edited by Joan Simon, 47–76. New Haven, Conn.: Yale University Press.

Mejri, Ouissal. 2010. "Women in Egyptian Silent Cinema: the 1920s Pioneers." Unpublished paper delivered at Women and the Silent Screen VI, University of Bologna, Italy.

Rancière, Jacques. 1994. *The Names of History: On the Poetics of Knowledge*. Trans. Hassan Melehy. Minneapolis: University of Minnesota Press.

Scott, Joan Wallach. 1996. "Introduction." In *Feminism and History*, edited by Joan Wallach Scott, 1–13. Oxford: Oxford University Press.

Simon, Joan. 2009. "The Great Adventure: Alice Guy Blaché, Cinema Pioneer." In *Alice Guy Blaché: Cinema Pioneer*, edited by Joan Simon, 1–32. New Haven, Conn.: Yale University Press in association with Whitney Museum of American Art.

Slide, Anthony. 1977. *Early Women Directors: Their Role in the Development of the Silent Cinema*. New York: Barnes.

———, ed. 1996a. *The Memoirs of Alice Guy Blaché*. Translated by Roberta and Simone Blaché. Lanham, Md.: Scarecrow.

———. 1996b. *The Silent Feminists: America's First Women Directors*. Lanham, Md.: Scarecrow.

———. 2012. "Early Women Filmmakers: The Real Numbers." *Film History* 24 (1): 114–21.

Smith, Sharon. 1973. "Women Make Movies." *Women and Film* 1: 77–90.

Stamp, Shelley. 2013. "Feminist Media Historiography and the Work Ahead." Unpublished keynote address, Women and the Silent Screen VII, University of Melbourne, Australia.

Steedman, Carolyn. 2002. *Dust: The Archive and Cultural History*. New Brunswick, N.J.: Rutgers University Press.

Veronesi, Micaela. 2010. "A Woman Wishes to 'Make a New World': *Umanità* by Elvira Giallanella." In *Not So Silent: Women in Cinema Before Sound*, edited by Sofia Bull and Astrid Soderbergh Widding, 67–79. Stockholm: Acta Universitatis Stockholmiensis.

White, Hayden. 1973. *Metahistory: The Historical Imagination in Nineteenth Century Europe*. Baltimore, Md.: Johns Hopkins University Press.

———. 1987. *The Content of the Form: Narrative Discourse and Historical Representation*. Baltimore, Md.: Johns Hopkins University Press.

———. 1992. "Historical Emplotment and the Problem of Truth." In *Probing the Limits of Representation*, edited by S. Friendlander, 37–53. Berkeley: University of California Press.

PART I

Searching for Sources, Rewriting Histories

CHAPTER 1

Scandalous Evidence

Looking for the Bombay Film Actress in an Absent Archive (1930s–1940s)

DEBASHREE MUKHERJEE

Bombay city in the 1930s was visibly modern. From its art deco high-rises and jazz clubs to its teeming factories and stock exchange, the colonial port city embodied the creative energies of a dynamic metropolis. One of the key markers of Bombay's modernity was the public woman. The woman who went about her business in the public domain was no longer confined to the factories, bazaars, or the red light districts of the city. Evidenced in newspapers, novels, and films of the time was a palpable excitement about a new breed of white-collar woman worker, encompassing a new range of profiles such as typist, telephone operator, nurse, journalist, photographer, and even anti-imperial political activist.[1] The film professional was one of these new public women.

It is common knowledge that since cinema was considered a socially dubious medium, the early South Asian film industries relied on male actors to play female parts. By the 1930s, however, women were participating in Bombay's rapidly expanding film industry in diverse capacities. Female film professionals such as the producer-director Fatma Begum, music composer Jaddan Bai, screenwriter-actress Snehaprabha Pradhan, and film critic Clare Mendonca directly contradict the widespread notion that the only women working in the early talkie industries of the subcontinent were actresses or extras.

This misperception is hardly surprising given the serious gaps in the official archives of South Asian cinema. The National Film Archive of India was only set up in 1964, and scores of early films are lost to us for reasons ranging from problems with flammable nitrate film, a hesitant film archival culture, and the politics of preservation. Moreover, primary sources that film historians in parts of Europe and the United States take for granted—such as studio papers—are practically nonexistent in India. Research on women in the early decades of Indian cinema is severely affected by these absences, and basic profiles of even leading actresses are scarce. My initial attempts to look for direct accounts of women's film practice repeatedly drew a blank. Instead, what I found in relative abundance were suggestions about actresses embroiled in scandals. In this chapter I seek to explore the historiographic productivity of such speculation and talk as an entry point into understanding the status and work of women in the early Bombay film industry. I have reconstructed specific scandal narratives in a jigsaw fashion using a variety of sources, including film magazines, biographies, creative nonfiction writing, fan letters, and interviews I conducted in Bombay from 2008 to 2013.

Dictionary definitions of the terms *rumor, gossip,* and *scandal* point to their narrative unreliability and their shaky epistemological status. However, if historicized, these discursive practices offer important clues about cinema as an industrial as well as imaginative form. Tightly framed within a discourse of morality, film scandals are not only about the individual acts condemned but are also attempts to articulate the unsettling of studio and social hierarchies, including gender relations. This chapter attempts to demonstrate how the film historian might use these "illegitimate" sources of history to approach lived histories of Bombay cinema's work culture.

I approach scandal as a discursive form that proliferates textually and orally rather than as a temporally contained mediatized event. Hints of scandal are available in film magazines, but layers of the same incident fold back on the rumored event through time via interviews with colleagues and published memoirs. Taking two star-actresses of the 1930s and 1940s, Devika Rani and Naseem Banu, as case studies, and moving outward from the initial scandal narratives, this chapter re-imagines the possibilities and pressures that actresses encountered in the film studio as well as in the public eye. Further, it suggests that the early film actress be seen as a manifestation of, and model for, the urban working woman in 1930s and 1940s Bombay.

Very early into the life of cinema in India it became apparent that this new phenomenon would generate talk. In its affective manifestations, cinema was able to circulate more freely and widely than the physical film object. Letters demanding biographical information about stars regularly swamped fan magazines and tabloids. The studios that were associated with these glamorous names became sites of intense speculation and wonder. The film studio was exciting both as an emblem of technological modernity and as a thrilling heterosocial work space that brought men and women together under intimate conditions. This combined excitement can be glimpsed in a *Filmindia* description of the new Ranjit Studio: "Ah, the new studio—the new Ranjit studio! It is big and beautiful with such perfect acoustics that even if the director tried a tête-à-tête in whispers with the heroine it would all come out on the sound track as distinct as the song of a lark" (Judas 1938, 14).

The most overwhelming narrative that emerged around women's presence in the Bombay film studio was that of respectability and moral danger, the constant subtext being an anxiety about female sexuality. Women in studios were caught in a professional paradox: not only were they likely to perform the seductive huntress on screen, but they were also susceptible to the seductions of the studio itself. The film studio became the site of much anxiety both inside and outside the film industry. The public sphere was rife with discussions about studio reform among so-called "concerned" citizens and journalists. The rapidly mushrooming parallel industry of fanzines and tabloids was driven by the unconventional work atmosphere of film studios and the risqué content often being shot inside. Actresses routinely made claims in these very fanzines about the "wholesome" atmosphere of film studios or protested that moral integrity was the ultimate defense of a working woman (see S. Devi 1993; C. Devi 1993; Sunita 1939). The participation of Muslim courtesan-singers and Anglo-Indian actresses in the film industry's workforce created a different frisson. Both communities of women were popularly viewed as sexually suspect, the former for their traditional professions and the latter due to their conspicuously westernized lifestyles. Women's sexuality in South Asia has historically been the preferred ground for waging politico-religious battles. As decolonization became a future certainty and talks of a faith-based "Partition" exacerbated communal tensions, actresses' bodies became contested territory. Studio bosses and celebrity journalists advocated a drive to recruit educated Hindu actresses who were tasked with changing the reputation of the industry and better embodying the nationalist ideal of the Indian woman on screen. Contemporary Indian film historians often argue that these hegemonic attempts at "improvement" were successful in their short-term aims (Majumdar 2009, Bhaumik 2001). However, the competing truths of film-scandal narratives complicate the dominant account of an industrial transition to "respectability." Rather, I hope to demonstrate that actresses from all social strata were equally interpellated by the challenge of respectability and that complex negotiations with urban modernity, fandom, and stardom were at play during this critical moment in the history of Bombay cinema.

Devika Rani (1908–1994)

The first of the "scandals" in this study took place sometime in 1935–36.

> When Najmul Hussain ran off with Devika Rani, the entire Bombay Talkies was in turmoil. The film they were making had gone on the floor and some scenes had already been shot. . . . The worst affected and the most worried man at Bombay Talkies was Himansu Rai, Devika Rani's husband and the heart and soul of the company. (Manto 2008, 447)

Details about the incident are reported in biographical sketches like the one above, in the innuendos of contemporaneous film magazines, and in memoirs. Bombay Talkies was founded in 1934 by the husband and wife team, Himansu Rai and Devika Rani, who had both spent many years learning film craft in Germany and England. Their ambition was to reconfigure the indigenous Indian film industry by introducing cutting-edge technology, an international team of technicians, a rationalized studio work model, and transparent financing sources. The studio's recruitment policies were explicitly class-conscious. To quote Devika Rani herself, "In Bombay Talkies we were all one class of people—all our recruits were from those sent by the Vice-Chancellors of various universities" (Kak 1980, 73). Similarly, in a pre–Bombay Talkies interview, it was reported that "Devika Rani has great hopes in assisting her husband in creating an Indian Hollywood in Bombay where she hopes to train educated young Indian ladies who are desirous of joining the Cinema Industry" (*Cinema Annual* 1933, 36).

It is clear that Rai and Rani were keen to distance themselves from the prevailing reputation of Bombay's film studios, a reputation not only of clumsy, ad hoc production and bazaar-type financing, but also of sexual immorality (see Bhaumik 2001, especially 151–64). Given the nature of Bombay Talkies' vision, how do we understand the scandalous elopement attempt by Devika Rani? Bombay Talkies' first film, *Jawani-ki-Hawa* (Osten 1935), had featured Najmul Hussain and Devika Rani, and they proved a hit pair. At the time of the elopement, they were shooting *Jeevan Naiya* (Osten 1936), and true to the cliché, the onscreen couple smoothly transitioned into an offscreen one. However, such matters rarely become hard facts that can be recorded in the annals of history. A co-actor remembers: "Something happened; what, no one knew for sure. There were stories, rumors. Perhaps only four persons knew the truth. The others could only conjecture" (Valicha 1996, 15). Devika Rani was finally tracked down in Calcutta and persuaded to return to Bombay. Najmul Hussain was fired. The popular appeal and longevity of this scandal narrative derives from its moral structure; two individuals fell in love, ig-

FIGURE 1.1. Devika Rani poses for a publicity still
on the set of *Vachan* (d. Franz Osten, pc. Bombay Talkies, 1938)
(Courtesy Wolfgang Peter Wirsching and Georg Wirsching, Goa)

nored the dictates of society or common sense, committed adultery, and had to repent. Might there be another way to view this history?

Born in 1908 into a privileged, upper-caste Bengali family, Devika Rani Choudhuri was famed as the grandniece of the poet-laureate Rabindranath Tagore. Her fans were well aware of key biographical details, including the fact that she had spent several years in Europe pursuing educational and vocational studies. In London she met Himansu Rai, a charismatic film entrepreneur who was sixteen years her senior. He offered her a position in set design for an international venture he was producing, *A Throw of Dice* (Osten 1929). In 1929 Devika Rani married Himansu Rai and moved with him to Germany "where he was a producer with the famous UFA studios" (Malik 1958, 33). At UFA Rani learned art direction, costume, and makeup in Erich Pommer's unit; magazines like *Filmfare* subsequently reported that she worked with Marlene Dietrich, G. W. Pabst, and Fritz Lang (Malik 1958, 35; Narayan 1977, 42). With Hitler's increasing power in Germany, Himansu Rai and Devika Rani moved to Bombay, complete with a German crew, and set up their own studio in 1934. Can these details of a meticulously planned, shared enterprise be reconciled with Rani's supposedly spontaneous decision to elope with a co-star? According to studio insiders, there was another, more practical angle to the elopement narrative (Pal 2004; Valicha 1996).

Najmul Hussain and Devika Rani, though on contract with Bombay Talkies, had been trying to join an established Calcutta studio, New Theatres, where they hoped to be signed on as a package deal. This was an era before freelance acting became the norm, and producers often enforced contracts through expensive legal battles and even by boycotting recalcitrant artistes. Devika Rani was technically a stakeholder in Bombay Talkies Ltd., but to abandon her new company as well as her producer-husband was a highly controversial decision. Relocating to another regional film industry, far from the immediate professional networks and production infrastructures of Bombay city, might have been the only way to stall social and legal censure. New Theatres, in the mid-1930s, was one of the leading film studios in the subcontinent. Run by B. N. Sircar, the studio was an efficiently managed, commercially successful, "respectable" organization much like the studio Rai and Rani envisioned for Bombay Talkies (Gooptu 2010). Agreement to sign on Devika Rani, who had set up shop in Bombay with her husband amid much fanfare, meant that Sircar was willing to risk the potentially scandalous repercussions. Also, it meant that Rani already had enough star value to justify such a high-stakes deal. Thus, the rival scandal narrative contains crucial information about studio competition, individual ambition, and the status of the actress as valuable commodity. In the earliest decades of cinema, the actress embodied the chief attractions of the movies. The leading studios of the day were, in the public imagination, inextricable from their representative female stars, employed under rigid contracts. New Theatres, at the time, had famous actresses like Kanan Devi and Jamuna on its payroll and was looking to augment its reputation by hiring Devika Rani, who had achieved rare success in the West.[2] The fact that Himansu Rai successfully brought Rani back to his studio and to Bombay also foreshadowed the displacement of Calcutta by Bombay as the new power center of Hindustani film production.

In her essay on the modern girl in Bombay cinema, Priti Ramamurthy (2006) argues that "for acting to be recoded as acceptable, the 'private' lives of the stars had also to be aligned as respectably modern. So, unlike Sulochana, whose breakup with her on-and-off-screen lover was posited as one cause for her decline, Devika Rani was posed gardening at home" (217). Nuancing such binary logic, I suggest that the production of respectability was a more complex process and that actresses performed modes of respectability and Indian femininity in strategic ways. It is striking that just a few months before the release of Rani's next film, *Achhut Kanya* (1936), gossip columnists avidly discussed Devika Rani's elopement attempt and its denouement. For example, "Miss Kamala" directly addresses the star thus: "And then came the news that you had run away from the Bombay Talkies and that we would have no chance to see your pictures for a long time to come . . . only to discover that you had gone for a short change to Calcutta and on return you will be working in *Jeevan Naiya*. We were relieved and glad" (1936, 28). Scandal thus becomes significant in the way it is mediated to a star's audiences in a context that is fraught with anxieties about actresses' virtue and family background. It seems that Devika Rani's elopement scandal hardly dented her star power; it might even have augmented it. Rani went on to star in some of Bombay Talkies' most enduring hits and was the first-ever recipient of the prestigious Dadasaheb Phalke national award.[3] The commerce of star-making works on contradictory impulses. Rani consistently played the demure, good girl in Bombay Talkies' films, even as she performed the role of the ideal Brahmin wife and partner to an influential studio boss, but her characters also flaunted fashionable sarees, Marcel-waved hair, and penciled eyebrows. Tradition negotiated with modernity as Rani performed conservative modes of feminine behavior while visually adopting transnationally circulating modern fashions. Her "Indianness" coupled with her lingering "foreignness" (betrayed in her enunciation of Hindustani dialogue with a distinct Anglicized accent) to create an exciting set of contradictions that fans could tut-tut about and simultaneously adore.

Therefore, to characterize the altering landscape of the Bombay film industry through identity-based oppositions between actresses is misleading. Women were caught in a vortex of local configurations of modernity pulling in different directions according to specificities of caste, class, race, and religion, while pressure to present an acceptable façade was uniformly felt. If fans asked, "Rose, I think is Anglo-Indian. What is her real name?" (Surinarayanan 1939, 35), they were equally curious to know if "Devika Rani [has] any children?" (Mahanty 1945, 14). I would argue that film journalism's constant production of a discourse of respectability not only emphasized conformity but also enabled many actresses to recast themselves through its new vocabulary. The virtue associated with being "cultured" could be retroactively ascribed by both cinema's canny publicity mechanisms and by ardent fans. Therefore, it was possible for one columnist to claim that "unlike so many other Indian actresses, Miss Kajjan . . . seems to create a new morality, a new freedom and culture in India" (Ahmed 1933, 22), or for another to include the popular Anglo-Indian actress, Sabita Devi née Iris Gasper, in the "recent introduction of some respectable, educated and well brought up society girls, with an inherent bent of mind into the Indian Films [sic]" ("Pictophone" 1933, 19). The respectability discourse had a real impact on studios' recruitment decisions, and actresses were pressured to align their private and public lives. Concerted efforts to prop up the respectability myth, combined with actresses' own work on their image, nevertheless had to contend with cinema's constant need for gossip production. The reception of star scandals points to spectators' desires that could not be limited by a nationalist conception of Hinduized femininity. As an anonymous magazine contributor put it, "These screen girls do not speak openly of their love and that alone has the secret of attraction" (*Cinema* 1939, 25).

Naseem Banu (1916–2002)

Between 1940 and 1941, scandal hit Naseem Banu, more generally known as *Pari-Chehra* or the Fairy-Faced One. *Filmindia* columnist Hyacinth (1942) commented: "Knowing her simplicity and sweetness it is hard to imagine how anyone could print slanderous posters about her. Those who know her were shocked to see large posters, crammed with falsehoods, pasted all over the city" (31). Naseem's first film was Sohrab Modi's adaptation of *Hamlet*, titled *Khoon ka Khoon* (1936), in which she played Ophelia. Her mother, Shamshad Begum, a well-known and wealthy Delhi classical singer and courtesan, also landed a part in the film as Queen Gertrude, ostensibly, a *Filmindia* columnist claimed, because Naseem was too shy to work by herself (Hyacinth 1942, 31). In another biographical sketch, the renowned Urdu writer Sa'adat Hasan Manto tells us that Naseem was referred to as the "Beauty Queen" of the Bombay film industry. Among her many suitors was the son of the Nizam of Hyderabad, Moazam Jah. Shamshad Begum, now acting as Naseem's full-time advisor and film agent, decided that the Nizam's offer was good enough for her to give up a career in films. Both women relocated to Hyderabad "as the prince's guests," but Shamshad Begum soon realized that "Hyderabad was like a prison, which would stifle her daughter" (Manto 2008, 595). Mother and daughter returned to Bombay and to films. It was at this point that a bitter Moazam Jah launched a unique smear campaign. In a highly cinematic flourish, the walls of the city were plastered with posters maligning Naseem's reputation. Her fans responded in like fashion (Hyacinth 1942, 33).

Crucial to this episode is Shamshad Begum's own professional history as a courtesan, a lifestyle and career that guided her choices for her daughter. The *tawa'ifs* of Allahabad, Lucknow, Calcutta, and Lahore were usually well read and expertly trained in the classical traditions of Hindustani dance and music. It was a matrilineal profession, with mothers or matriarchal figures grooming girls from an early age. These women survived on patronage from the aristocratic class and were invited to perform concerts at private and public gatherings. While many were exploited by patrons, mentors, or relatives, others also enjoyed a sexual freedom unheard of at the time. These factors led to a contradictory play between professional fame and social notoriety, a conflict that doggedly shadowed many actresses' careers. Veena Oldenburg has suggested that tawa'ifs be seen not as victims of patri-

FIGURE 1.2. Naseem Banu is the main attraction in this poster for *Ujala* (d. K. M. Multani, pc. Taj Mahal Pictures, 1942) (author's collection)

archal power structures but as women who chose a lifestyle that resisted conventional institutions like marriage in favor of financial independence. It is noteworthy that in the nineteenth century, tawa'ifs were perhaps the only female professionals who owned property and paid taxes (Oldenburg 1990, 259). Given that the Nizam of Hyderabad was considered the "richest man in the world," it is significant that Shamshad rejected his patronage and embraced the film industry as a career for her daughter (*Time* 1937). In Shamshad Begum's lifetime the courtly system of patronage went through serious decline and a prescient few turned to new, urban avenues of sustenance such as the gramophone and radio industries (Farrell 1993). While the Nizam was an exception among this dying breed of feudal lords, cinema work presented a concrete option that could support a performer's aspirations for a lavish lifestyle and provide her a way out of dependence on capricious male support.

Financial gain was one of the main attractions that drew workers to the cinema industry and helped many men and women overlook the question of the profession's perceived reputation. Salaries of actresses were so high by contemporary standards that they became a matter of urban folklore. Readers would often write to magazines curious about individual pay packages. More than one actress, including Naseem Banu, claimed that her salary rivaled that of the governor of Bombay. Many of these declarations were designed to bolster the aura of luxury necessary for the star image. Nevertheless, judging from trade journals, autobiographies, and government surveys, it is evident that cinema acting was a highly lucrative profession for women. In 1942 the leading heroines of the day averaged an income of Rs. 2,000 to 3,000 per month (Judas 1942, 10). This was a time when a French chiffon saree cost Rs. 9, a brand new imported Studebaker cost Rs. 6,000, and an average salaried person made Rs. 200 per month (Kazim 2005, 145). More interesting was the fact that, at least until the 1940s, top-billed actresses were often drawing higher salaries than their male counterparts. Perplexed by this deviation from the social norm, a reader asks the editor of *Filmindia*,

Q: Why are actresses paid more than the actors?
A: Because the industry is run by men.
(September 1940, 16)

The editor's flippant reply nonetheless acknowledges the salary disparity as a fact. Since the silent days, the film actress was a symbol of cinema's glamour, with actresses like Patience Cooper and Zubeida ruling the marquee. Film advertisements of the 1930s and 1940s regularly gave heroines top billing. Film journalism depended on actresses whose color photographs adorned magazine covers and drove advertising revenues and sales (Shah 1950, 143). It was the actress, again, who had "the power of endorsement," and many leading cosmetics, toiletries, and textile manufacturers started to exploit the screen goddess's brand value in their advertisements (Shah 1950, 153). The industry may have been "run by men," but it was being powered by women.

Naseem Banu's decision to work in the film industry paid off. By 1941 she had acted in a series of successful big-budget historicals and social melodramas. She was also drawing a hefty salary. In an interview in January 1942, Naseem was quoted as not being "terribly anxious to get married but if she meets a good and attractive man she might consider changing her name" (Hyacinth 39). Not many women in those days had the luxury to make such a statement. The same interview went on to describe Naseem as "simple but extravagant," earning "over Rs. 2500 a month [meaning she] can well afford to buy real stones"; she "has over a thousand sarees and continues to buy more" (33). Such fairytale descriptions sold dreams of a high-end consumer lifestyle, but lest these luxuries be seen as obscene hedonism, the actress's economic superiority was validated through a nationalist work ethic: "Naseem works hard for her large salary and although she is exhausted after her work at the studio she still manages to fit in a daily three-hour dancing lesson" (33). Thus, the actress's life was presented as a mix of toil and consumerist pleasure. Such descriptions of an actress's private life offered her as an aspirational model for the modern woman. In a parallel with Devika Rani's career, images of global fashion and consumption, a frisson of risk, and cosmopolitan lifestyles became crucial aspects of the star image and the dispersed pleasures of cinema. The scandal involving Prince Moazam Jah was casually dismissed by Naseem Banu at the time. She is reported as saying: "I don't care very much what they write about me. I'm sure my fans will not believe anything so horrible" (Hyacinth 1942, 33). Even if they did, the incident was so wildly romantic, involving Nizams and princes in an age of mass picketing and secretarial pools, that it is likely to have added to Naseem's otherworldly appeal.

Naseem's career trajectory highlights how the old-world courtesan lifestyle informed the industry by creating a unique work culture. As noted, this was a strictly female lineage, which understood the value of individualized star auras long before stardom was perceived as an essential part of cinema's industrial mechanisms. The courtesan background also complicated prevalent notions of respectability, since the tawa'if bridged the domains of high culture and social stigmatization. The film actress similarly generated mixed responses from her publics, representing success and talent at the same time as sexual transgressiveness.

Scandal and disrepute attempt to censor transgressive behavior, but they also help circulate defiant imaginations and acts. Be it Devika Rani or Naseem Banu, we see a typically ambivalent fan response to the Bombay actress, delighting in gossiping about star affairs while also awed by the actress's wealth, refinement and sophistication. This was a time when fans, across sexes, frequently wrote to magazines asking direct and practical questions about an actress's salary, the route to a career as an actress, even retirement ages (*Filmindia* 1942–1946). By 1946 "college educated" girls were sending in "Jobs Wanted" advertisements to film magazines, a practice hitherto restricted to male aspirants and thus indicating the newfound social acceptance of acting as a career for women (see *Filmindia* August 1946, 47). These examples suggest that alongside onscreen fantasies of freedom and mobility, the film industry and its employees also materially influenced the cityscape. Audiences were watching and consuming and desiring not just stars but new urban lifestyles.

Scandal narratives, as layers of discursivity, help interpret a crucial juncture in Bombay's urban and cinematic history. At the same time, such relative discursive fecundity is available to researchers only in the case of stars. While actresses represent the most visible face of early talkie cinema, almost all other female work roles remain obscured, due both to industrial factors (such as the lack of rationalized work structures and uncredited labor) and to historiographic reasons (such as the archival marginalization of women's work). Other methods and sources will need exploration in order to approach histories of Muslim women director-producers like Jaddan Bai, anonymous Anglo-Indian "extras" and background dancers, European makeup artistes like Madame Andree, and Parsee screenwriters like Frene Talyarkhan. Nevertheless, the specific case studies of actresses in this chapter illuminate aspects of the work environment in the Bombay studio that would have formed the context for all female film practitioners.

Multiple marginal identities lingered and thrived among Bombay's galaxy of film stars well into the late 1940s. Both Devika Rani and Naseem Banu negotiated cinematic modernity using the skills of their communities and individual genealogies while also resisting community conventions. The modern urban woman similarly used a variety of strategies to negotiate spaces within and alongside frameworks of capitalism, patriarchy, and nationalism. By taking nontraditional sources like scandal narratives seriously, the film historian is able to follow tangential leads that suggest untold and peculiarly local contestations of gender and modernity. We are reminded that a direct application of theories of Western modernity is likely to miss the spectrum of modernities wrought within South Asia's historical, cultural, social, and political specificities. We are also able to reclaim stories of women as active historical agents and participants in the dream of the cinematic modern.

Notes

A section of this chapter appeared in "Notes on a Scandal: Writing Women's Film History against an Absent Archive," *BioScope: South Asian Screen Studies* 4, no. 1 (2013): 9–30. I would like to thank Ranjani Mazumdar, Christine Gledhill, and Ravi Vasudevan for their close readings of and comments on the earliest draft versions. Many thanks also to Sabeena Gadihoke, Ira Bhaskar, Shohini Ghosh and Geeta Patel for their insightful observations at a presentation organized by the American Institute of Indian Studies at IIC, New Delhi (July 2013).

1. With overt titles like *Miss 1933* (Chandulal Shah, 1933), *Indira M.A.* (Nandlal Jasvantlal, 1934), *Shaher ka Jadoo/ Lure of the City* (K.P. Ghose, 1934), *College Girl* (Jayant Desai, 1935), *Dr. Madhurika or Modern Wife* (Sarvottam Badami, 1935), *Madam Fashion* (Jaddan Bai, 1936), and *Educated Actress* (Imperial, 1938), these films tackled the advantages as well as fallouts of a swiftly modernizing city with its attendant sociocultural transformations.

2. A number of British publications, including the *The Star, The Observer, The Lady, Daily Dispatch,* and *Birmingham Post* eulogized Devika Rani's performance in the English-language *Karma* (J. L. Freer-Hunt, 1933). The *Morning Post* said, "Without the slightest doubt . . . the leading actress is one of the greatest stars that the talk-films have yet produced" (see Malik 1958, 37).

3. Najmul Hussain, on the other hand, was forced to quit the Bombay film industry altogether and starred in a handful of movies in Calcutta and Lahore, even changing his screen name to the brief "Najam."

References

Ahmed, Nazir. 1933. "My Impression of Miss Kajjan." *Cinema* (November): 22–23.
An Admirer. 1939. "Devika—Darling of the Indian Screen." *Mirror* (June 11): page nos. missing.
Bhaumik, Kaushik. 2001. "The Emergence of the Bombay Film Industry." PhD diss., Oxford University.
Cinema Annual. 1933. "Short Life Sketch of Devaki Rani [sic]," 36.

Cinema. 1939. "Beware of These Screen Nymphs." December, pp. 25–28.

Devi, Chandravati. 1993. "What I Actually Think of the Screen." In *Indian Cinema: Contemporary Perceptions from the Thirties*, edited by Samik Bandopadhyay, 103–5. Jamshedpur: Celluloid Chapter. Originally published in *Filmland* 1931.

Devi, Sabita. 1993. "Why Shouldn't Respectable Ladies Join the Films?" In *Indian Cinema: Contemporary Perceptions from the Thirties*, edited by Samik Bandopadhyay, 111–14. Jamshedpur: Celluloid Chapter. Originally published in *Filmland* 1931.

Farrell, Gerry. 1993. "The Early Days of the Gramophone Industry in India: Historical, Social and Musical Perspectives." *British Journal of Ethnomusicology* 2:31–53.

Gooptu, Sharmistha. 2010. *Bengali Cinema: An Other Nation*. New Delhi: Roli.

Hyacinth. 1942. "Naseem Thinks Shantaram Wonderful!" *Filmindia* (January), 31–39.

Judas. 1938. "Bombay Calling." *Filmindia* (February), 9–14.

———. 1942. "Bombay Calling." *Filmindia* (January), 9–11.

Kak, Siddharth. 1980. "The Colossus and the Little Flower from India." *Cinema Vision* (April), 70–73.

Kamala. 1936. "Letters from Kamala." *Filmindia* (May), 22, 28.

Kazim, Lubna. 2005. *A Woman of Substance: The Memoirs of Begum Khurshid Mirza, 1918–1989*. New Delhi: Zubaan.

Mahanty, Prabha. 1945. *Filmindia* (January), 14.

Majumdar, Neepa. 2009. *Wanted Cultured Ladies Only! Female Stardom and Cinema in India, 1930s–1950s*. Urbana: University of Illinois Press.

Malik, Amita. 1958. "Padma Shri Devika Rani: An Interview with the First Lady of the Indian Screen." *Filmfare* (March), 33–43.

Manto, Saadat Hasan. 2008. "Ashok Kumar: The Evergreen Hero," "Naseem: The Fairy Queen," "A Woman for All Seasons." In *Bitter Fruit*, translated and edited by Khalid Hasan, 447–60, 594–606, 270–78. New Delhi: Penguin.

Narayan, N. 1977. *Filmfare* (November 11), 42–47.

Oldenburg, Veena. 1990. "Lifestyle as Resistance: The Case of the Courtesans of Lucknow." *Feminist Studies* 16 (2): 259–87.

Pal, Colin. 2004. *Shooting Stars*. Mumbai: Screenworld.

"Pictophone." 1933. "Naughty Sabita Revealed." *Cinema* (June), 19–21.

Ramamurthy, Priti. 2006. "The Modern Girl in India in the Interwar Years: Interracial Intimacies, International Competition and Historical Eclipsing." *Women's Studies Quarterly* 34 (Spring–Summer): 197–226.

Shah, Panna. 1950. *The Indian Film*. Bombay: Motion Picture Society of India.

Sunita. 1939. "Morality and Films." *Mirror* (May 14), 7.

Surinarayanan, T. G. 1939. *Filmindia* (May), 35.

Time. 1937. "Hyderabad: Silver Jubilee Durbar." February 22. Available at http://content.time.com/time/magazine/article/0,9171,770599,00.html (accessed June 6, 2013).

Valicha, Kishore. 1996. *Dadamoni: The Authorized Biography of Ashok Kumar*. New Delhi: Viking.

CHAPTER 2

Reading between the Lines

History and the Studio Owner's Wife

MICHELE LEIGH

As a historian of early cinema, one of my favorite courses to teach is a graduate-level class titled Historical Research Methods. Students come to the class not quite sure what to expect and without a clear understanding of how history will serve their research agendas; in other words, they don't see themselves as historians of film or television. After reassuring them that we are all historians, I often compare the labor involved in historical research to the work done by those now-famous television crime scene investigators. As in the television shows, rarely does one find a history/case where all the clues are readily available and the subject/criminal is waiting to tell his or her story.

More often than not, the work of the historian/CSI involves hunting down clues, some obvious, some obscure, and some that lead nowhere. The historian/CSI soon learns that sometimes it is the seemingly small or insignificant bits of information that shed light on or unravel the mystery. The clues, of course, when they are found, do not of themselves make up a road map; they require careful and sometimes ingenious piecing together until the full picture can be seen. Martha Howell and Walter Prevenier (2001) call this the "central paradox" of our profession, commenting further that "historians are prisoners of sources that can never be made fully reliable, but if they are skilled readers of sources and always mindful of their captivity, they can make their sources yield meaningful stories about the past and our relationship to it" (3). By emphasizing that historians piece together information to create meaningful stories, Howell and Prevenier inadvertently point out how the historian (especially the film historian) and the CSI are primarily different: the result.

The CSI is looking for a logical connection between the clues that will reveal THE answer as to who committed the crime. The historian, on the other hand, realizes that sometimes the puzzle is not solved, that the stories created, while meaningful, cannot be complete. As investigators we are held captive, not only by our "never fully reliable" sources but also by the seeming lack of sources. This is especially true for historians working to uncover details about women working in the film industry during the silent era. Film scholar Radha Vatsal (2002) notes that, as many of us know, not only are the films made by women in the silent era difficult and often impossible to see, but, perhaps more important, the "textual documentation [of their work] is extremely idiosyncratic," as it was not common for women to receive proper credit in title sequences that were, in any case, inconsistent as to roles acknowledged, whether by men or women (120). Vatsal's article is in essence a call to action; she asks us as historians to embrace the uncertainty and instability of the industry itself—and by extension, its documentation—and to foreground this as part of our research.

In some national contexts this means that uncertainty and idiosyncrasy are all the historian has to work with. Such is the case in Russia, where the fledgling cinema, which began in 1908, was just gaining a foothold as a new art form when the country was plunged into a world war and a revolution; documents, if they existed in the first place, were either destroyed by war and ignorance or were squirreled away in special collections and deemed dangerous because of their bourgeois associations. What researching Russian cinema from 1908 to 1917 has taught me is that sometimes histories must be pieced together and told, not through a chain of primary sources and personal documents but rather through a mindful attention to a series of asides and offhand comments.

My interest in early Russian cinema and the A. Khanzhonkov and Company film studio began in graduate school with three casual comments made by my professor, Yuri Tsivian: that while male actors in prerevolutionary Russian cinema were relatively interchangeable, the actresses were the real stars; that Khanzhonkov's studio had more famous actresses than any other pre-1917 studio in Russia; and that Evgenii Bauer was often referred to as the "woman's director." I am grateful for this course for several reasons: it piqued and solidified my interest in early Russian cinema, but it also taught me the importance of the offhand remark, the comment made as an interesting aside but perhaps not the focus of discussion. I realized that sometimes the most interesting and fruitful research may be sparked by those less-than-significant comments, by the space found between the lines of discussion. Thus began the research and thinking that led to my project exploring the significance of Evgenii Bauer's role as a women's director.

While captive to sources for Bauer and perusing *Silent Witnesses* (Usai et al. 1989) in search of his extant films among the credits for the Khanzhonkov studio, I came across names of several women who worked there not only as actresses but also as screenwriters, editors, and even directors. Regardless of this fascinating discovery, I put the information aside to focus on writing about Bauer. With that out of the way, I was finally able to return to these women, among them Zoia Barantsevich, Vera Popova, Olga Rakhmanova, and Antonina Khanzhonkova, who have become the foundation of my research on female industrial practice in early Russian cinema.

Of these women, one in particular stands out as exemplifying the caprices and idiosyncrasies of conducting research in the silent era, and she is Antonina Khanzhonkova, the first wife of studio owner Alexander Khanzhonkov.[1] I first realized that Antonina was more than the studio owner's wife through Tsivian's comment during my class that Khanzhonkov and his wife frequently worked together to write scenarios. At the time, I thought it interesting and mentally filed it away for possible use later. Then while conducting my research on Bauer I found among his directorial credits a 1917 entry that listed Antonina Khanzhonkova as one of the editors for the film *Nabat* (The Alarm) (Usai et al. 1989, 410).[2] I became very curious as to how the wife of the studio owner came to edit a film by one of the studio's leading directors, but again I put the information aside.

Later, in an attempt to learn more about women working as screenwriters, directors, and editors in the early years of the Russian film industry and, more particularly, to find information about Antonina Nikolaevna Khanzhonkova, I began looking to see what other scholars had uncovered about her. What I found, or rather didn't find, led me to understand further that sometimes historians must pursue offhand comments that seem initially to lead nowhere. What follows records my somewhat meandering journey through various historical texts and sources, all in an attempt to flesh out the details of this woman who piqued my curiosity.

After searching for entries (in English and in Russian) on Antonina Khanzhonkova in books on silent cinema, in histories of Russian and Soviet cinema, and, in case new archival materials might have surfaced, on the internet, I was able to piece together a few basic biographical details. I then searched Antonina's husband's autobiography in an attempt to corroborate what I learned about her (this too proved futile, but more about that later). She was born Antonina Nikolaevna Batorovskaia in the Rostov region, an area of Russia bordering eastern Ukraine. Her father apparently owned a shop that sold Singer sewing machines.

She married Alexander Alekseivich Khanzhonkov sometime between 1898 and 1900, and they had two children, Nikolai and Nina (Orlova 2007, 16–17).[3] She died some time between 1922 and 1923, most likely in Germany while the Khanzhonkov family was in exile after the Revolution. In 1922 Alexander was invited to return to Moscow to work in the fledgling Soviet film industry; he accepted the offer and Antonina chose to stay in Germany.[4] This information is compiled from a variety of sources, ranging from Soviet-era histories and memoirs to a film festival program and contemporary histories of Russian and Soviet film (all listed in the references herewith). When she is mentioned, it is more often than not as the wife of Alexander Khanzhonkov, with a few exceptions outlined below. Not one of these sources, even her own husband's memoir, refers to Antonina as a filmmaker in her own right. In fact, most recent histories do not mention her at all, let alone attribute any agency to her in helping to shape the Russian film industry.

Rather than giving up under the assumption that Antonina's possible editorship of *The Alarm* was an anomaly, the CSI in me kicked into gear. No one source was able to provide a decent account of her life or her hypothetical film career; but this preliminary scouring of histories of Russian cinema made me particularly curious as to why past and current texts have relegated her to the periphery of history. For, by piecing together various scraps of information and casual asides, one begins to suspect she played a larger role than any one source gives her credit for.

One of my first encounters with a cursory mention of Antonina was in Jay Leyda's seminal text on Russian cinema, *Kino: A History of Russian and Soviet Film* (1973). For an English-speaking scholar of Russian cinema, this is often one of the first places to consult as grounding for research. In his discussion of prerevolutionary Russian cinema, Leyda mentioned Antonina only once, in passing, noting that in the early 1910s both the Pathé and Khanzhonkov companies were competing to see which studio could sign screenwriting contracts with the largest number of great literary figures. For both companies, this was a concerted effort to increase their respective prestige and to draw in audiences familiar with popular literature (57). According to Leyda, "Khanzhonkov signed contracts with Arkadi Averchenko, Osip Dymov, Fyodor Sologub, Amfiteatrov, Chirikov, Alexander Kuprin and Leonid Andreyev—but it soon appeared that the majority of these were to contribute no more than their names, for, as Mr. Dymov has said, Madame Khanzhonkova did all the real scenario work" (57–58). What appears as a throwaway comment turns into a significant piece of information. In other words, in addition to her role as wife of the studio owner, Antonina Khanzhonkova may have significantly contributed to the studio's production roster by ghostwriting the scenarios for popular male authors. For the historian/CSI this is an exciting lead, but also a dangerous one. We can now compile a list of films supposedly penned by popular authors, which may in fact have been penned by Antonina. The danger comes, of course, in the verification process; without corroborating evidence it may be difficult to say definitively that she in fact was the actual screenwriter.

Another reference to her possible writing career was found on the Web site *Chastnyi Korrespondent* (Private Correspondent) in a short biographical piece on Alexander Khanzhonkov by Maxim Medvedev (2011), who notes, again as an aside, that "one of Khanzhonkov's best known companions was his wife who was especially strong-willed and enterprising. She was busy with the organization of the company and she wrote together with her husband under the pseudonym Antalek; they wrote scenarios and made films."[5] So in addition to ghostwriting for popular authors, a fact that is tough to corroborate, the pseudonym Antalek—a portmanteau of their two names: Ant(onina) plus Alek(sander)—credits Antonina as co-scriptwriter with her husband. It turns out that there are at least two films (non-extant) directed by Evgenii Bauer, *Irina Kirsanova* (1915) and *Iamshchik, ne goni loshadei* (Stagecoach Driver, Don't Rush the Horse) (1916), with scenarios credited to Antalek. Interestingly, the pseudonym is not arranged alphabetically, and so Antonina gets first billing, perhaps alluding to her larger role in the partnership. One other issue raised by this article but frustratingly not elaborated is the mention of Antonina's being busy with the organization of the company, thereby implying that her role as writer was just one of the many she played for Khanzhonkov and Company.[6] The reference also implies that she had some power within the company if she was involved in its organizational structure, meaning she may have exercised significant influence in the production of the company's films, a very intriguing clue.

Another clue as to the extent of Antonina's involvement in the fledgling film industry can be found in S. Ginzburg's 1963 history, *Kinematografiia dorevoliutsionnio rossii* (Cinema of Prerevolutionary Russia). Ginzburg (1963) mentions Antonina only once in passing, in regard to a collective of filmmakers who hoped to create a permanent governing body for entrepreneurs in the film industry. This group was composed of:

> V. Akhramovich-Ashmarin (a worker for A. Khanzhonkov), Agranovich (from the Society of Filmworkers), M. Brailovskii (film critic), V. Viskovskii and N. Turkin (from the Union of Workers of Artistic Cinema, "SRKhK"), A. N. Khanzhonkova, editor and publisher of "Sine Fono," S. Lur'e, M. Trofimov (the owner of the film studio "Rus'"), P. Antik (industrialist and theater owner), theater owner Shlezinger, distributors Khapsaev, Kerre and Shchigel'skii. (332)

There is no further mention of Antonina N. Khanzhonkova or her involvement in the group; however, her inclusion brings up some interesting points. First and foremost, she is the only woman included in the group. While we know that other women were making films during this period, her involvement in the group is possibly a testament to the influence and power she may have held within the industry. Second, she is the only person listed who is not qualified in some way by what work she/he does or what business she/he owns. On the one hand, this marks her as not having one identifiable job within the industry or not owning a film-related business. On the other hand, perhaps she needed no further qualification. Finally, this text was published in the Soviet period under Khrushchev, when all things prerevolutionary were taboo and one had to tread carefully. The fact that she is mentioned at all is a testament to the fact that she was more than she seemed to be. It would have been easy, if not advantageous, to ignore the bourgeois wife of a bourgeois businessman, especially one who emigrated after the Revolution and never returned. This suggests that perhaps among these male power players she was well known and her opinions respected. Not to mention the fact that, as one of the two representatives from Khanzhonkov and Company and the wife of Alexander Khanzhonkov, Antonina perhaps held the most decision-making power.

Antonina's involvement in decision-making within the Khanzhonkov film studio is corroborated in a series of casual remarks by two people working in the Russian film industry at the time, Zoia Barantsevich and Alexander Khanzhonkov himself. While conducting research on film actress-cum-screenwriter, Zoia Barantsevich, I came across in her autobiographical musings "Liudy i vstrechi v kino" (People and Acquaintances in Film) a brief remark about Antonina Khanzhonkova (in Barantsevich 1965). The first time Zoia met Antonina was when Zoia was invited to sign her contract with Khanzhonkov and Company film studio, not at the studio offices but rather at the home of the owner, Alexander Khanzhonkov. Zoia notes: "When I went there, I was pleased to meet a tall, beautiful brunette dressed in black, with a very energetic appearance and pleasant high voice—this was Antonina Nikolaevna Khanzhonkova" (158). Holding this first meeting at their private residence with Antonina present probably put a very young actress at ease, therefore making it easier to get the eighteen-year-old Zoia to sign a three-year, exclusive contract. While this reference does not overtly speak to Antonina's role in the company, it does imply that Khanzhonkov saw no need to keep his business dealings separate from his home life and his wife. A further implication is that perhaps meeting at the residence made it easier for his wife to participate in the decision-making process while at the same time caring for their two children.

Alexander Khanzhonkov himself also briefly mentions his wife Antonina's involvement in the company in his memoirs, *Pervye gody russkoi Kinematografii* (The First Years of the Russian Cinematograf) (1937). Unfortunately, his comments, too, are nothing but an aside in his account of his own role in Russian film history; Antonina is randomly mentioned twice and never addressed again. These comments serve to titillate as well as frustrate by both acknowledging her importance to the company and burying that importance with claims about the great accomplishments of the men who worked for Khanzhonkov and Company. Khanzhonkov noted that his wife was "elected to the board of members, but not because she was the person closest to me. In the opinions of all our employees, she was an active worker in our firm, she knew the work well, having participated in all stages (of film production)" (64). Antonina, it seems, served on the board of directors for Khanzhonkov and Company. Her election to the board speaks volumes about the level of her involvement in her husband's company and the value that his employees placed on her opinions. Yet Khanzhonkov felt it necessary to qualify her involvement, reassuring posterity that she was not chosen to be a board member just because she was his wife: she actually had extensive knowledge of the business.

Khanzhonkov elaborates briefly on Antonina's involvement in the company, providing some details about her abilities and explaining what he means by her "participation" in all stages of production:

> She especially brought her artistic influence to the process and worked with enthusiasm, developing scripts with directors and ensuring the correctness of the filming and so on. . . . She was indispensable, since I was buried under the commercial and organizational side of the business and had to frequently travel around Russia and abroad. (64)

Despite the brevity of these two comments, Khanzhonkov proves himself invaluable, since he corroborates almost all the information I gleaned from other sources. He reinforces Antonina's role as writer and basically implies that she oversaw all film productions for the company. In other words, while her husband was occupied with the commercial side of the business, Antonina controlled the creative side. Khanzhonkov's business acumen was legendary, and by the early 1910s he had built one of the most successful film companies in Russia. While he downplays Antonina's role—he was busy and she was not, so she was able to help out—being the business person he was, he would not have left her as the de facto head of production of his lucrative production company had he not trusted and valued her creative decision-making skills. Additionally, one issue that Khanzhonkov's comments seem to gloss over is that his successful venture, while vertically integrated—meaning the company not only produced films, it also distributed and exhibited films (its own and other companies')—relied on the quality and success of its films on the big screen. Khanzhonkov himself would not have been quite so busy if his wife were not so successful at running the creative side of the business.

So while I hoped that Khanzhonkov's memoirs would prove a gold mine of information and perhaps provide insight into the mystery that is Antonina Khanzhonkova, I was not so lucky. He did corroborate much of the information I had deduced from other sources, but he also left me with more questions. The above-mentioned citations are just the beginning and in no way exhaust the search for details about Antonina's role within the Russian film industry. Not referenced are the numerous texts, both old and new, that do not mention her at all when discussing the prerevolutionary period in Russian film history, most notably works published within the last twenty years by film scholars/historians such as Birgit Beumers, Yuri Tsivian, and Denise Youngblood. This is not to discredit these scholars, as each has made immeasurable contributions to the field of Russian and Soviet film history; instead, it is a reminder of the fact that there is still much to do to recuperate Antonina's and other women's labor in early Russian cinema.

The scarcity of information about Antonina and other female film workers is both infuriating, though par for the course in silent-cinema research, and intriguing. Conducting research on the silent era in general is often an exercise in frustration, caused in part by a lack of respect at the time for this budding form of mass entertainment, by inconsistent recordkeeping, and, of course, by destruction of records during various wars. These issues are compounded when one attempts to uncover details about women working in the industry, many of whom worked behind the scenes. This includes women like Zoia Barantsevich and Olga Rakhmanova, who began their careers as actresses and then transitioned to other roles in the industry. Their work behind the camera is often forgotten or pushed to the periphery in favor of their more visible and therefore verifiable work in front of the camera. Occasionally, the behind-the-scenes work was done by women who chose to avoid the limelight, women like Vera Popova, whose work as editor for director Evgenii Bauer remains largely uncredited. And finally, work by women like Antonina Khanzhonkova and Elizaveta Vladimirovna Theimann,[7] whose work was quite literally pushed behind the scenes, subsumed by their more famous/more vocal husbands or partners. This situation, of course, is not singular to Russia; it is a common occurrence in other countries as well, that women's work gets lost or hidden behind the work of a male protégé.[8] What interests me most in this respect is how one goes about indentifying the level of female agency in an industry and a history that was and is dominated by men.

As a historian interested in the elusive female industrial worker in the silent era, I myself embrace my inner crime scene investigator. The crimes in question revolve around: women not receiving the acknowledgements and credits for their labor; men unjustly being given or taking credit for the work of their female counterparts; and historians unwittingly or willfully perpetuating the crime by repeating the suppression of women's contributions to the industry. Very rarely in silent cinema research does one find a source or archive that provides all the necessary information for reconstructing the crime/history. More frequently, we are required to don the white gloves, figuratively and literally, as we get dirty in dusty archives, mired in our sources that are never as neat and succinct as we would like them to be. This is part of the "central paradox" discussed by Howell and Prevenier in the passage I quoted earlier; the historian and CSI are often held prisoners by the sources/clues that "can never be made fully reliable" on their own. It is only through careful/skilled/scientific reading of the clues that we are able to free ourselves from their hold on us in order to piece together meaningful histories/recountings of the crimes in question. We, historians/CSI, must embrace the unconventional sources—the asides, the off-hand comments, and even the omissions—because sometimes they provide us with important clues. Sometimes what is left out of a history provides us with insight into not only the historian but also the moment in which the history was written, which in turn helps to explain the omission. Seen separately, then, these details often appear insignificant. However, when taken together, as in the example of Antonina Khanzhonkova, they paint a more complete and visible picture of the woman Russian film history left—and still leaves (?)—in the periphery.

I am reminded again of Radha Vatsal (2002), when she asks scholars to utilize the footnote as a means of recording and sharing the idiosyncrasies, the red herrings, and even the dead ends of silent-cinema research; for as she suggests, your red herring may be the linchpin to my meaningful history (120–40). As a researcher and educator, I couldn't agree with her more. To expand the CSI analogy, each crime/history is not solved by one person alone. It sometimes takes a constellation of experts in different fields, from different moments in time and with different theoretical perspectives, piecing together their clues, in order to recreate a history that has yet to be written. Let the case of Antonina Khanzhonkova—wife, mother, welcoming face, ghostwriter, representative of the film industry, board member, line producer, creative director and head of production—be our inspiration.

Notes

1. Alexander Khanzhonkov was married twice, first to Antonina Nikolaevna and then later, in 1923, to Vera Popova, one of his former film editors.

2. The citation notes that the film was re-edited by Antonina Khanzhonkova and Vera Popova. There is currently no evidence to suggest that Antonina worked as an editor; however, Alexander Khanzhonkov's second wife, Vera Popova, edited almost every film made by Evgenii Bauer. Despite that fact, this is one of the only films for which Antonina is given credit—but that is part of my larger research project.

3. The Khanzhonkovs' granddaughter, Nina Orlova, published a book titled *A Life Dedicated to Cinema*, intended to highlight the greatness of Alexander's career, and, as such, some of the details about Antonina are a little vague. For instance, the year of their marriage is my estimate based on details provided by Orlova. During his military service Khanzhonkov was promoted in 1897, then served four years in the capital as an officer. At some point during this time he met, courted for six months, and then married Antonina; their son was born one year later and their daughter was born after another five years.

4. Currently this is the end of the trail for information about Antonina's life.

5. (My translation.) Ironically, the article mentions how little is known about Alexander Khanzhonkov and the difficulty of finding archival materials. Unfortunately, it does not directly cite any of its sources, though it does mention that Khanzhonkovs' granddaughter, Irina Alexandrovna Orlova, cobbled together memoirs from a variety of sources to make her documentary *Slave of Love*, about her grandfather's contribution to Russian film history. I have not yet managed to track down the film.

6. While not cited, this little tidbit was probably deduced from Khanzhonkov's own memoir, which I will discuss in more detail later on.

7. Elizaveta Theimann was the wife of studio owner Pavel Theimann of Theimann and Reinhardt, and like Antonina, she too managed the creative side of her husband's production company (Youngblood 1999, 29).

8. A case in point is Jill Nelmes's work on the screenwriting team of Muriel and Sydney Box, presented at the 2011 Doing Women's Film History conference, University of Sunderland, UK.

References

Barantsevich, Zoia. 1965. "Liudy i vstrechi v kino" (People and Acquaintances in Film). *Kino i vremia; Biulleten* (Film and Time: Bulletin) 4:153–62.

Beumers, Birgit. 2009. *A History of Russian Cinema*. Oxford: Berg.

ETVnet. "Aleksander Khanzhonkov: Rab kinematografa v sadu raskhodiashchikhsia tropok" (The Slave to the Cinematografin the Garden of Forking Paths). Available at http://etvnet.com/blog/aleksandr-hanzhonkov-rab-kinematografa-v-sadu-rashodyaschihsya-tropok/717 (accessed March 10, 2011).

Ginzburg, S. 1963. *Kinematografiia dorevoliutsionnoi rossii* (Cinema of Prerevolutionary Russia). Moscow: Iskusstvo.

Howell, Martha, and Walter Prevenier. 2001. *From Reliable Sources: An Introduction to Historical Methods*. Ithaca, N.Y.: Cornell University Press.

Khanzhonkov, Alexander. 1937. *Pervye gody russkoi Kinematografii* (The First Years of the Russian Cinematograf). Moscow: Iskusstvo.

Leyda, Jay. 1973. *Kino: A History of Russian and Soviet Film*. Princeton, N.J.: Princeton University Press.

Medvedev, Maksim. "Aleksander Khanzhonkov: Rab kinematografa v sadu raskhodiashchikhsia tropok" (The Slave to the Cinematograf in the Garden of Forking Paths). Available at http://www.chaskor.ru/article/aleksandr_hanzhonkov_rab_kinematografa_v_sadu _rashodyashchihsya_tropok_19002 (accessed March 10, 2011).

Orlova, Irina. 2007. *A Life Dedicated to Cinema*. Donetsk: TOV "VPP Promin."

Tsivian, Yuri. 1994. *Early Russian Cinema in Russia and Its Cultural Reception*. London: Routledge.

Usai, Paolo Cherchi, Lorenzo Codelli, Carlo Montanaro, and David Robinson, eds. 1989. *Silent Witnesses: Russian Films 1908–1919/Testimoni Silenziosi: Film Russi 1908–1919*. Research and coordination by Yuri Tsivian. London: BFI/ Pordenone: Edizioni Biblioteca dell'Immagine.

Vatsal, Radha. 2002. "Re-evaluating the Footnote: Women Directors of the Silent Era." In *A Feminist Reader in Early Cinema*, edited by Jennifer Bean and Diane Negra, 119–40. Durham, N.C.: Duke University Press.

Youngblood, Denise J. 1999. *The Magic Mirror: Moviemaking in Russia, 1908–1918*. Madison: University of Wisconsin Press.

CHAPTER 3

Imagining Women at the Movies

Male Writers and Early Film Culture in Istanbul

CANAN BALAN

Cinema-going as a public experience began as early as December 1896 in the Ottoman capital.[1] The initial public *cinematographe* shows were organized by a French painter, Henri Delavalle, and shortly after, the shows became a regular part of the spectacle of modernity in Istanbul at the turn of the twentieth century. Sources such as newspaper reviews, consulate reports, trade records, memoirs, and novels written from the 1890s to the late 1930s reveal a changing culture of spectatorship. This occurred concomitantly with the sociopolitical transition from the declining Ottoman Empire to the rise of the Turkish nation-state. During this period, Turkish society endured a defeat in World War I and the occupation of Istanbul and other big cities; the rise of nationalism and a war of independence; the foundation of the Turkish Republic along with new lifestyles and cultural practices. One of the most significant social shifts was the increasing public visibility of women. Arguably, it was the resulting change in gender politics that triggered the new anxieties we find creative writers projecting onto the activity of filmgoing.[2]

In this chapter, I focus on the construction by male writers of cinema-going women in early twentieth-century and postwar Istanbul. My main intention is to analyze gendered concerns about spectatorship emerging in the patriarchal imagination of that time. Thus the reactions I investigate are not the recorded responses of actual women in the audience; rather, they represent literary versions of young female spectators, written in the 1920s and 1930s. Novels—for example, by Peyami Safa (in particular *Sözde Kızlar*) and Mehmet Rauf (*Genç Kız Kalbi*)—offered troubling depictions of films as hostile cultural products and as a result provoked further anxiety about their influence on the morals of the young. These concerns may be traced not only in novels but also in newspaper reviews by the quasi-liberal journalist Sermet Muhtar Alus; in a short story by Fahri Celal Göktulga; and in the mid-1930s poetry of Nâzım Hikmet, who viewed American cinema as objectifying the female body and harming heteronormative relationships in Turkey. These sources explicitly or implicitly reveal a nationalistic and patriarchal attitude toward the films of the Great Powers (mostly French and Italian productions) while in the context of an occupied Ottoman Empire in decline embodying a problematic relationship to gender. The reception of early cinema in Turkey can be examined through a variety of other sources, of course. However, novels, poems, and newspaper reviews enable us to understand the cultural status of cinema among the Ottoman/Turkish intelligentsia and the gender politics surrounding it.[3]

The Film Market in Post–World-War I Istanbul

Following the first public cinematograph show in the Ottoman capital on December 11, 1896,[4] film shows took place in circuses, coffeehouses, and beer halls until the early movie theaters were established in the mid-1900s. Early Turkish films were made mainly in support of and by the Ottoman army.[5] However, European films—in particular German and Austrian films before and during the initial years of World War I, and French and Italian in its later years—attracted large audiences in the city. Film shows also occurred in other big cities such as Thessaloniki, Beirut, Damascus, İzmir, and Amasya, yet Istanbul remained the hub of the global film market for the Ottoman Empire.[6]

Soon after occupying Istanbul at the end of World War I, the Entente Armies ordered the Ministry of Internal Affairs to ban films from Germany, Austria, Hungary, and Bulgaria (Özuyar 2007, 28). The same year, the Turkish *Mürebbiye* (Ahmet Fehim 1919), which was considered a resistance film, was censored for its negative representation of French women. Turkish filmmaker Cemil Filmer recalls the difficulties he experienced when making films for the National Army Film Center. Once, he was sent to shoot a public speech given by Halide Edip Adivar (a female novelist and nationalist) against the Occupation forces, yet he had to hide his camera while filming because the British Army banned any recordings (Filmer 1984, 100). A few months after this incident, the National Army Film Center, the only remaining film production company in the country after the war, was also abolished by the Entente Forces. Yet by hiding their equipment the manager of the center and his crew managed to found another company. Such constraints during the occupation not only included the scrutiny of films but also of movie theaters. The movie theater that Fuat Uzkinay and other veterans had been running on the Asian side of the city was shut down by the Entente Forces (Filmer 1984, 107).[7] Afterward, Cemil Filmer recalls, he could not find a job even as a projectionist, since most theater owners were short of funding (108).

Female Spectators Depicted by Male Authors

Under these circumstances, the Turkish people were largely consumers of cinema, exposed to films by the occupation countries, particularly Italian melodramas and the diva and vamp films that became popular during the Great War. Most penmen in this period saw their audiences as female. While it is possible to find depictions of cinema as metaphors for mental processes or for colonialism (Altuğ and Balan 2015), more striking is the particular moralistic attention given to cinema's negative influence on women.

Diva and vamp films also foreground the popularity of film stars. Novels and stories of the 1920s and 1930s emphasize identification with Italian divas as sources of attraction for Turkish/Ottoman women. Before delving into such creative fictions, it is worth noting the sarcastic depictions of Turkish fans of Pina Menichelli, Mary Bel, Gabrielle Robinne, Francesca Bertini, and Lyda Borelli in journalist Sermet Muhtar Alus's weekly column. He thought the most imitated was Menichelli (see figures 3.1 and 3.2): "Her fame was felt everywhere; all the young girls and ladies were copying her. If they adopted a lustful pose it would be Pinaesque; the décolleté would slip off one shoulder; immediately accompanied by hysterical gestures, mouth half open and eyes half closed" (Alus 2001, 64). There is a condescending tone here toward women, whom Alus thought lost their individuality by succumbing to the allure of film stars.

Fahri Celal Göktulga's short story *Pina Menikelli* (1921) exemplifies this depiction of Turkish/Ottoman audiences carried away by identification with film stars to the point of giving up their own identities. The story is centered on a love affair between a woman and a man who look and act just like Menichelli and Alberto Nepoti in *Tigre Reale* (Pastrone, Italy, 1916). As the story unfolds, we realize that resemblance goes beyond mere looks. The woman, as in *Tigre Reale*, has difficulties in committing to relationships due to her tragic past. The narrator, who is also the main male character, tells the reader that he succeeded in approaching the woman by following the film's example. Seeing her walking along the road while he was with another woman, he—like the hero in the film who spots Menichelli traveling alone—left his friend to chase after her. The story ends with the heroine

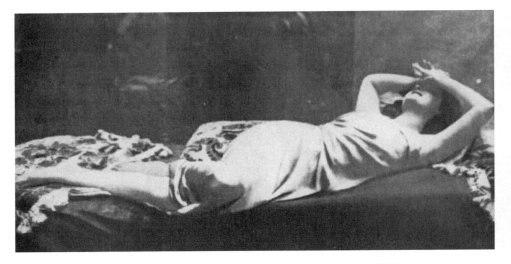

FIGURE 3.1. Pina Menichelli, in "lustful pose." *Tigre Reale* (1916)

FIGURE 3.2. Pina Menichelli's "hysterical gestures." *Tigre Reale* (1916)

resting her head on his shoulder as in the film's finale that unites the lovers. Both Alus and Göktulga view Menichelli as a figure significantly close to the hearts of Istanbul's women. However, while Alus devalues women's imitation of her looks, seeing this as a loss of authenticity and an opportunity for mockery, Göktulga's male narrator-hero seems not only to believe in the female character's melancholy attachment but also to be fascinated by the affinities between her and the star. In this respect, Göktulga addresses his readers' familiarity with Menichelli's films in a playful manner and bows to women's interest in her.

A second novel that deals with the fascination of Istanbul women with the Italian divas is *Sözde Kizlar* (The Would-Be Girls), written by Peyami Safa (2007). The story takes place in Istanbul in 1919 and seems far crueler than Göktulga's fiction in its depiction of the "corruption" of women by metropolitan life brought about by the end of World War I. Furthering the binary oppositions, "debauchery versus patriarchal values," "modern versus traditional," and "Entente Powers versus resistance," Safa sets romantic affairs and entertaining life depicted in films in opposition to traditional gender roles. One of the main antagonists, Behiç, is an upper-class, womanizing dandy and cynic who has previously traveled and lived in Western Europe and now tries to seduce a naïve young Anatolian girl, Mebrure. His ex-lover Belma, on the other hand, is a frivolous Istanbulite who adores Italian melodramas and aspires to be a film actress.

Mebrure, coming to Istanbul from her village to look for her lost father, a war veteran, moves into the house of her "decadent" cousins, Behiç and his fashion-queen sister, who the disapproving author depicts as inexorably preoccupied with the look of film stars. She tells Mebrure, "If I don't put the eye shadow on top of the eye liner it would not seem natural. All actresses use this style of make-up" (35). To criticize this obsession, the author sets this scene against a backdrop of war, occupation, and poverty.

Belma is another victim of glamour who suffers from moral troubles created by her desire to be an "artiste" and by her aspirations for a richer, more liberated life. At parties, Belma performs scenes from various films in order to demonstrate her talents. "She decided to be an actress even before she was an adolescent due to the influence of the movie halls in Şehzadebaşı. Since then she has performed monologues or copied famous actresses. Her *weakness* for cinema and film stars was so great that once she admitted that she could sacrifice anything to be an artiste" (50, my emphasis added). At one of these parties, in order to lighten the heavy atmosphere created by sad news about the war, Belma imitates a scene played by Lyda Borelli. But such an act is felt inappropriate by the novel's responsible and patriotic characters. Cinema in this context is reaffirmed as escapism from the spirit of a national struggle, which demands alert minds, undistracted by the fascination or influence of the movies. From the novel's moralistic perspective, Belma is turned into a "fallen woman" by the snobbish Behiç—who promises that he will introduce her to famous Viennese actresses—and by the "indecent" melodramas she adores. Even Belma's brother blames the film theaters in Şehzadebaşı (a district in Istanbul famous for early movie halls) for her troubles. Belma gives birth to an illegitimate child, an unacceptable act for a single woman who belongs to a modest, middle-class family. While attempting to save naïve Mebrure from the "dirty hands of Behiç," Belma pinpoints for us the role her passion for cinema has played in her downfall.

> I looked down on my family's humble way of life. I don't know why, maybe because of the films I saw . . . I had this dream of a glamorous future, which would be fulfilled by my becoming an actress! Becoming an actress! Oh, spectacular! An actress is so free, her life is full of amusement and comfort! If she can act in a film she can go to Paris, see America, make money, become a celebrity, everyone adores her, applauds her . . . perfect . . . perfect . . . that man Behiç told me about the actresses' lives in Vienna, he showed me their autographs and postcards in their own handwritings. (155)[8]

Behiç kills the illegitimate baby to hide Belma's sin from the bourgeois public of Istanbul. This leads her to commit suicide, for which Behiç is blamed by her brother. In order to wash his hands of any responsibility, Behiç highlights Belma's desire to be an actress: "This [death] was foreseen. Belma always told me she wanted to die like Pina Menichelli in the pictures" (182). Indeed, her story resembles Menichelli's films; for example, in *La Storia di una Donna* (Eugenio Perego 1920) Menichelli is seduced by a rich man like Behiç, her death after losing his baby placating a society dominated by middle-class moral values. Mebrure, overwrought, watches Belma on her deathbed, wanting to help her and crying for her, despite her previously cold response to Belma's alienating allure. Arguably, Safa positions Mebrure in relation to Belma in terms that echo widespread conceptions of female spectators emotionally identifying with the suffering movie heroine. Mebrure, while she dislikes cinema, is seemingly Safa's favorite character, but here she reacts like the stereotypical female spectator whom the author describes critically throughout the novel.

Ironically, *Sözde Kızlar* was adapted to cinema in 1924 by Muhsin Ertuğrul; however, no copies of the film appear to have survived in the Turkish Film archive. Yet if the issue of female spectatorship was problematized by the film as in the original source, a paradoxical self-reflexivity arises, since the novel opposes the values offered by the cinema. On the other hand, since the only types of films the novel's characters appear to enjoy are Italian and French melodramas—from Safa's perspective, escapist films made by the occupation countries—viewing this film as a local production perhaps negated the story's ostensible critique of cinematic identification; young female audiences watched a national film in which fictional young women were "corrupted" by European melodramas.[9]

Another novel relevant here, *Genç Kız Kalbi* (Young Girl's Heart) by Mehmet Rauf, posits cinema less as a source of corruption than as misleading guide. The heroine, Pervin, opposing her father's wishes, goes to Istanbul from Izmir in search of the fascinating European life styles she has witnessed in cinema and literature. Unlike Peyami Safa, Rauf shows some sympathy toward his free-spirited female character; however, in the end, tragically, it seems there is no happiness for a girl who goes against patriarchy. Because of her humble background, Pervin is abandoned by her lover, a member of the Westernized intelligentsia. In her journal she records her disillusionment arising from the dissimilarity between the life she had seen in films and the life she experienced in Istanbul, which for her embodies the "European dream" (1997, 8). This time the punishment for the disobedient woman is not death but return to a modest and thereby less illusion-filled life with her family in Izmir.

Studies of diva films in Italian silent melodramas reveal stories similar to those of Belma and Pervin, if not involving the dangers of cinema depicted by Safa (see Dalle Vacche 2008). Therefore, we may assume that the Turkish novelists, while severely critical of these films, must have seen and examined them in order to posit their literary characters as absorbed and strongly influenced by the filmic protagonists. Safa's novel *Sinema Delisi Kız* (The Girl Who is Mad about Cinema [1931]) speaks explicitly about the negative effects of cinephilia on young women. The story depicts Sabiha's troubles caused by her passion for cinema-going. Her love life and understanding of the world are directed by films and film stars. Sabiha stages imaginary films at home, making her mother, cousins and grandmother act for her. She also plays the leading role in her films and tries to imitate Clara Bow and Marlene Dietrich. One day, upon leaving a movie theater, she meets a supposedly French film star, André Roanne, who turns out in reality to be a Turkish man taking advantage of her by promising both romantic love and leading roles in French movies. He frequently takes her to his studio flat, where he stages imaginary films on the pretext of testing her acting abilities. In the meantime, her best friend's brother, Pertev, for whom she had previously developed affection, returns to Istanbul. Sabiha would give him another chance, if only he could share in her love for cinema. In the meantime the man she still thinks is André Roanne tempts her to elope to Paris with him, where, he promises, they will marry and make films together. Completely unaware of his daughter's plans, Sabiha's father complains that "after the cinema emerged, it has become increasingly difficult to raise a daughter" (45). She thinks her brother is the only person who understands her feelings, but even he disapproves of her wish to become an artist, though not out of "conservatism" but because "Turkish people are incapable of making good films" (48). Almost succumbing to the deception, Sabiha discovers that André Roanne is actually an old school friend of Pertev's. At the end of the novel, Safa, influenced by an orthodox understanding of Islam, makes his leading character regret her passion for cinema: "Cinema blinded my eyes, I ceased seeing [the world as it is]." Ultimately Sabiha declares: "All the evil that exists in this country comes from the cinema!" (120).

Thus Peyami Safa's main concern lay in his belief that his characters, and therefore young female readers, were mesmerized by cinema's blurring of boundaries: cinema as a modern apparatus weakened the borders between public and private spheres, between the safe home and dangerous modern cities, and ultimately between traditionally conceived gender roles of men and women. Yet according to Safa, the real danger was not cinema itself but the lifestyles it offered that were becoming increasingly evident in everyday life, misleading young people and naïve women, who needed education and discipline.

Nurdan Gürbilek argues that the novelists of this period projected their own anxieties onto their characters (2004, 17–50). Female characters thus appear open and vulnerable to "Western influences" such as cinema. Therefore, the imaginary female spectators in these novels may not be about women at all but may indeed be about the male novelists' fears of cultural influence.[10] Given this context, the gendered significance of "cultural influence" needs addressing. Cultural history in Turkey has long been dominated by a narrative of Westernization (circulated by those who both celebrate and criticize it), implying that Turkish culture is a passive receiver of its more sophisticated and forward counterpart, the West. This discourse is preoccupied with "cultural influence" as an unequal relationship, one understood by Cemal Kafadar (with reference to the intercultural exchange between the Ottoman State and the Byzantine Empire) in terms of a sexual act. "The influencer is like the one who penetrates and is proud, and the influenced is like the one who is penetrated and thus put to shame. If one was influenced by others . . . one acted like a 'passive' partner in intercourse and was 'inseminated'" (1996, 25). In the context of occupation literature, an anxiety about Western *influence* prevailed in most of the Turkish novels of this period and perhaps generated a castration anxiety among the Ottoman/Turkish intelligentsia, which is then projected onto the female audience, reinforcing compensatory patriarchal dominance.

Nâzım Hikmet, who is probably the most famous Turkish poet of the twentieth century, references cinema in his poems frequently.[11] His major theme is film as metaphor, making consciousness intelligible; his second, cinema spectatorship as it shapes the subject's mind, body, and performance in the social arena. While such parallels between cinema and consciousness involve class perceptions, the overwhelming influence of cinema is thematized in terms of gender—as, for example, in his 1925 poem, "Mountain Air," written in the voice of its heroine, Leman:

> You know how much I like cinema,
> To burn with excitement while watching a wild movie . . .
> As adventures charge one after another
> I lose myself in its course
> The crazy dream of adventures is born in me
> Here is what lies before me today:
> This journey, this train, Anatolia, Ankara . . .
> Already, I'm flung into the wind
> A wind that knows no end, no calm!
> (. . .)
> I travel as if going to a film
> A film that seems to end when only at the beginning.
> (Nazım Hikmet, 2010, 1987–8).[12]

"Burning with excitement," "losing oneself," "adventure's wild dream," being "thrown into the wind" depict a young woman experiencing the world and her country in overwhelmingly cinematic terms. Later, she leaves the film behind, meets the mountain air—in other words, local, solid reality. Snow blocks the railway, and hence, Leman has to get off the train and travel to the village, where Süreyya, a young man she met on the train, lives. Her cinematic perception of Süreyya's mother, the village, and a hunting expedition slowly changes as the mountain air and the reality of the locale come to define her experience. Recalling the journey from the train to the village, she realizes how much her life resembles a movie. Her mind slips back into the cinematic realm when Süreyya opposes her wish to join him in a hunting expedition: "Isn't it murder to cut in half / a thrilling film that's in its course?" (2002).

Leman finds her adventure when she is abducted during the hunting trip. However, after she is rescued, she begins a new life. As she moves from the fake realm of cinema into the reality of nature, "wild ideas" recede and "solid ideas take root" (2006). The poem turns into a story of endenization after she marries Süreyya and leaves Istanbul behind. Here cinema figures as an illusion that prevents the subject from relating to reality. Authenticity means overcoming illusory representations. Cinema acts like a layer of skin that separates the young woman from reality, translating experience into cinematic imagination. However, toward the end of the poem, the skin-like layer between subjectivity and experience, the curtain between the eye and reality—the cinematic worldview—disappears, and an authentic state of affairs reigns.

The woman who loses herself under the influence of cinema is frequently thematized in Nazım Hikmet's 1930s newspaper articles published under the pseudonym Orhan Selim. In these texts the influence of cinema represents distance from reality and an indulgence in appearances rather than truth. For example, Hikmet's piece, "Girl, I'm Telling You . . .," published in the newspaper *Akşam* on December 9, 1934, utilizes cinema to criticize a fourteen-year-old girl, her dress, gestures, and characteristic features, while asserting that he is a free-thinking individual and not a "bigot." Her hat, worn at a rakish angle, "imitates who knows what kind of a devilish coquetting film star." She does not know Madame Curie but she "knows by heart the film stars with their thin and pointed moustaches" (2007, 207). In another article, "You Show Too Much, My Woman," published in the same newspaper on December 15, 1934, he focuses on women at a wedding ceremony. Hikmet's tone toughens when he writes that one of the guests is called the Marlene Dietrich of Turkey. The woman, whom he likens to Blonde Venus,[13] is "the wife of a respected man, a woman with two children who belongs to a well-reputed lineage." A film star for Nazım Hikmet may act as a meat seller if the role necessitates it. "However, there is nothing artistic about showing her flesh solely to titillate/tickle *us*." Implying that female fashion is directed at the male "us," he continues, "Even being an artist cannot be an excuse for confusing shame with butchery, meat selling." He finishes with the statement, "You show too much, my woman" (2007, 213).

In Nazım Hikmet's opinion, cinema not only imagines a woman readily inclined to exhibitionism and ostentation, it also influences relations between women and men. In his article "Compliment" (*Akşam*, December 25, 1936) Hikmet criticizes a young man who compares a woman's beauty to Cleopatra's, referring, however, to the role played by Claudette Colbert in Cecil B. DeMille's 1934 film. Such a compliment confuses reality and fiction as well as a historical figure with an actress (2007, 102). In "New Style Love Declaration" (*Akşam*, May 16, 1935), a couple takes the era's renowned film lovers Gustav Fröhlich and Camilla Horn as a model for lovemaking. The writer is upset that "cinema, a *pointless, malicious* business, meddles in love affairs," blurring the division between reality and fiction (2007, 121 [emphasis added]).

In *Akbaba* (November 16, 1935), Nazım Hikmet's article, "Today's Issue Is 16 Pages," criticizes newspapers for publishing photos of film stars instead of dealing with actual news. Constructed as a dialogue, this text ostensibly criticizes the way female sexuality is exploited. However, a closer examination shows that the main speaker is not entirely against such a use. On the one hand, he is upset that the private life of a film star depicted in a photo covering half a page is used to draw attention from the conflict between China and Japan. On the other, he claims that such photos cannot quench the thirst of "nudity aficionados": "I'd go purchase a film magazine with glossy paper, and watch with a *cleaner conscience* the thighs that appear in a swimsuit." However, he claims also that "even if there were 100 Mary Pickfords, Claudette Colberts and Marlene Dietrichs smiling at me and undressing in front of me, they would not make the 'heart-darkening' images of Mussolini disappear from my mind" (2007, 360–361).[14]

It would be incorrect to assume that Nazım Hikmet or the other authors discussed in this chapter found cinema essentially bad. Hikmet himself wrote film scripts, and Safa tends to emphasize cinema's *healing* role in helping people forget worldly problems. Certainly, however, they accuse Italian diva films and Hollywood's star system for being overly commercial and culturally colonizing/imperialistic. These accusations stem from the "anxiety of influence," fuelled by cinema perceived as a foreign (Western) form, a perception revealed by the male writers either in the way they caricatured the West and Westernized, largely middle-class women characters, or in the way they reflected feelings of guilt, inadequacy, loss, and mourning for the mother country as national allegory. While the sociocultural status of cinema among the Ottoman/Turkish intelligentsia cannot be restricted to female participation in the audience and cinema's "foreign" status, these imaginary constructions, spreading across a range of fictional and journalistic writings, suggest a general cultural (male) anxiety emerging from the perceived relationship between cinema and women.

Notes

All translations from novels and articles are mine except where stated otherwise. I would like to offer my gratitude for the help I received from Fatih Altuğ and Suna Kafadar throughout the process of writing this chapter.

1. My title borrows the term "early film culture" from Zhen Zhang (2005, xviii–xix) in recognition of the different periodization of film histories across the world and so to avoid attributing belatedness to Turkish cinema culture when compared with developments in Western Europe or North America.

2. This very briefly summarizes the findings of my doctoral work (2010).

3. Yuri Tsivian (1994) similarly examines Russian literature in order to understand cultural reception of cinema.

4. Reported in *Stamboul*, December 12, 1896, 3.

5. On the propaganda films of the Ottoman Army see Cemil Filmer (1984); Mustafa Özen (2008, 145–57); Ali Özuyar (2007; 2013, 101–15).

6. *Annuaire Oriental du Commerce de l'Industrie, de l'Administration et de la Magistrature* (Istanbul: 1914).

7. Uzkınay was a former officer in the Ottoman Army, in charge of the Central Army Cinema Unit and allegedly made the first Turkish film, *The Destruction of the Russian Monument*, in 1914 (see Kaya 2007).

8. The disillusion that comes with aspirations to an artiste's life is echoed in Miriam Hansen's description of 1930s Shanghai films whose plots turn on the "glamour, decadence and tragedy that comes with stardom and success" (2000, 14). Parallels could be drawn between cinema's appeal to women during the Ottoman experience of Western occupation and Shanghai's experience of semicolonialism. Hansen's focus is on the ambivalent role of Hollywood, which offers signs of a liberating modernization for women while also disrupting—often with tragic results—traditional social structures.

9. I have yet to come across any reviews or other primary sources related to this film.

10. However, it should be noted that such practices of female spectatorship are not entirely the imagination of the novelists; they also relate to actual women audiences. Several women's magazines of the 1920s reveal an ambivalent approach to cinema, emphasizing its "eye-opening" effects for women while also finding it a little dangerous (see Türe 2007). Another important source recounting the cinephilia of actual female spectators is provided by letters from a young woman to her lover, written from the occupation of Istanbul in 1920 to the ending of the War of Independence in 1922. The lovers usually meet in movie theaters along with a group of their friends. She frequently mentions how tired she is because of the films she saw during previous nights and recommends to her lover new films she has recently seen. She reports that her mother says they love cinema so much that "we will soon be martyrs of cinema" (İstekli 2013). Also indicative are advertisements for luxurious movie theaters announcing films showing the latest fashions from Paris: "Chic women of Istanbul are advised to go to Elhamra and see films with the latest fashions before they go for their winter shopping" (Mahir 2005).

11. For analysis of cinematic themes in Nazım Hikmet's poetry see Altuğ and Balan (2015).

12. All quotations from Nazım Hikmet are translated by Suna Kafadar.

13. Marlene Dietrich plays Blonde Venus in the film of that name by Joseph Von Sternberg (USA, 1932).

14. Nazım Hikmet notes the objectification of the female body and film star when he remarks sarcastically on Fay Marbe's insurance of her legs (*Akşam*, March 22, 1936).

References

Altuğ, Fatih, and Canan Balan. Forthcoming 2015. "'Kaybederim Kendimi Ben Filmin Gidişinde': Nazım Hikmet'te Sinema İzleği." In *Vatan, Dünya ve İnsanlık Şairi Nazım Hikmet*, edited by Nilay Özer. İstanbul: Yapı Kredi Yayınları.

Alus, Sermet Muhtar. 2001. *Eski Günlerde*. İstanbul: İletişim.

Annuaire Oriental du Commerce de l'Industrie, de l'Administration et de la Magistrature. 1914. Istanbul.

Balan, Canan. 2010. "Changing Pleasures of Spectatorship: Early and Silent Cinema in Istanbul." PhD diss., University of St. Andrews, Scotland.

Dalle Vacche, Angela. 2008. *Diva: Defiance and Passion in Early Italian Cinema*. Austin: University of Texas Press.

Filmer, Cemil. 1984. *Hatıralar: Türk Sinemasında 65 Yıl*. Istanbul: Emek Matbaacılık.

Gürbilek, Nurdan. 2004. *Kör Ayna Kayıp Şark*. İstanbul: Metis.

Hansen, Miriam. 2000. "Fallen Women, Rising Stars, New Horizons: Shanghai Silent Film as Vernacular Modernism." *Film Quarterly* 54 (1): 10–22.

İstekli, İ. Bahtiyar, ed. 2013. *Fatma Cevdet Hanımdan İhsan Beye Yakılmamış Mektuplar*. İstanbul: İş Bankası Yayınları.

Kafadar, Cemal. 1996. *Between Two Worlds*. Berkeley: University of California Press.

Kaya, Dilek. 2007. "The Russian Monument at Ayastefanos (San Stefano): Between Defeat and Revenge, Remembering and Forgetting." *Middle Eastern Studies* 43 (1): 75–86.

Mahir, İkbal Elif. 2005. "Fashion and Women in the Istanbul of the Armistice Period (1918–1923)." Master's thesis. İstanbul: Boğaziçi University.

Nazım Hikmet. 2007. "Kızım Sana Söylüyorum...." In *Yazılar (1924–1934)*, edited by Güven Turan, 207–8. İstanbul: YKY.

———. 2010. "Dağların Havası." In *Bütün Şiirleri*, edited by Güven Turan and Fahri Güllüoğlu, pp. 1987–2008. İstanbul: YKY.

Özen, Mustafa. 2008. "Visual Representation and Propaganda: Early Films and Postcards in the Ottoman Empire, 1895–1914." *Early Popular Visual Culture* 6 (2): 145–57.

Özuyar, Ali. 2007. *Devlet-i Aliyye'de Sinema*. Istanbul: De ki Basım Yayım.

———. 2013. *Türk Sinema Tarihinden Fragmanlar (1896–1945)*. İstanbul: Phoenix.

Rauf, Mehmet. 1997. *Genç Kız Kalbi*. İstanbul: Arma Yayınları.

Safa, Peyami [Server Bedii, pseud.]. 1931. *Sinema Delisi Kız*. İstanbul: Semih Lutfi Basimevi.

———. 1995. *Fatih-Harbiye*. İstanbul: Ötüken Yayınları.

———. 2007. *Sözde Kızlar*. İstanbul: Alkım Yayınevi.

Tsivian, Yuri. 1994. *Early Cinema in Russia and Its Cultural Reception*. New York: Routledge.

Türe, Fatma. 2007. "Images of Istanbul: Women in the 1920s." PhD diss., Boğaziçi University, Istanbul.

Zhang, Zhen. 2005. *An Amorous History of the Silver Screen: Shanghai Cinema, 1896–1937*. Chicago: University of Chicago Press.

CHAPTER 4

When Iris Skaravaiou
Met Iris Barry

The First Greek Film Reviewer
and West European Modernity

ELIZA ANNA DELVEROUDI

The beginning of film literature in Greece remains obscure, as press and editorial developments in the country during the 1920s are still underexplored and need thorough study. Inaccessibility of main sources, such as particular magazines and newspapers, and lack of personal or public archives explain the absence of histories of the Greek popular press during that period. Thus, the feeling that research questions regularly lead to dead ends is not surprising.

My own research focuses on the emergence and editorial development of film literature in Greece in the 1920s and is closely tied to related popular journalism. Here, my scope is twofold. First, I will present the activities and early professional life of a woman reviewer, Iris Skaravaiou. Then, attempting to establish links between Skaravaiou and women critics and cinéphiles of the 1910s and 1920s in France and the United Kingdom, I seek to connect the cultural centers, where intellectual fashions are produced, to the periphery, with its local exploitations and adaptations; to relate Greek to West European film literature.

Skaravaiou's signature figures repeatedly among texts collected in a recent anthology of late 1920s writings on Greek cinema (Soldatos 1994). As the only woman included, her gender triggered my research. Who was she, and how did she become involved with film journalism?[1] Having started writing about film in the mid-1920s, Skaravaiou moved on to broader journalism and worked on a daily basis for a major Athens newspaper. By the turn of the 1930s, she had an extended professional life. Yet her name is absent from every history of feminism and women's journalism in Greece during that period, and no biographical entries, even shorter mentions, exist in dictionaries or encyclopedias. I soon realized that, with the sole exception of a reference in Aglaïa Mitropoulou's book on Greek cinema (1980, 122), Skaravaiou was almost completely unknown; she even seems to be forgotten by the post–World War II generation of film critics and journalists, among whom she could have been working. I then supposed that she died young, after a short but intense career in the 1920s, without leaving a memory to her colleagues. A key question was emerging: Why is a woman, who probably was among the first to work in the daily press and whose contribution to the history of Greek film criticism is highly important, missing from both our collective memory and written history?

In Greece, academic interest in the silent era is limited, and relevant research did not emerge until recently (Delveroudi 2012b). West European literature on the subject had already been booming since the 1990s. This produced remarkable studies on women's film writings of the 1920s (Lant 2006; Marcus 2007), on the magazines concerned (Donald, Friedberg, and Marcus 1998; Slide 2010), as well as on the women who took an interest in cinema and contributed to cultivating both film criticism and cinephilia in their own special ways—Colette (see Virmaux and Virmaux 1980), Iris Barry and the co-editors of *Close Up*, H. D., and Bryher (see Maule and Russell 2005), for example. The studies conducted by Maggie Humm (2003), Leslie Kathleen Hankins (2004), and Haidee Wasson (2002, 2006) suggest that Skaravaiou's writings should be examined in the light of a form of modernism that legitimated personal expression and was not aligned with the male canon.

Barry, H. D., Bryher, and Virginia Woolf enjoyed a prominent position in the modernist circles of their times. Through both their writings and their participation in clubs and production of experimental films, they contributed immensely to cinema's conception as a form of art. Ultimately, as Maggie Humm points out, they developed an alternative style of writing about cinema: a nonnormative style, allowing the inclusion of elements of personal observation or doubt, making space for audiences and their reactions, not imposing on them the image of an omniscient film critic.

When I delved into Iris Barry's track record, I was enthralled by the possibility that Iris Skaravaiou might have been inspired by her. The initial hint was the name "Iris." Both Iris and the surname Skaravaiou are quite unusual among Greek names. My hypothesis that Iris Skaravaiou was a pen name was confirmed by Mitropoulou, who referred to her as Elli Inglessi (1980, 122). Moreover, Mitropoulou compared Skaravaiou to Iris Barry: "She and Iris Barry from Birmingham are the international cinema's first women critics. . . . Skaravaiou [. . .] predated Barry's appearance as a critic in 1924 for the *Spectator.*" Mitropoulou also claimed that

Kinimatografikos Astir (Cinema Star, hereinafter *Astir*) (1924–1970) was not the first magazine Skaravaiou had been writing for. Mitropoulou, a second-generation film reviewer, probably had the opportunity to gain information from Skaravaiou herself, underlining at Iris's own suggestion her contribution to film reviewing and cinephilia but not providing details concerning her life and work. The two women could actually have met: my research shows that Skaravaiou lived a long life.

Until recently, I had not been able to locate any traces of Skaravaiou in the form of autobiography, diaries, or letters. Her texts contain hardly any references to herself. Nevertheless, some public files have been revealing. The members' file of the Journalists' Union of the Athens Daily Newspapers (ΕΣΗΕΑ [ESIEA]) proved to be precious.[2] Skaravaiou's own registration offered up important new evidence. Her file contains an undated "Personal Journalist's Sheet" and a letter written in her hand. The first, probably redacted on her instruction, confirms her actual name, "Kalliopi Inglessi," her father's name, "Nikolaos," her birth date—"1909 September," and a blurred number referring to the day; her birthplace, "Kavala"; her workplace, that same Journalists' Union; her activity providing "reports, investigations, translations, etc."; her foreign languages—"French, some English"; her high school diploma, home address, office telephone number, year of her registration with the Union ("full member, 1936"), and previous work experience, "*I Vradyni, Elliniki,* etc." Some fields in this sheet are not completed: wage, family status, participation in other professional unions, and other works ("books, press offices, past and present reports, etc."). However, this "Personal Journalist's Sheet" confirms Mitropoulou's naming her Elli (probably a nickname derived from her first name, Kalliopi) Inglessi. This—one and only—use of the nickname shows a kind of familiarity between the two women.

In the Journalists' Insurance Fund (ETAM-MME) she figures in the digital database, but her file has been discarded and is not available. She started drawing from the fund in "December 1986," and her pension was "suspended on September 1, 1991."[3] Assuming that was her death year made possible an investigation in the Athens registry office.[4] There, the exact date of her death, August 14, 1991, is stated, and her birth year and place are crosschecked. Her long life and relatively recent death are not compatible with the fact that nobody remembers her, either among film critics or the older members of the Journalists' Union, who have a close relationship with the union's everyday life. This mystery has probably to do with a premature retirement, due to a bereavement or infirmity, which compelled Skaravaiou to abandon active journalism and live on the margins of the union. The letter, saved in her Union file, insinuates such an explanation, noting "the extreme solitude in which I am condemned by my infirmity."[5] Her start in life promised a different future.

Finding such evidence shows how necessary is this time-consuming and tortuous route through the archives, as one source complements another. In fact, further sources have to be investigated, as the collected data does not fully answer questions about Skaravaiou's family, education, and initial connection to journalism. This biographical sketch must remain provisional, a fact that reflects her minor status in her professional environment, and, at the same time, testifies to the fragmentary condition of the archives. One question I was continually asked during this project was whether Skaravaiou was an important-enough subject for such research. This speaks to the difficulty of investigating new, not-yet-validated topics, working with questions and possible answers rather than with certainties.

Skaravaiou's birthplace, Kavala, was an Ottoman city in 1909. Her birth does not figure in the locality's Greek registry office.[6] This means that her father was not a Kavala citizen. We do not know how long she lived there nor where she went to school. Nevertheless, she finished high school and, if as a journalist she was translating from French and English, she must have received a good education, probably in a private (boarding) school. Investigation of schools' archives of the 1910s has not yet been possible. To this point in my research the lack of information about her father's profession and social status reduced the possibility of situating her clearly within a social milieu. Was she a young woman working of necessity or by choice?

Of the long list of questions concerning Skaravaiou's biography and professional life, the following were of critical importance: When did she start writing, and where had she first published? Two film periodicals circulated before *Astir*, the weekly *Kinimatografos* (Cinema, 1923–1924), the first Greek film magazine, and the fortnightly *Kinimatografiki Vivliothiki* (Cinema Library, 1923–1926). My hypothesis had been that Skaravaiou took her first steps into film journalism in *Kinimatografos*. To my surprise, *Kinimatografos*'s "founder and owner," as noted in its title, was N. P. Inglessis. To the present, we know little about him other than that his name is connected with three more publications of that period: the daily *Efimeris tou Hrimatistiriou* (Stock Market's Newspaper) 1920–1957; *Neai Arhai* (New Principles) 1922; and the weekly magazine *Eva* 1923–1924. Otherwise, N. P. Inglessis's presence in Greek press history remains unremarked.

Until recently, my efforts to establish some relationship between N. P. Inglessis and Kalliopi/Elli Inglessi, alias Iris Skaravaiou, had borne no fruit, although I knew her father's first name was Nikolaos. Similarly, I had not been able to locate any of her family members. Finally, however, during the process of writing this chapter, I made a new discovery in the Historical Archive of the National Bank of Greece. The editor N. P. Inglessis was a former employee and continuing client of the bank (then known as the Bank of Athens), which has kept records of their financial relationship. Among these are some legal documents testifying that Kalliopi was his daughter and that she was born on September 8, 1909.[7] We can then assume she followed her father in his professional permutations as a manager in the bank's branches in Smyrna (December 1909) and Amissos, Pontus (October 1910), until they settled in Athens in 1912.[8] In 1918 Inglessis was dismissed. As an executive officer of the Bank of Athens, he was in a position to identify gaps in the field of publishing and probably felt that he had the necessary knowledge to respond to existing needs. He subsequently became owner and editor of the newspapers and magazines mentioned above. At thirteen years old, Kalliopi was presumably already a cinema fan and knew the film press, so, it seems, her father asked for her help, resulting in his publishing *Kinimatografos*.

This discovery, then, illuminates the interesting information that appears in *Eva*'s 5th issue (March 17, 1923), under the headline "The youngest newspaper manager": "Miss Kall. Inglessi, only twelve years old, manager of our companion magazine *Ellinismos* (Hellenism), published since last year (1922), has sent us the following announcement, that we are publishing with pleasure: 'The fortnightly magazine *Ellinismos* is going to be reissued on April 1st, with attractive material and extensive reports from the Thracian front.[9] Any voids will be filled by artists and intellectuals and by a special fashion reporter. We are hoping that these re-forms will be favorably commented on'" (13). The style of this notice indicates a cordial relationship between Kalliopi and the founder-owner-manager of *Eva*, N. P. Inglessis, whom we now know to be her father.

No trace of *Ellinismos* has been detected in any public library. However, the "twelve years old" given as the manager's age matches Skaravaiou's birth date: born in September 1909, she would be thirteen in March 1923, twelve in 1922. To us, she may seem too young for such work. One might question the information given some decades later in her "Personal Journalist's Sheet," supposing she altered her birth date to appear younger. But in 1923 why should she reduce her age? Besides, although no formal evidence of her birth has been located, 1909 also figures in her death certificate. Her youth substantially alters my initial approach to and interpretation of her work, as well as demanding reconsideration of how the capabilities of the young during that period were evaluated. This last question awaits detailed examination in an international context.

She was about twelve years old, then, when she entered the profession, not as a young journalist but as manager of what was probably a popular publication, addressed not to children but to adults concerned with activity on the Thracian Front and with fashion, to men—soldiers and their families—and to women. The reference to her actual name in *Eva* increased the possibility of encountering her in *Kinimatografos*'s pages. Moreover, it enforced the hypothesis of kinship with the publisher N. P. Inglessis, now known to be her father, drawing his precocious young daughter into the family business.

Most of *Kinimatografos*'s articles are not credited, and a few are pen named. By comparing some of these short pieces on stars' lives to similar but more extended ones published later in *Astir* and signed by Skaravaiou, one could argue that, at age fourteen, she was their author.[10] In addition, these short pieces could represent only a part of her writing for this magazine. Her possible contributions to *Eva* have also to be detected, since this magazine informed its readers about film releases and stars in every issue. We can speculate, then, that *Kinimatografos* gave her the opportunity to engage with American and French fan magazines, which would have provided necessary information for her work, and to combine her cinephilia with writing about the cinema.

The pen name "Iris Skaravaiou" appears first in *Astir*, in the "Our Correspondence" column. Through the magazine's respectful reply to a letter from her, we gather that she had sent in a couple of her articles, which suggests some form of editorial collaboration. The column is unsigned, but probably the owner and editor Iraklis Ikonomou himself is answering her, thanking her, confirming the reception of the articles and describing their prospective collaboration as "valuable" (July 20, 1924: 8). Perhaps due to her young age, this peculiar method of communication was imposed by Skaravaiou for at least two more years and allows us to have some insight into her relationship with the magazine. Indeed, her first signed work is published in the same issue: "Those who have gone. Amleto Novelli," introducing a series of presentations on late actors and actresses, such as Suzanne Grandais, a famous French actress killed in a car crash in 1920, or Eva May, daughter of the German director Joe May and star Mia May, who had committed suicide in April 1924. Her initial articles refer also to Douglas Fairbanks and Mary Pickford ("From Spain: Douglas and Mary," August 10, 1924: 11), the Talmadge sisters (September 7, 1924: 10), Natalia Kovanko and France Dhelia ("Our Visitors," September 7, 1924: 13). In the latter she introduces a special focus on information particularly interesting to Greek readers, such as France Dhelia's visit to the Acropolis in 1920 to film René Le Somptier's *La montée vers l'Acropole*.

These first articles already frame an important aspect of Skaravaiou's writings, the presentation and commentary on international film stars, more often on women than men. During this period her texts become longer and she is forming a personal style, consisting of first-person narrative, quite self-confidently written, and playfully addressing the reader. For the extensive documentation of her articles, she certainly consulted sources that could only be the cinema pages of foreign magazines and newspapers: my general impression is that the Greek press of the period was extremely poor in providing such information. Besides, in her texts there are specific mentions of foreign magazines of the time; the French *Écran* and *Mon ciné*, the Italian *Cine-fono*, the American *Photoplay*. Additionally, she must have had an excellent memory, or a documentation system constructed like a personal archive, or, at least, a diary, recording her moving theatre visits and screenings.

Skaravaiou's presence in *Astir* is linked to its innovations—she introduces new columns but soon abandons them for new propositions. Other collaborators such as the equally young Vion Papamichalis work along her lines but in a more stable and systematic way. The reasons for Skaravaiou's volatility are not clear at present. In what follows I discuss her most obvious innovations; the possibility of others, unsigned or signed with other pen names, is not discussed here.

Skaravaiou's column "Silhouettes" (November 9, 1924: 13) offers information quite close to that provided in *Kinimatografos*, with capsules on stars' lives, such as Alla Nazimova, Agnes Ayres, Pola Negri. She often comes back to Pola Negri, and she confesses she understands her not only as an actor but also as a person, since Negri "is proud, bright and extremely stubborn" ("Artists' Silhouettes: Pola Negri-Gloria Swanson," January 25, 1925: 23). One could interpret this preference as a sign of Skaravaiou's identification with the star, a precious and scarce self-portrait. A further step toward her implication in film personalities' biographies is her method of interviewing through a form of correspondence (for example, "Conversations with Artists: Jean Angelo in *Astir*; An Interesting Interview with Our Contributor Iris Skaravaiou" [November 22, 1925: 25–26], and "Germaine Dulac for *Astir*" [December 20, 1925: 1–2]). She responds to readers' requests by sending questions to the actors, asking, for example, about their relationships with their colleagues, scriptwriters, and directors, and whom they preferred to work with. One standard question asks for their opinions about Greece and whether they would like to visit the country. The uniformity of the questions and answers is remarkable, and the whole interview process needs to be further examined and compared with international fan magazines' practices. It is not clear whether Skaravaiou's choices are personal or are linked with the promotion of French cinema in Greece. In this regard her relationship with particular distribution companies should also be investigated.

Through some of her texts we can access the interests of the otherwise silent audience: in an article on Italian star Italia Almirante Manzini (*Astir*, October 26, 1924: 32) she focuses on female characteristics, suggesting these are more important for her audience than the actress's talent. Her close relationship to female and male readers is detected through a new column introduced to *Astir*, "The Inquiring Column" (October 19, 1924: 24). Although uncredited, a hint as to its authorship is given in the previous issue ("Not Only a Sleepers' Club," October 12, 1924: 24), where she promises that she will answer any readers' queries about stars' ages and supply their full biographies.

Eventually, she signs her first film review, under the headline "Reviewing Notes: *La Garçonne; Pulcinella*" (January 4, 1925: 5–6). According to Skaravaiou, the 1923 film *La Garçonne*, adapted from Victor Margueritte's novel and directed by Armand du Plessy, caused a scandal at its international release. It was, she says, banned in London, along with confiscation from bookstores of its source novel, and censured in Athens. Contrariwise, the film was permitted in Paris, Bucharest, and Turkey. Skaravaiou argues that the novel and film comment critically on the depravity of the family and social mores after World War I and insists on the unfairness of their near-universal disapproval.

Her reviewing practice follows international patterns, adjusted to local needs. She always refers to actors' performances, to their previous films that Athenians had already the opportunity to view, to their evolution from one film to another, and, over time, to the interaction between actors, directors, and scriptwriters. Skaravaiou comments on technical matters, on the découpage and visual composition of scenes, on institutional and social responses to the films in other countries. She seems to be fascinated by what she calls "realism," the representation of "real" social situations like drug use or prostitution.

She is informed not only about the films themselves but also about writers and novels. She points out literary sources of film adaptations, showing a good knowledge of foreign literature. Though she does not consider herself to be qualified enough to write literary reviews, she consistently makes detailed comments on the original literary work being adapted. It becomes obvious that she is an educated young woman who has read widely, seen lots of films, and keeps her information up to date. Coinciding with the films' distribution, her articles exemplify journalistic choices and adjustments necessary to the local market. Her reviews are condensed, conforming to the restricted space allowed to the column. As she gets older, her topics and arguments are enriched by broad cultural reference, including her predilection toward modernism.

She is particularly fond of the French director Germaine Dulac, whose films and professional and artistic development she meticulously tracks and records. Dulac is her idol. She emphasizes the symbolism in her films and suggests how lucky Dulac was to have been born in France, in a country where she seems to be honored by her male colleagues and where gender is no obstacle to the recognition of her work.[11] Skaravaiou later travels to France as a correspondent of the daily newspaper *I Vradyni* and has the opportunity to meet Dulac (recorded in a front page article "What Germain Dulac Says about a Greek Artist" [the well-known actress Eleni Papadaki], May 19, 1931). A record and photograph of this meeting exist in Dulac's archive, held by the Paris Bibliothèque du Film. Skaravaiou sent Dulac the articles she published about her in *Astir* and *I Vradyni*. She claimed also that she wrote a scenario, which would have been directed by Dulac, but of this she has left no trace. Certainly, she had a small part in the 1928 Greek film *Maria Pentayotissa* by Achilleas Madras. This involvement with film practice is another point shared between her and her Western peers.

Like Iris Barry in the 1920s, Skaravaiou, in her concern for the future of cinema, looked to Europe rather than Hollywood. She regarded Hollywood as an industry

FIGURE 4.1. Iris Skaravaiou meets Germaine Dulac in Paris;
photo in the Greek newspaper *I Vradyni*, May 19, 1931

whose sole target was profit, suppressing artistic vision for the sake of increasing return on investment. Her preference for French filmmaking lies in the quality of the scripts employed. In the United States, Skaravaiou argues, scripts are churned out as end products of a process resembling an industrial assembly line, dividing the creative process among various specializations. French filmmakers opt for adaptations, which, although incurring copyright payments, ensure the quality as well as publicity that well-known plays entail; for example, in "Literature and Scripts" she mentions Pierre Benoit and playwright Maurice Dekobra, authors respectively of *L'Atlantide* and *Koenigsmark* (*Astir* December 25, 1927: 5).

From 1927, Skaravaiou was regularly concerned with developing Greek cinema, trying frequently to persuade Greek playwrights to engage in writing film scripts. Her main question was how Greece could nurture competent production companies, which could make an on-equal-terms contribution to cinema within the internationally established framework of the time. She was convinced that if a reliable production company were to be created, it would have to employ foreign artists. In the following years she closely watched the production of Greek films with both optimism and sternness, the latter often expressed in harsh remarks and conclusions. For instance, she often encourages theater actors to turn to cinema—yet sometimes, concerned at the incompetence of some Greek directors, she warns them against doing so.

Two more of her activities are worth noting. The first concerns her (probably unpaid) collaboration with the periodical *Protoporia* (Avant-Garde) during its existence from 1929 to 1931, for which she wrote film reviews. In the same field we can include her contribution to other short-lived magazines, youthful ventures comprising a total of no more than three or four issues each. The second field of activity concerns her work for the daily nationwide newspaper already mentioned above, *I Vradyni*. As early as 1929, Skaravaiou starts contributing to this newspaper by writing articles not only about cinema but also on diverse subjects such as social problems or sports, always focusing on women.[12] Finally, in 1932 she launches into managing a weekly newspaper, *To Thavma* (The Miracle), only one issue of which is retrievable (February 7, 1932).

Combined with ongoing research findings, this recently discovered evidence of Skaravaiou's early professional activity suggests a woman who fought hard to claim a place in Greek journalism and to establish cinema as the newest form of twentieth-century art. Though several analogies can be drawn between Iris Skaravaiou and her West European peers, there is a fundamental difference. Her international peers benefited from institutional or cultural support for their ventures: publishers themselves twice offered Barry the post of cinema critic, and she held an on-equal-terms role in the London-based Film Society. H. D., Bryher and the other cinéphiles of *Close Up* were also members of an international cinema-oriented community, which supported their self-expression in writing for the public. Neither should their social and financial status be underestimated as a contributing factor. Bryher was daughter to a shipping magnate; Colette had already established a place for herself in her country's literary culture and was merely adding her interest in cinema to her repertoire. The work of all these women was encouraged, acknowledged, and widely accepted in their countries' intellectual circles. It was also welcomed by following generations.

Skaravaiou, on the other hand, did not find favor with her contemporaries, mainly because she lived, worked, and expressed her creativity within more actively resistant patriarchal structures. She engaged in cinema culture, which Greek literary elite had not yet recognized as a form of art. She did not have any visible social links to the upper class or any access, apparently, to the intellectual circles that set the literary rules of the time. These facts should not obscure Skaravaiou's link with the imagined community of West European modernist women, who found in writing about cinema a brand new space to express themselves in the public sphere—a space not already fully occupied by male canons, which permitted several strands and styles of writing to co-exist, putting theory of art side by side with popular interests and curiosities: other people's lives, confessions of personal reactions to films, and the experience of shared leisure at the movies. Skaravaiou dared to participate in these discussions from a distant place, as a parallel voice. She was not just informed by the foreign press but, working through what it offered, adapted ideas to the local market. Her innovative introduction of new columns to the press, inspired by her Western fellows' example, enriched considerably its content. In addition, she promoted the profiles of "new women," pointing to their modern achievements. She was a pioneer of cinema culture during the first years of its establishment as the most popular entertainment in her country. She actively contributed to the process of modernizing Greek society through cinema and to changing women's social roles. She served the popular, not the highbrow, press, and the forfeit has been her work's marginalization. A reconsideration of silent cinema history in Greece, based on neglected but important sources, should welcome Iris Skaravaiou as a crucial contributor.

Notes

I would like to warmly thank Eleni Liarou, who initiated me into the DWFH world, for her strong encouragement and suggestions. I thank my friends and colleagues who patiently supported me during the incubation process. I am grateful to Konstantina Stamatoyannaki of ELIA, Athens, Vassiliki Tsigouni of the National Library of Greece, and Valdo Kneubühler of the Bibliothèque du Film, Paris, who made possible several aspects of this research, for an earlier report on which see Delveroudi 2012a.

1. Richard Abel (2006) asked similar questions concerning Gertrude Price, a 1911 film reviewer in several U.S. publications.

2. My thanks to the journalist Aris Skiadopoulos, who searched for Skaravaiou's file in ESIEA and suggested I follow her in the Journalists' Insurance Fund (ETAM-MME) archives. Access to the ESIEA library and archives is now suspended.

3. Oral information, Journalists' Insurance Fund, visited June 5 and June 28, 2013.

4. My thanks to Zacharis Bobolakis for his investigation at the Athens registry office.

5. Greetings letter addressed to the ESIEA Management Board, dated January 4, 1984.

6. My thanks to Ypakoi Chadzimichail and Kyriakos Lykourinos of the General State Archives in, respectively, Athens and Kavala, for emails March 6, 2013.

7. See certificate of the Municipality of Athens no. 64620, January 2, 1942, NBG Historical Archive, ΑιΣ40Υ45Φ61.

8. See Inglessis's suit against the bank, August 1, 1918, NBG Historical Archive, ΑιΣ36ΥΦ984/2, p. 1.

9. Until the Treaty of Lausanne was signed on July 24, 1923, the Thracian Front remained active. Greek soldiers were an important readership of popular periodicals, as we can observe in *Eva*'s correspondence column (e.g. June 9, 1923: 19; June 16, 1923: 19).

10. Unsigned, "What Film Stars Are Thinking about Their Husbands," *Kinimatografos* (December 30, 1923), 5; Iris Skaravaiou, "What American Leading Film Actresses Are Thinking about Their Spouses," *Astir* (May 17, 1924), 10–11, with reference to *Photoplay*. For further documentation see Delveroudi 2012a, notes 42–45.

11. Dulac had been publicly honored by the *Légion d'Honneur* and was active in the press and in committees promoting cinema both as a profession and as culture. For Dulac see Tammy Williams (2014).

12. The newspaper's volumes between October 1929 and June 1930 are missing in the National Library of Greece and the digital Library of Parliament. No traces of its archive exist.

References

Abel, Richard. 2006. "Fan Discourse in the Heartland: The Early 1910s." *Film History* 18 (2): 140–153.

Delveroudi, Eliza Anna. 2012a. "Otan I Iris Skaravaiou synantise tin Iris Barry, tin Colette kai ti Germaine Dulac" (When Iris Skaravaiou met Iris Barry, Colette and Germaine Dulac). In Society for the Study of Modern Greek Culture and Education, *Theatre and Cinema: Theory and Criticism*, 341–70. Athens: Author.

———. 2012b. "Silent Greek Cinema: In Search of Academic Recognition." In *Greek Cinema: Texts, Histories, Identities*, edited by Lydia Papadimitriou and Yannis Tzioumakis, 115–28. Bristol: Intellect.

Donald, James, Anne Friedberg, and Laura Marcus, eds. 1998. *Close Up, 1927–1933: Cinema and Modernism*. London: Cassel.

Hankins, Leslie K. 2004. "Iris Barry, Writer and Cinéaste, Forming Film Culture in London 1924–1926: The *Adelphi*, the *Spectator*, the Film Society, and the British *Vogue*." *Modernism/Modernity* 11 (3): 488–515.

Humm, Maggie. 2003. *Modernist Women and Visual Cultures: Virginia Woolf, Vanessa Bell, Photography and Cinema*. New Brunswick, N.J.: Rutgers University Press.

Lant, Antonia, ed. (with Ingrid Periz). 2006. *Red Velvet Seat: Women's Writings on the First Fifty Years of Cinema*. London: Verso.

Marcus, Laura. 2007. *The Tenth Muse: Writing about Cinema in the Modernist Period*. Oxford: Oxford University Press.

Maule, Rosanna, and Catherine Russell. 2005. "Another Cinephilia: Women's Cinema in the Twenties." *Framework* 46 (1): 51–55.

Mitropoulou, Aglaïa. 1980. *Ellinikos Kinimatografos* (Greek Cinema). Athens: Thymeli.

Slide, Anthony. 2010. *Inside the Hollywood Fan Magazine: A History of Star Makers, Fabricators, and Gossip Mongers*. Jackson: University Press of Mississippi.

Soldatos, Yannis. 1994. *Ellinikos Kinimatografos, Dokoumenta 1: Mesopolemos* (Greek Cinema, Documents 1: The Interwar Years). Athens: Aigokeros.

Virmaux, Alain, and Odette Virmaux. 1980. *Colette at the Movies*. New York: Ungar.

Wasson, Haidee. 2002. "Writing the Cinema into Daily Life. Iris Barry and the Emergence of British Film Criticism in the 1920s." In *Young and Innocent? The Cinema in Britain, 1896–1930*, edited by Andrew Higson, 321–37. Exeter: Exeter University Press.

———. 2006. "The Woman Film Critic: Newspapers, Cinema and Iris Barry." *Film History* 18 (2): 154–62.

Williams, Tammy. 2014. *Germaine Dulac: A Cinema of Sensations*. Urbana: University of Illinois Press.

CHAPTER 5

Searching for Mary Murillo

LUKE McKERNAN

In 2009 I was invited to speak at an event about women and British silent cinema at the BFI Southbank in London. I was interested in the work being done by the Women and Silent British Cinema project to investigate all traceable women working in the British film industry in the silent era and to share that research via their Web site. For my talk I offered to take on a scriptwriter about whom little was known, Mary Murillo, to demonstrate the research process and some of the online sources available. I published my findings in the form of a blog post on *The Bioscope*.[1] This chapter, based on that post, traces the journey I took, retaining the original premise of providing advice on how to research such a subject when starting with little more than a name. It concludes with additional information found since then. All the online sources consulted and discussed below are listed at the end of the chapter with their URLs.

Who Was Mary Murillo?

Mary Murillo did not turn up in any current motion picture encyclopedia or reference book. Her name was absent from all of the histories of the silent-film era that I consulted (bar a film credit or two) when I began my research, yet she was a significant screenwriter in American film for ten years, then worked in British films for six or more years, where her name brought prestige to three different film companies, before she moved to work in French films at the start of the talkies. The fact that she had almost disappeared from dominant film-history narratives says much about how women filmmakers have been allowed to slip out of the history of early film and about the low status of scriptwriters generally. So, how to go about recovering that history?

Type Her Name into Google

Typing "mary murillo" into Google produced 15,500 hits.[2] Initially, this seemed very promising, but I quickly discovered that the same film credit data has been lifted from one or two sources to be reproduced on numerous filmographic and DVD sales sites, and useful information about her was very thin on the ground (I also found many sites that refer to paintings of the Virgin Mary by the Spanish artist Murillo).

The search results included Wikipedia, which at that time had a one-paragraph biography of Murillo, a filmography, and a couple of links.[3] The biography told us that she was born in Britain, wrote for the Fox, Metro, and Stoll studios (the latter in Britain), that most notably she wrote for Theda Bara and Norma Talmadge, and that she was Irish by nationality, though some sources identified her as Latina. This was because, unfortunately, the major piece on Mary Murillo then available online, "Mary Murillo, Early Anglo Latina Scenarist" by Antonio Ríos-Bustamante, made the fatal assumption that her surname meant that she was of Latin American extraction, despite evidence that she was born in Bradford.[4] The writer had uncovered some useful information but, having made a wrong turn at the start, went off in the wrong direction. There were other errors, notably in the filmography, and one is better off with her credits on the Internet Movie Database—more than fifty titles—yet one should never accept the IMDb as being accurate or complete, especially for the silent-film era, when credits can be difficult to determine (particularly for scriptwriters). Certainly she had made more films than were listed there.

Family History Sources

For a proper grounding in biographical film research, it is essential to use family-history sources. This is where some small investment is necessary, because apart from the volunteer-produced FreeBMD (births, marriages, and deaths in the United Kingdom, roughly to 1900), the major sources—Ancestry.com, Findmypast.com, and the like—require payment.[5] Ancestry.com, however, is essential, offering not just births, marriages, and deaths, but census records, shipping registers, military records, and much more. "Mary Murillo" was a problem, however, because it was an assumed name. Her real name was Mary O'Connor. She was of Irish parentage, which was a further problem because there are few Irish family-history resources online, and most pre-1901 census records were destroyed in 1922 during the civil war. However, Murillo/O'Connor was born in Bradford (explained below) in 1888, yet I could find no official birth record—the first indication of what seemed to have been an unconventional childhood.

Shipping Records

These are essential. One of the great boons for biographical research recently has been the publication of shipping records, particularly between Britain and the United States before 1960, which give access to passenger registers, or manifests, that contain much biographical information, as well as certain dates. Ancestry .com has some, Findmypast.com provided Ancestors on Board using records from the National Archives (the Ancestors on Board site is now defunct and its records absorbed within Findmypast itself), but best of all for Mary Murillo was the Ellis Island site online, a free database with digitized documents of New York passenger records from 1892 to 1924.[6] From Ancestry.com's shipping records I discovered that Mary first went to America in 1908, under the name Mary de Murillo, when she was nineteen years old, that she was Irish but living in England, that she was born in Bradford, was an actress, and was traveling with her stepsister, Isabel Daintry.

The existence of a stepsister seemed a wonderful clue, though it proved to be a bit of a dead end. I was unable to trace a family history for Daintry, who was an actress herself, appearing in a few films in the early 1910s before fading from history, leaving just a photo in the Billy Rose Theatre Division at New York Public Library. I discovered also from the shipping record that Murillo did not give a family member as contact back in England, instead naming a Mrs. Henderson of Eton Avenue, London, as her friend. It seemed reasonable to assume, therefore, that her parents were dead. I learned as well that she was 5' 4" tall, with fair complexion, fair hair, and brown eyes, and that she was in good health.

Databases

Why was Murillo traveling to America? Well, she was calling herself an actress, and she was looking for work. Among the several handy databases one can employ to find biographical information for those in the performing arts is the particularly useful and free Internet Broadway Database, which lists production credits for all stage performances on New York's Broadway. Sure enough, there in early 1909 was Mary Murillo appearing alongside Isabel Daintry in the chorus of a musical, *Havana*. It was not a notable dramatic career—she had three further credits on the IBDb in 1912 and 1913, from which I could infer that she was on tour in stage productions during this period. As newspaper and theater records reveal, she was a member of Annie Russell's Old English Comedy Company, performing way down the cast list in plays such as *She Stoops to Conquer* and *The Rivals*. This correlated with shipping records, because I found she sailed again from Britain to New York in October 1912, this time on her own, revealed by the manifest for her departure (on Ancestors on Board) and for her arrival (on the Ellis Island site), with the useful information that her previous stay in the country had lasted for three-and-a-half years.

Census Records

Census records are the bedrock of biographical research. These give a person's age, place of birth, family members, occupation, place of residence, and incidental information that one can glean, such as social status. Mary Murillo/O'Connor proved difficult to locate at first, but she did turn up in the 1910 New York census, where she was recorded as a lodger in Manhattan, born in England, profession stage actress, no other family member with her. Something to be wary of—the electronic versions of such data, in this case Ancestry.com, are based on transcriptions, and often the names have been written down incorrectly: for the 1910 census, Ancestry.com had her name as "Mary Minter" and only by reading the image of the original document could I confirm that it was she. Later census records have not yet been made publicly available.

Newspapers

At some point in 1913 or 1914, Mary Murillo sold a film scenario to the husband-and-wife production team of Phillips Smalley and Lois Weber. Her career as a stage actress had not taken off, and like many others before her she looked to the movie industry as a way out, though in her case it was through her pen. She clearly had talent, because within two years she was one of the leading film scenarists in the American film business, becoming chief scriptwriter at Fox in 1915. This rise to fame one can trace through the best source for any online research of this kind, newspaper archives. There are many of these, though few are free, so either you pay a subscription or you hope your local library subscribes. Major resources include NewspaperArchive.com (for American papers), the British Newspaper Archive, The Times Archive and The Guardian Archive. Free resources include the National Library of Australia's Trove database, National Library of New Zealand's Papers Past, and a private archive of American papers, Old Fulton New York Post Cards. Film publicity departments sent out supporting information worldwide, and you can find Mary Murillo's name scattered all over the place, because such was her prominence that her name was frequently mentioned as a leading feature—in reviews, advertisements, and posters.[7]

Mary Murillo specialized in exotic melodrama and wrote five scripts for Theda Bara, Hollywood's archetypal vamp. The films were *Gold and the Woman*, *The Eter-*

nal Sapho, East Lynne, Her Double Life, and *The Vixen* (all 1916). From an article titled "The Scenario Writer" in the *New York Clipper,* May 1, 1918 (found at Old Fulton's New York Post Cards), I learned this:

> Even as late as the year 1914, there were few companies who deemed the writer worthy of mention on the screen and as for proper financial reward, many an excellent five reeler brought the magnificent sum of seventy-five dollars. Slowly but surely, however, the big film producers have come to realize the importance of the scenario writer in the general scheme of things with the result that from being one of the most poorly paid individuals connected with the industry, the men and women who create the successful screen plays today, now receive monetary recompense of substantial proportions. Mary Murillo, for example, a scenario writer, who made over twenty-five thousand dollars last year, sold her first script for twenty-five dollars, four years ago. She is but one of many scenario authors, who unsung and ignored but a few years back, are now reaping similar big rewards in the scenario field.

Quite a leap from a modest stage career to $25,000 a year in just four years. Newspaper records also revealed that Murillo left Fox at the end of 1917 to go independent, working for Metro, among others, before joining the staff of Norma Talmadge productions in 1919, where she scripted such titles as *Her Only Way* (1918), *The Forbidden City* (1918), and *The Heart of Wetona* (1919), plus others such as *Smilin' Through* (1922), where her name did not turn up on official credits but where she seemed to have been a script doctor—a role she performed many times, making her exact filmography a difficult subject on which to be precise.

Murillo ended her American film career in 1922. Why this was I could only speculate. Perhaps she wanted new challenges, perhaps her penchant for high-flown romanticism was starting to go out of fashion, or perhaps it was related to a revealing report in the *New York Times* of March 18, 1923, where I learned of the seizure by a deputy sheriff of a five-story building at 339 West Eighty-Fifth Street leased by Miss Mary Murillo, "a scenario writer, now said to be in Hollywood." She had defaulted on her payments. Among the goods seized were "tapestries alleged to be valuable, a mahogany grand piano, phonograph and a quantity of records, a lot of silver and a leopard skin." Mary had been living the movie life, and how.

Contemporary Movie Guides

It is worth remembering that there were reference guides produced from the early 1910s onward that provide biographical information on those in front of and behind the camera in the film business. Often the personal information provided needs to be taken with a pinch of salt, but it is always a handy starting point. Some of these are available on the Internet Archive: for example, Charles Donald Fox and Milton Silver's *Who's Who on the Screen* (1920), and the 1921 edition of William Allen Johnston's *Motion Picture Studio Directory and Trade Annual*. The latter had the following entry on Mary Murillo, which seemed to be wholly accurate:

> **MURILLO, Mary**; b. Bradford, Yorkshire, Eng.; educ. Sacred Heart Convent, London; screen career, wrote for Lois Weber, Philip [sic] Smalley, Herbert Brenon and Edgar Lewis. Chief writer for Fox, having written or adapted fifty Fox productions until 1918, for Theda Bara, William Farnum, etc. Since 1918 free lancing, writing for Norma Talmadge "The Forbidden City," "The Secret of the Storm Country," "The Heart of Wetona." Wrote for Metro, Emily Stevens, Ethel Barrymore, Madame Nazimova, Harold Lockwood, also for Clara Kimball Young and "The Panther Woman" for Petrova, Frank Hall "The Other Man's Wife." Ad., Hotel Algonquin, N.Y. (291)

Trade Papers

There was plenty to be found about Mary Murillo from American newspaper sources, even if mostly of a superficial nature. Once she moved to Britain, the on-line sources dried up, because she had little mention in the digitized British newspapers. She started writing for Stoll Film Productions, the major British studio of the early 1920s, resulting in five films: *The White Slippers* (1924), *The Sins Ye Do* (1924), and *A Woman Redeemed* (1927), plus two (possibly three) titles for other studios. Information on these is best found in film trade papers, such as the *Bioscope* and the *Kinematograph Weekly*, which do not exist online and need to be located at the BFI Reuben Library, at the British Library (which has produced a useful list, available online, of British and Irish cinema and film periodicals that it holds), or on microfilm sets at film research centers. There are no indexes to such resources— you just have to scroll through them and hope to strike lucky, though the BFI's online database provides many references. One trade journal that does have a handy index is the American *Moving Picture World*, and it was from Annette M. D'Agostino's invaluable *Filmmakers in the Moving Picture World: An Index of Articles, 1907–27* that I found an article titled "Mary Murillo, Script Writer Extraordinary" from March 16, 1918 (p. 1525)—though only after looking twice, because her name was indexed as Murrillo (remember never to trust indexes implicitly—always look laterally, and be prepared for misspellings and other errors). From that I got the only photograph of her (figure 5.1) that I was able to trace, and some tantalizing biographical information, including her schooling at a convent in Roehampton, near London. (By the way, the American journal *Variety*, which is available online in its entirety via a subscription service, does publish indexes, for film titles, and an obituaries index, but only in printed form.)

Ask People

Of course, asking people is a hugely important part of research. It is always best to do a bit of research yourself rather than expect others to do all your work for you, but armed with some information you have been able to gather, turn to the experts. Having taken my research so far, I posted a query on the classic film forum Nitrateville, which is full of knowledgeable people only too willing to help. It so happened that none knew anything about Mary Murillo directly, but one or two respondents came up with excellent leads. One used Google Books, which enables

FIGURE 5.1. Mary Murillo, "Script Writer Extraordinary," in *Moving Picture World*, March 16, 1918

you to search through snippets of texts from books old and contemporary, and found a mention of Murillo in a Belgian memoir—more of that below. Another looked in the Irish Times Digital Archive, a subscription site, and found that there seemed to be an article on her in 1980. I was able to access the site at the British Library (which provides a list online of all full-text, word-searchable newspapers and journals available electronically on its premises) and discovered that the article— "A Dun Laoghaire Film Connection"—was a piece by Irish film historian Liam O'Leary on the director Herbert Brenon, with whom Murillo worked. O'Leary, as an aside, revealed the precious information that her real name was Mary O'Connor and that she came from Tipperary.

Tipperary and Bradford? Something odd there, but the Liam O'Leary papers are held in the National Library of Ireland, where former cameraman and known walking encyclopedia of Irish film history, the (now late) Robert Monks, had care of the papers. Monks kindly looked up Liam's card index for me and found reference to an article on Murillo in the October 1917 issue of *Irish Limelight*, a short-lived film trade journal. Fortunately, the British Library has *Irish Limelight*. From this article (on page 9), titled "A Successful Irish Scenario Writer: Mary Murillo Talks about Herself," I learned that her family came from Ballybroughie—although that presented a problem, as there is no such place as Ballybroughie (the location was probably Ballybrophy in County Leix). Her early years were spent near Tipperary, though as she and her sisters were born in Bradford, the family clearly moved around a bit. She mentioned her father (no name) but not her mother, boasted of her great musical gifts when young, said that she chose the name Murillo because she was compared when young to a Murillo madonna painting, and described how tough it was to find work as an actress.

She also mentioned the convents she went to—St Monica's in Skipton, Yorkshire, and Convent of the Sacred Heart School in Roehampton. The latter is now Woldingham School, and the archivist there told me that Mary O'Connor (born January 22, 1888) and her sisters Philomena and Margaret were at Roehampton for a year (1903–4) before deciding that its tough regime was not for them. The parents' (parent's?) address was given as Thomas Cook c/o Ludgate. He was overseas, or they were (the travel agents Thomas Cook's main offices were in Ludgate Circus, London). In the 1901 census Margaret, Philomena, another sister Winifred, and Mary were given as boarding at St Monica's, ages three, four, seven, and twelve. What were the first two doing in a boarding school at that age? Were the absent parents touring performers or involved in international (Empire?) business, or just plain neglectful?

Having the names of the sisters, I could revisit Ancestry.com and see what further clues might be uncovered. This was not as easy as it might have seemed (there were more Philomena O'Connors than you might expect, and in some cases the surname had been transcribed as O Connor with the O classed as a second forename) but I pinned down Winifred's birth records and ordered a copy of her birth certificate from the General Register Office (for which payment is required). From this I got the names of the parents: Edward O'Connor, an Irish commercial traveller, and Sarah Mary, née Sunter, previously married to someone named Peacock.

Mary Murillo turned up in a couple of British newspapers in the late 1920s when her name was used by two film companies issuing prospectuses in the hope of investment. In an advertisement in the *Times*, November 29, 1927, the British Lion Film Corporation (with backing from the author Edgar Wallace) announced that its grand plans included "a contract with Miss Mary Murillo, whereby she is to write two complete Film scenarios for the Company during the year 1928." It also made the surprise claim that she wrote the script for *The Magician* (1926) by Rex Ingram (Irish himself, of course), something not otherwise recorded in any source.

She also turned up in the prospectus of the Blattner Picture Corporation—found in the *Daily Mirror*, May 21, 1928, available from pay site ukpressonline—where it declared that "the company will from its inception have expert technical assistance, and in particular Miss Mary Murillo (formerly Scenarist for the Metro-Goldwyn Corporation, Messrs Famous-Players Lasky, Mr D. W. Griffith, Miss Norma Talmadge &c.) will write Scenarios for this Company's first year's programme."

This was useful, though only a couple of films seem to have come out of Murillo's association with British Lion, and none with Blattner. She made some films in France, apparently working on English versions of French releases, though she was credited for the script of the 1930 classic *Accusée, levez-vous!* Her last film credit was as a co-writer of the British film *My Old Dutch* in 1934. Then what? Well, the Belgian source I mentioned above was *Les Méconnus de Londres* (2006), the memoirs of Tinou Dutry-Soinne, widow of the secretary to the Belgian Parliamentary Office in London, which cared for Belgian exiles during World War II. She met Mary Murillo in London at that time and provides a sketch of a lively, interesting character with a fascinating history in film behind her who was keen to help Belgian exiles. An e-mail to the obliging people at the Belgian embassy in London got me Mme. Dutry's address, and she wrote me a most friendly and detailed letter with all the information she could find on her social contact with Mary Murillo up to October 10, 1941, the last time she saw her. Murillo wanted to do what she could to help the Belgian cause (she seems to have spent some time in Belgium before the war), but suddenly disappeared from the scene.

Archives

And then what? I had no idea. She just seemed to vanish. I had found no record of a marriage or children. I could find no death record, though admittedly as common a name as Mary O'Connor was not easy to research. But for the film researcher, the biographical information, though a necessary backbone, is not the main business. She was a scriptwriter, and we want to find her surviving scripts and surviving films. First we need reliable film credits. I have said that IMDb is a good start, but always double-check with at least two other sources. The filmography I compiled for the original blog post came from a combination of the IMDb, references in newspapers, the *Library of Congress Catalog of Copyright Entries: Motion Pictures 1912–1939* (available from the Internet Archive), the American Film Institute Catalog (which makes its records for silent films accessible for free online), Denis Gifford's *British Film Catalogue 1895–1985*, and the BFI online database.[8] There were some uncertain titles in the filmography—as already noted, Murillo seems to have tidied up others' scripts at times, or to have developed scripts that were then completed by other hands, so determining what is her work outright is not easy.

There is no register of all extant film scripts, and one has to search in multiple places (while also being aware that scripts adapted from novels may also be cataloged under the original author's name). I found two Murillo shooting scripts in the indexes of the BFI Reuben Library in London (*The Sins Ye Do*, *A Woman Redeemed*). The Margaret Herrick Library of the Academy of Motion Picture Arts and Sciences has a Motion Picture Scripts Database, from which I found nine scripts, held by UCLA and AMPAS itself: *Ambition*, *The Bitter Truth*, *The Little Gypsy*, *Love's Law*, *The New York Peacock*, *A Parisian Romance*, *Sister against Sister*, *Two Little Imps*, and *The Vixen*. Some of these scripts are held also in the Twentieth Century-Fox archives. WorldCat, the union catalog of world libraries, lists two scripts available on the microfilm set *What Women Wrote: Scenarios, 1912–1929*. All in all, a remarkable fourteen Murillo scripts survive, a gratifyingly high number.

Finding what films exist in archives—as opposed to the DVD store (only two of Murillo's films are currently available this way, *The Forbidden City* [1918] from Grapevine and *Accusée, levez vous!* [1930] from Pathé,[9] but Silent Era Films on Home Video is the place to check)—is not easy. Again, no central register exists, and not all film archives publish catalogs of their holdings, let alone online catalogs. The International Federation of Film Archives (FIAF) provides a list of world film archives. A useful first source for checking whether a film survives and where (chiefly American titles, though) is the Silent Era Web site, which remains an essential source for information on silent films. Otherwise, you just have to check a lot of catalogs and ask in a lot of places (once again, specialist fora such as Nitrateville or the Association of Motion Picture Archivists [AMIA] discussion list are home to many experts, archivists, and collectors).

Roundup and a Few Tips

This chapter documents some of the avenues down which I traveled over a period of a few weeks as I tried to uncover information on one film scriptwriter from the silent era. It was not a typical research inquiry, but then what such inquiry ever is? It shows that you tend to start out with some basic sources and some key questions to ask, but will then find yourself led down all sorts of unexpected avenues, because people are unexpected. And I had much more to try and find out somehow about Mary Murillo. What was her connection with D. W. Griffith? What films did she write for Nazimova? Did any other photographs of her exist? When did she die? The quest would go on.

A few tips. Never trust any source on its own—always try to verify the information in two or three other places. Remember that people tell lies about themselves. Official documents such as birth certificates, census forms, and shipping registers tell us much, but they can also mislead (sometimes deliberately—people lie about ages and other personal information) and the electronic databases suffer from mistranscriptions. Always think laterally. Remember when searching for female subjects that names usually change on marriage, and of course with Mary Murillo we have someone who lived under an assumed name. Beware also of people sharing the same name—there was a second Mary O'Connor, full name Mary Hamilton O'Connor (1872–1959), who was a scriptwriter for American films in the 1910s and worked for a time in British films in the early 1920s (our Mary seems to have used Murillo professionally and a mixture of Murillo and O'Connor personally). Do not expect to find everything online, do not expect to find everything immediately, and be prepared to spend a little money for valuable resources that have taken a lot of expense and effort to compile.

Postscript

Happily, more information has emerged about Murillo since I first investigated her in 2009. Color film historian Simon Brown has discovered that in 1936 Murillo formed a company, Opticolor Ltd., to acquire the British rights to a French color film system, Francita. Sadly, the business turned out badly after a disastrous demonstration of the system caused investors to withdraw. Another company, British Realita, was set up to acquire the rights, but a dispute with Murillo and Opticolor greatly hindered the system's further commercial development.[10]

New research resources have also appeared online since 2009, and by far the most significant is the Media History Digital Library, which offers access to many hundreds of classic film journals (mostly American, and including *Variety* 1905–1941), all freely available online. In August 2013 it introduced a search mechanism across all titles, which currently reveals no less than 141 mentions of Mary Murillo. In addition, I wrote an article on Murillo's life, with filmography, for the Women and Silent British Cinema Web site, and an article has been written by Amy Sargeant on one of Murillo's British silent films, *A Woman Redeemed* (1927).[11]

Then in 2014 I made contact with her family after I came across the unexpected information that she might be the daughter-in-law of French film pioneer Gaston Velle and did some name-searching on Ancestry.com, which had fresh information added since I had last visited it. Indeed her partner (they never married—hence there was no marriage certificate to be found) was Maurice Velle, cinematographer on a few French feature films in the 1920s, and son of Gaston. He was also the person behind the development of the Francita color film process. They had two daughters, born in 1929 and 1931, both still alive at the time of writing.

Family contacts are both a blessing and a challenge. They yield much precious primary information, but there are also stories handed down which may have altered in the telling over the years and whose veracity is difficult to establish. Was Mary Murillo thrown out of America after trying to organize other women film workers against unfair labor practices? So the family had been given to understand. No supporting evidence for this has been found, and it is likely that the story had its roots in film news reports on Murillo being in dispute with studios over back payments in 1924.[12] Did she see her money troubles as being rooted in institutional sexism, at a period when women filmmakers were becoming increasingly marginalised by the American studio system?

I found also that she died on February 4, 1944, in Ickenham, near London, of breast cancer (her elusive death record was under the name Mary Velle). I have been able to pass on information that had been lost to the family. Indeed, one of the particular joys in conducting such research is that you can sometimes make contact with descendants, who often know little more than that their ancestor was involved in films somehow, and pass on your discoveries and understanding of the history back to them.

Finally, and most recently, I have found an 1891 census record indicating Mary was illegitimate, born to Sarah Mary Sunter but with an unknown father whose surname may have been Gordon. If true, she was an O'Connor only by adoption (Edward O'Connor and Sarah Sunter married in 1894) and had no Irish ancestry. Therefore, she went through life with at least four surnames, assuming different masks while putting on a series of grand performances, all part of a remarkable, independent life.

More can always be found to gain access to a past life and to question the film history we have inherited. The astonishing range of online research resources that have been opened up in recent years should encourage us not simply to reaffirm our knowledge of the familiar but to seek out that which has been lost hitherto. Historiography begins with the evidence, and there is so much evidence now available that will enable us to take our film history research—and particularly research into women's film history—in new directions. Mary Murillo is just one name among hundreds of women who played a significant role in the development of cinema and film culture in its early years. All you need is a name that intrigues and the will to start searching.

Notes

1. This is a blog dedicated to the subject of early and silent cinema that I wrote and administered between 2007 and 2012. It is no longer active but is being kept online as an archive (see http://thebioscope.net/about).

2. This was the case in November 2009; by the time of writing (October 2014) the figure had risen to 36,900.

3. The Wikipedia entry has since been amended and now references my research.

4. Antonio Ríos-Bustamante, "Mary Murillo, Early Anglo Latina Scenarist." Although the article is no longer available via its original URL, it can be traced via the Internet Archive's Wayback Machine, at http://web.archive.org/web/20091110085550/http://tell.fll.purdue .edu/RLA-Archive/1995/Spanish-html/Rios-Bustamante,Antonio.htm.

5. For a guide to family history sources and film research, see http://thebioscope .net/2007/09/30/family-history-for-film-historians.

6. The site has since been amalgamated with others to form http://www.LibertyEllis Foundation.org.

7. For a general guide to newspaper sources online, see http://thebioscope.net/2011/02/09/ discovering-newspapers.

8. Available at http://bioscopic.files.wordpress.com/2009/11/murillo_filmography.pdf.

9. *The Forbidden City* is available from Grapevine Video (http://www.grapevinevideo .com), while *Accusée, levez-vous!* is available from Amazon's French site.

10. Simon Brown, "Technical Appendix," in *Colour Films in Britain: The Negotiation of Innovation 1900–1955*, by Sarah Street (London: BFI/Palgrave Macmillan, 2012), 281–82. The papers of investor Sir Thomas Bazley, Bt. at Gloucestershire Archives, contain much information on Francita and Mary Murillo's ill-fated involvement.

11. Amy Sargeant, "The Return of Mata Hari: *A Woman Redeemed* (Sinclair Hill, 1927)," *Historical Journal of Film, Radio and Television* 30 no. 1 (2010): 37–54.

12. See, for example, "Miss Murillo's Particulars," *Variety*, November 12, 1924, p. 21, regarding a $23,200 suit for damages she issued against R-C Pictures.

Online Resources

While many online resources appear to have become permanent fixtures on the internet, some can move to different Web sites with new URLs—as happened with two of the resources used in my original 2009 research—or simply become unavailable, either temporarily or permanently. The list below is correct at the time of writing (October 2014).

American Film Institute, Silent Film database (http://www.afi.com/members/catalog/ silentHome.aspx?s=1&bhcp=1)

Ancestry.com (family history, http://www.ancestry.com)

Association of Motion Picture Archivists (discussion list, http://lsv.uky.edu/archives/amia-l .html)

BFI Database (film and TV works, books, journals, press cuttings, scripts, and the like, http://collections-search.bfi.org.uk/web)

The Bioscope, "Discovering newspapers" (http://thebioscope.net/2011/02/09/discovering-newspapers)

The Bioscope, "Family History for Family Historians" (http://thebioscope.net/2007/09/30/family-history-for-film-historians)

The Bioscope, "Searching for Mary Murillo" (http://thebioscope.net/2009/11/05/searching-for-mary-murillo)

British Library, "News Media" (http://bl.uk/subjects/news-media)

British Library Newspapers, "Cinema and Film Periodicals: British and Irish" (http://www.bl.uk/reshelp/findhelpsubject/artarchperf/film/britirishfilm/index.html)

British Newspaper Archive (http://www.britishnewspaperarchive.co.uk)

Ellis Island (New York inbound immigrant, passenger and crew lists, 1892–1924, http://www.LibertyEllisFoundation.org)

Find My Past (family history records from USA, Canada, UK, Australia, New Zealand and beyond, http://www.findmypast.com)

Fox, Charles Donald, and Milton Silver, eds. *Who's Who on the Screen*. New York: Ross, 1920. Available at https://archive.org/details/whoswhoonscreen00foxc.

FreeBMD (births, marriages and deaths in the UK, roughly to 1900, http://www.freebmd.org.uk)

General Register Office (national archive for births, marriages and deaths from 1837, http://www.gro.gov.uk)

Google Books (http://books.google.com/books)

The Guardian Digital Archive (http://www.theguardian.com/info/2012/jul/25/digital-archive-notice)

International Federation of Film Archives (FIAF) (http://www.fiafnet.org)

Internet Archive (includes Web sites, texts, video and audio, https://archive.org)

Internet Broadway Database (Mary Murillo, http://www.ibdb.com/person.php?id=54089)

Internet Movie Database (Mary Murillo, http://www.imdb.com/name/nm0613943)

The Irish Times Digital Archive (http://www.irishtimes.com/search)

Johnston, William Allen. *Motion Picture Studio Directory and Trade Annual 1921*. New York: Motion Picture News. Available at https://archive.org/details/motionpicturestu00johnrich.

Library of Congress, *Catalog of Copyright Entries: Motion Pictures 1912–1939* (https://archive.org/details/motionpict19121939librrich)

Margaret Herrick Library (http://www.oscars.org/library/index.html)

Mary Murillo filmography (http://bioscopic.files.wordpress.com/2009/11/murillo_filmography.pdf)

Media History Digital Library (classic film journals, mostly American, http://mediahistoryproject.org/collections)

Moving Picture World (http://mediahistoryproject.org/collections)

National Library of New Zealand's Papers Past (newspapers and periodicals, 1839–1945, http://paperspast.natlib.govt.nz/cgi-bin/paperspast)

New York Public Library, Billy Rose Theatre Division (http://www.nypl.org/locations/lpa/billy-rose-theatre-division)

New York Times Article Archive (http://www.nytimes.com/ref/membercenter/nytarchive.html)

NewspaperArchive.com (American newspapers, plus other countries, http://newspaperarchive.com)

Nitrateville (classic film discussion list, http://nitrateville.com)

Old Fulton New York Post Cards (New York State historical newspapers, http://fultonhistory.com)

Silent Era (http://www.silentera.com)

Silent Era Films on Home Video (http://www.silentera.com/video/index.html)

The Times Archive (http://www.thetimes.co.uk/tto/archive)

Trove (Australian newspapers, diaries, letters, archives, http://trove.nla.gov.au)

UKpressonline (British newspapers archive, http://www.ukpressonline.co.uk/ukpressonline)

Variety (1906 to present, http://www.varietyultimate.com; and 1905 to 1941, http://mediahistoryproject.org/collections)

Wikipedia, "Mary Murillo" (http://en.wikipedia.org/wiki/Mary_Murillo)

Women and Silent British Cinema (http://womenandsilentbritishcinema.wordpress.com)

Women and Silent British Cinema, "Mary Murillo" (http://womenandsilentbritishcinema.wordpress.com/the-women/mary-murillo/)

WorldCat (catalog of world library collections, http://www.worldcat.org)

PART II

Feminism, Politics, and Aesthetics

CHAPTER 6

Alice Guy's Great Cinematic Adventure

KIMBERLY TOMADJOGLOU

> The head of the business, the originator of
> it, the capitalist, the art director, is a refined
> French woman, Madame Alice Blaché.
>
> —Louis Reeves Harrison, 1912, 1007

This chapter suggests a new framework for thinking about Alice Guy's legacy. Much of what we know about Alice Guy comes from previous scholars, devoted to ensuring she is not forgotten: Anthony Slide, Victor Bachy, Alison McMahan, Francis Lacassin, André Gaudreault, and Guy's family members, daughter Simone and daughter-in law Roberta Blaché. Feminist scholars have a particular investment in restoring Alice Guy to the historical record, much as she herself tried to do in her memoirs. The ongoing recovery and preservation of films attributed to Guy directly and/or as participant, recent retrospectives and conferences, and several documentaries and DVD releases all shape our general understanding of world cinema's first woman director and studio head. Yet the figure of Alice Guy still presents us with a host of unanswered questions: Was she a feminist? Was Herbert Blaché responsible for the failure of their company, Solax? Was she omitted from standard film histories because she was a woman? Did she create the first story film? And more recently, did she direct *La Fée aux choux* (The Cabbage Fairy), which she recalled was her first film, made in 1896, but in the Gaumont Film Company catalog is listed as made in 1900? Even her name—should we use Guy or Guy Blaché?—is a point for discussion.

Finding Alice Guy

How do we attempt to answer these questions? Are they relevant to Guy's legacy? I suggest we begin by interrogating the "feminist" image of Guy first proposed more than a decade ago by filmmaker Alison McMahan in *Alice Guy Blaché: Lost Visionary of the Cinema* (2002). McMahan writes that she was looking for a woman filmmaker who could serve as a role model in her own search for a feminist filmic language. "I had to invent Alice Guy before I could find her. [. . .] I drew a profile of what this role model might be like." McMahan looked for her role model in Europe rather than in the United States "because that would put her at a further remove from what became classical Hollywood narrative" (xxv). Inspired by 1980s feminist film theory and Tom Gunning and André Gaudreault's "cinema of attractions," *Lost Visionary* is shaped by McMahan's perspective as an independent feminist filmmaker, drawing on ten years of archival research. McMahan's invaluable contribution helped jump-start feminist historiography; she created Alice Guy for us and, more important, gave us access to her in ways that other male historians had not.

In her paper "Are They Us?" Jane Gaines (2007) suggests that we often construct historical women in our own image: "We find what we would be but not what we would not be." In this context, McMahan's expressed desire to recreate Guy suggests a fantasy figure, enabling McMahan to reaffirm her own practice as a feminist filmmaker, a fantasy we share through our mutual desire to locate historical role models "like us." This may be why Alice Guy is so attractive and at the same time so problematic. Guy fulfills our need to have history's most important woman director of the twentieth century recognized; but what kind of role model does she offer us? *Lost Visionary* situates Guy within a feminist framework that valorizes her as both a film pioneer and a progressive, modern woman ahead of her time. McMahan covers a range of historical "first" cinematic accomplishments by Guy—first woman director, first woman to own and operate her own studio plant, innovator of the "first dramatic close-up"—in order to argue that Guy was ahead of the men, including, in the latter case, American cinema's patriarch, D. W. Griffith. By situating Guy within a reactive feminist framework (against history's centering on great men), McMahan, and we as well, encounter contradictions— ambiguous and unsettling depictions of race, ethnicity, and gender, or unwelcome suggestions that Guy was a conservative, capitalist entrepreneur—contradictions not easily reconciled with contemporary feminist perspectives, which we either hesitate to address fully or completely ignore.

For example, was *La Fée aux choux* (The Cabbage Fairy) Guy's directorial debut, as she claimed? Guy's assertion was largely unchallenged by feminists, until recent research by Maurice Gianati (2012) revealed that Guy directed her first film in 1902, the two-shot *Sage-femme de première classe* (First Class Mid-Wife), before which possibly she wrote scenarios. To reframe cinema past and future we need to acknowledge such revisionist scholarship in order to properly historicize our research. In fact Guy frequently confused *La Fée aux choux* with *Sage-femme de première classe* and their dates of production. The close resemblance between the two films and their depiction of the cabbage-patch baby motif may have contributed.[1]

Transnational and Networking Frameworks

In her autobiography Alice Guy describes sailing with her mother across the Strait of Magellan to join her father in Chile.[2] Years later, in 1907 and newly married, Alice Guy Blaché made another landmark voyage, traveling with her husband Herbert from her native Paris across the Atlantic to Cleveland, then to New York, leaving a successful and rewarding career at Gaumont behind. This new adventure would ultimately change the course of Alice Guy's life and career, as a new name, identity, husband, country, and culture shaped the woman we now celebrate as world cinema's first female director. Rather than continue to immortalize Guy's cinematic firsts, we might use this journey across the ocean to begin reframing her legacy. The fracturing of Guy's career across two continents is one reason it has been difficult to properly assess her cinematic achievements. Alice Guy was a multidimensional figure and throughout her life played a range of roles: secretary, director, screenwriter, producer, distributor, manager, and art director, not to mention mother. Yet her legacy is overdetermined by the title "first woman director." A transnational framework enables us to contextualize Guy's entire career, bridging two important eras and two continents: the earliest period of invention, innovation, and diffusion of moving images in France through 1907; and the transitional period of the 1910s in the United States, as new modes of production, distribution, and exhibition, the advent of feature filmmaking, and the star system radically transformed the industry and art of moving images internationally. A flexible transnational approach may reveal more, not only about Alice Guy but also about the broader historical, social, and cultural milieu in which she and other pioneers participated in early cinema's intense cosmopolitan internationalism of the 1910s.

Describing the early French film industry, Alan Williams seeks to avoid the great men (and women) theory of history by focusing on filmmakers in their industrial context, adapting a biographical format to compile multiple, interlocking, creative career histories. Rather than crediting a single "auteur," Williams's method addresses a "film community"—a "network of individuals" (1992, 3–4). Thus he deals with the specific historical context of the French industry, as well as the social context of those working in it. Guy's network consisted of Gaumont's business associates, the inventors Demeny and the Lumières, her friend and secretary, Yvonne Mugnier-Serand and her sister Germaine, her trainees, Louis Feuillade, Ferdinand Zecca, Victorin Jasset, and finally her set designer Henri Menessieur and cameraman Anatole Thiberville. In describing Guy's network, Williams argues that there was "a sympathy" (*sympathia*) between her and Leon Gaumont. Furthermore, with her "convent education and good royalist connections," Guy was an asset to the company, not only in her efficiency and dedication but also socially:

> Guy's bourgeois background and her many travels must certainly have helped fit in with the firm and its generally wealthy sophisticated clientele. Her ambition to re-enter the bourgeoisie from which she had fallen would have endeared her to the enterprise's new owner. She and he both combined the drive and the flexibility of the *parvenue* (self-made upstart) with the cultural and intellectual values of the bourgeoisie. (55)[3]

Alice Guy's cosmopolitan, bourgeois work and social environment at Gaumont differed from that of Madame Blaché in the United States. Now manager and part owner of Solax, an independent film studio in Fort Lee, New Jersey, Madame Alice Blaché entered a business partnership with her younger, American husband, Herbert. Richard Koszarski (2011) informs us that Solax's ownership was divided between Alice, president of Solax, and Herbert, president of the New Jersey Company that owned Solax's real estate. The reasons for this division are unknown, but Koszarski suggests that while some historians ascribe the creative side of Solax to Alice and the business side to Herbert, the "peculiarities of American contract law of the time" were likely a contributing factor (2). Married women were still treated as a distinct class with regard to property ownership.[4] However, if Guy had more autonomy at Solax, did her approach as a producer and manager differ from Gaumont's?

The Blachés belonged to a cosmopolitan French American community that included Henri Menessieur, Anatole Thiberville, Alberto Capellani, Maurice Tourneur, and Emile Cohl. We know that Madame Blaché and her compatriots spoke French on set, collaborated on productions, and also socialized together. Richard Koszarski's 2004 study describes how these French immigrants helped establish Fort Lee as a film town by constructing studios and factories, utilized by filmmakers making regular trips across the Hudson River from New York. Yet with the exception of Alan Williams's work, Alice Guy's bourgeois French legacy seems to be understated or ignored in the literature. For example, while McMahan (2002) emphasizes Leon Gaumont and the Lumières' reputation as bourgeois "right-wing" conservatives exercising paternalist domination over work environment and employees (29), she argues that Solax functioned along American lines, with less a hierarchical structure and more a family-friendly atmosphere (120).[5] What, then, does this say about the impact of Alice Guy's formative years on how she ran Solax? Was Guy any less a bourgeois capitalist entrepreneur than her French associates? Given Williams's point that Guy's background helped her fit in at Gaumont, is it possible that Madame Blaché's maternal approach at Solax played a similar role to Leon Gaumont's paternalism? Trade-journal interviews recounting visits to Solax often commented on the warm, family-like atmosphere of the studio and note how many Solax employees composed entire families. Madame is portrayed as a strong, even-tempered matriarch, a capable and organized business manager (as McMahan emphasizes), but she is also president of the company, a "capitalist." One gets a sense from this publicity that Madame ran Solax as if it were her factory-household. Is it then possible that Solax resembled the patriarch-led familial, social, and business networks of Gaumont and the Lumières described by Williams and McMahan?

As a young secretary, Miss Alice convinced Leon Gaumont to allow her to make her own films, and he not only granted her the opportunity but also provided a studio on the outskirts of town for her to play at directing while also managing his company. Only a capable, organized, and efficient individual like Guy could balance both activities. However, while the family structures and work environments of Gaumont and Solax may not have been exactly the same (the one patriarchal bourgeois, the other maternal), both shared a familial atmosphere in which work and play combined. Correspondingly, the employees of both companies appear to have maintained a high degree of respect for and confidence in the authority figures (Leon Gaumont, the patriarch, and Madame Blaché, the matriarch) overseeing their work and their play. Whether Guy herself was responsible for fostering this environment at both companies is unclear, but Williams suggests "it was presumably Alice Guy who created and nurtured the mood of excitement and sheer aesthetic pleasure" visible in Gaumont's prewar films and those made after Guy's departure from France (1992, 57).

Solax: A French American Company

A visitor to Solax commented, "It is not only the agreeableness of the place and of the people one meets there that one notices, but the smoothness and order with which the work is carried on" (Guy Blaché 1996, 135). If Leon Gaumont was a kind of father-figure boss, we know also that young Miss Alice was an independent self-starter, and, showing great initiative, quickly rose up the ranks of a male-dominated workplace. Forward looking, Guy demonstrated ingenuity, resourcefulness, and creativity as a manager (Williams 1992, 55–57).[6] Williams says the cinema was a "process of discovery" for Guy and that she welcomed its challenges (57). McMahan emphasizes how Guy pioneered a form of studio management at Gaumont that traveled with her to Solax and later evolved into the classical Hollywood mode of production. She shows how two divergent modes of production, collaborative and hierarchical, co-existed at Gaumont (2002, 119). Guy managed Gaumont's *phonoscène* studio, synchronizing images of performers with their prerecorded voices, which utilized a more factory-like division of labor, while her silent film production was more collaborative. However, McMahan draws on successive production models debated between American film historians Janet Staiger (1985) and Charles Musser (1996) to argue that at Gaumont Guy passed over the cameraman phase of production and launched immediately into direction. Whether this has any bearing on Guy's legacy as "the first woman director"—in the modern sense of auteur—is not the point. The problem is the limitation of Guy's diverse roles as director, producer, and manager to a single category that is interpreted as more advanced and attributable to either French or American practice. From a transnational perspective, Solax's mode of production and organization is more usefully understood as a hybrid form in which different national systems synergized. So while Solax claimed that it was exclusively American, we might consider its French-American character.[7]

At Solax, Madame Blaché seems to have utilized the European metteur-en-scène system familiar to her at Gaumont, where she hired and trained a number of men to handle a diverse range of genres that distinguished the company's product.[8] In both Italy and France, the term *metteur-en-scène* described those who oversaw and/or supervised the direction, coordination, and details of each production. Typically, the metteur-en-scène specialized in a genre or genres, and most production companies employed a number of such staff. While it is difficult to generalize from country to country and from firm to firm with regard to the early silent period, we know that the majority of productions involved less a strict division of labor than loosely functioning collaborative teams in which the players and technicians could perform different roles. Williams (1992) notes that it is difficult to attribute many early Gaumont films to a single individual. Alice Guy and Romeo Bozzetti, for example, share directorial credits for *Le Matelas alcoolique* (1906). A number of Bozzetti's comedies share stylistic features with Guy's films. Thus applying to Guy's own films the term *metteur-en-scène* rather than *auteur*, I would argue that in the total body of work she produced for both Gaumont and Solax, and later as an independent director, we recognize a developing signature studio style and form of narration: namely the Solax 'house' style that seems consistent, whether or not Madame Blaché was the metteur-en-scène herself, or wrote and/or

The Woman Picture Maker

Madame Blaché, the Distinguished Producer, Tells Townsend Black of Her Wonder Work

THOUGH it smacks somewhat of the paradoxical, Mme. Alice Blaché, the foremost woman producer of motion pictures in the world, and one of the ablest directors of the silent drama, is—

Mme. Blaché is a notable exception to her own rule does not alter it a whit, in her opinion, although many would doubt the assertion once they had seen this energetic little woman at work in the Popular Plays and Players' studios at Fort Lee, N. J., where she has produced many of the finest—her finger tips. Not only does she write scenarios and direct the production of them, but she personally superintends the making of a picture until it is released a finished product. She directs her camera men, and indeed, has taught them many

MME. ALICE BLACHÉ

FIGURE 6.1. Mme Blaché's "wonder work" as producer of *The Sewer* (1913) is celebrated in a contemporary fan's collage of image and text derived from trade and fan magazines of the time.

produced a work that others directed. Guy was one metteur-en-scène among others at both companies, specializing in comedy and melodrama at Solax. Thus Madame Blaché's overall role was closer to an executive artistic director's, performing for Solax as trainer, director, and visionary managing director.

If we reconceive Guy's role in matriarchal bourgeois familial terms, crossing between French and American production systems, we may better understand some of the disturbing and unsettling class and race attitudes captured in her films. In this respect, the lack of clear period boundaries between one mode of production and another is equally true of cultural attitudes, making a figure like Guy forward looking in one direction and regressive in another. The transitional era (roughly 1908 to 1914, depending on country) was marked by uneven and discontinuous production methods as single-reel films were gradually replaced by feature-length productions, the American film industry consolidated and film became an industrial product of mass media entertainment identifiable by national standards. Cultural attitudes, then, played into such broad industrial changes in the drive to "Americanize" the American cinema described by Richard Abel (2006). The transnational context of this process of Americanization is key to reframing Guy's legacy. It forced independents out of business and foreign producers out of the United States, while the development of an American star system focused attention on female actresses (and male actors), increasingly more visible and accessible to the public through advertising, the press, and fan magazines, further diminishing the appeal of foreign produced films. Meanwhile, despite identifying itself as American, Solax remained tied to France and to Gaumont—at least through December 9, 1911, when Solax moved from Flushing, New York, to Fort Lee.[9] At that time Gaumont lost its position as a licensee of the Motion Picture Patent Company Trust (MPPC) and the benefits of participating in the

General Film Company distribution network. Solax was also adversely affected when independent and foreign producers were squeezed out of the U.S. market. Solax's failure, then, as McMahan points out, cannot be attributed to Herbert Blaché's inability to manage the company.[10]

Cultural attitudes, however, contributed further to undermining Solax's position within an Americanizing film industry. Solax's films were sent to France to be developed, and since many of the intertitles were originally composed in French, like other foreign-produced films of the time, they were awkwardly translated into English. Moreover, beyond the obvious expressive and interpretive differences between French and English, a broader context of culturally diverse and class-informed values distinguished French (or European) films from American films. In a *Photoplay* article of March 1912, H. Z. Levine, a publicity manager for Solax, explained how the French notion of art and realism informing Madame Blaché's work was often at odds with American views on morality:

> Having been born and bred in an artistic environment [Madame Blaché] always demands the very highest artistic values from her directors and actors. Sometimes what she in Paris would have considered classic art, the Board of Censors here insist is objectionable. Madame cannot reconcile Parisian training with American prudishness.

And he quotes Madame Blaché:

> Here, contrary to all established precedents of art, we find conditions such that the showing of a revolver or the jimmying of a desk or the cracking of a safe is objectionable. Such a point of view is primitive. I believe, as others, that the flagrant exhibition of crime and the glorification of vice are a menace to society; but the exhibition of crime to bring home a moral lesson with a dramatic climax, and the achievement of a period in the true development of a character should be permissible. Pantomine is the most difficult form of expression, and to limit it to mere namby-pamby, milk-and-water themes manacles its chances of development in this country (37–38).

The period's "film as art" discourse comes into play here, as does the role of publicity in transmitting a range of cultural, class, social, and national discourses, important for assessing the entirety of Guy's career. Madame appears a forward-thinking and progressive European in an American climate wherein reformist and religious groups opposed the cinema on the grounds that it was a low-class novelty and socially disruptive form of amusement. Guy was caught between two value systems as well as two production systems, so not only is her career fractured, but she cannot easily be fitted into a national history and is largely misjudged or underrecognized by both French and American film historians.

Conversely, recalling our question "Was Alice Guy a feminist?" Madame Blaché's interviews emphasized that America offered her opportunities not possible for a woman living in France:

> Perhaps I should not have been able to accomplish so much in any other country, particularly in France. . . . It is so different here and never once have I been sorry that my husband brought me with him—to live, to associate and to grow among such nice, cosmopolitan people. They talk of French chivalry. Yes, it does exist, but mostly it is superficial. So long as a woman remains in what they term, her place, she suffers little vexation. Yet, let her assume the prerogative usually accorded her brothers and she is immediately frowned upon. The attitude toward women in America is vastly different. . . . An American gentleman, on joining my company, presumes that I know what I am doing and that I have a right to be where I am. It is a constant conflict when a woman in a French studio attempts to handle and superintend men in their work. They don't like it, and they are not averse to showing their feelings. (Quoted in Gates 1912, 28)

Guy's comparison of French and American attitudes toward the role of women within the public sphere of employment seems to contradict her earlier comment on "prudish American morality"—clearly a response to censorship. As Solax studio head, Madame Blaché was an ambitious and powerful figure, free to use publicity to express her personal opinion and point of view—a privilege denied in France. We may say Madame Blaché prefigured the modern-day celebrity and cultural spokesperson. In this sense, Alice Guy can be a feminist when she has social power and has control of her female identity. This wanes when, as we shall see, she becomes a single, divorced mother with two children, and her identity is fractured.

Fantasy, Play, and a Feminist Historiography

If, as Gaines suggests, McMahan represents herself (and us?) as much as Guy in her filmmaking practice and scholarship, then we might consider what role fantasy plays in creating a feminist historiography or a feminist Alice Guy. Lynn Hershman-Leeson's film on the 1960s feminist movement, *!Women Art Revolution—A Secret History* (2010), devotes considerable screen time to the significance of "role playing" for feminist artists, including herself. Hershman-Leeson narrates that "performance art" was specific to women—they actually created it as "the best way for them to act out." Play or acting out and humor provided vehicles for Hershman-Leeson and her peers to create new identities, expressing ways their personal lives were political. For example she reveals that she funded her film with earnings from personal artwork that had been unmarketable until she wrote a rave review using an alias! Hershman-Leeson writes herself into history much like Alice Guy did in her autobiography. While the two situations are not identical, we may ask why in the 1990s a feminist artist like Hershman-Leeson had to resort to such a ruse, and what her action tells us about the history of women's labor, be it creative or otherwise.

In a series of interview sessions with Victor Bachy from November 1963 to June 1964, the then-ninety-year old Alice Guy, silent for years, vocalized why she thought her work was overshadowed by her male colleagues:

> I can assure you that I am not the least bit vain about what I accomplished. I was there at the right time, I began my career then, and I had a fair amount of imagination. . . . I wrote—that amused me—and . . . I was the daughter of a bookshop owner and I could read whatever I chose, or rather almost everything. I loved it. (Bachy 1985, 34)

If this appears defensive, her initial response to Bachy's question was: "Why, I cannot say. I have children."[11] This slip of the tongue suggests Guy had unresolved regrets about putting her children before her career after her failed marriage. In a recent revisionist essay on silent women filmmakers, Anthony Slide accuses Alice Guy of being "weak" by "packing herself and her children off to her native France after her divorce," leaving the United States and a possible independent directorial career behind (2012, 120). While Slide acknowledges Herbert Blaché's infidelity, he blames Alice Guy for being "incapable of moving beyond a Victorian concept of marriage and family" (120). Slide's comments remind us of the weight of Guy's bourgeois legacy, as does his observation that Guy's inability to embrace the promise of liberation offered to the twentieth-century new woman was the result of her conservative Catholic upbringing. Furthermore, Slide challenges the feminist notion of mutual support between women filmmakers, referencing Guy's comment in her memoirs, "Americans pretend [Weber] was the first woman director" (120). While Slide's observations diminish the appeal of Alice Guy as a role model of female independence, they also underline the extent to which we have imagined Guy's feminist leanings by ignoring her bourgeois and conservative outlook. What kind of role model does Alice Guy offer us? Louis Reeves Harrison wrote in 1912: " This is the woman's era, and Madame Blaché is helping to prove it" (1007). Paradoxically he then states that Madame Blaché "only favors universal suffrage when satisfied that women are ready for it." While Alice Guy may have accepted the challenges of balancing family and career, she was not ready for divorce, the fracturing of her identity, and loss of the real-life fantasy of the cinema she constructed and enjoyed as Madame Alice Blaché.

In "An Alliance between Film History and Film Theory," Heide Schlüpmann addresses the question of a specifically female culture in cinema's transitional period, offering the notion of "play" originating in the "Haus" (the bourgeois home) as a means to understand cinema's transitional years. "Play," as a specifically historical phenomenon, allows for an intermediate zone in the space of the cinema "in which film and its audience find their place and where their separation, together with the hierarchy that is usually associated with it, has no decisive importance" (2008, 10). Play thus mobilizes the private and intimate within the public sphere. I'd like to take up the notion of "play" to suggest how we might use Alice Guy's Gaumont and Solax comedies to interrogate the concept of "female identity." The cinema itself seemed to offer Guy a fantasy-life where she could creatively combine work and play, helping her shape her own female identity. Indeed, she fondly described the cinema as "my own prince charming" (1996, ix).

Her first film, *Sage-femme de première classe* (1902), is a narrative centered on a young woman's "fantasy" of purchasing/having babies, directed and performed by a young Alice Guy with female friends who appear to be curiously at "play." Babies and children were a consistent motif throughout Guy's career, as seen in films like *Sage-femme*, *Mixed Pets* (1911), and the *Coming of Sunbeam* (1913). Yet it is possible that the fantasy of having children, once realized, may not have fulfilled Guy's hopes. At Solax Madame Blaché seemed to revel in both worlds—the home and the studio.

If contexted within French Grand Guignol traditions, much of the sometimes vulgar or crude humor of Guy's Gaumont and Solax comedies—producing contradictory and ambiguous representations of sex, gender, class and ethnicity—can be seen to derive from her own class background. At the same time cross-dressing, dressing up, disguise, and mistaken identities constitute playful humor as well as devices to motivate action. Thus in *Mixed Pets* a dog is confused with a baby. The bourgeois Mrs. Newlywed wants a pet dog, against her husband's wishes. The butler and maid are secretly wed and must hide their baby. When at his wife's prompting Mr. Newlywed goes to the cupboard, he finds the baby rather than the dog. Here, the playful mixing of dog and baby equalizes heterosexual union between class-differentiated couples.

As in Guy's earlier film, *Sage-femme de première classe*, babies function like material objects. In *Sage-femme* the cabbage fairy has a stall where she sells babies, and in *Mixed Pets* domestic servants hide their baby from their employers, while the newlywed wife wishes to displace baby by dog. In both films an ironic tone, whether deliberate or unconscious, underscores the subject of infants (selecting them in *Femme*, mixing them with animals in *Mixed Pets*) that is the motivation for the narration (see figures 6.2 and 6.3). As in many of Guy's films, an unsettling undercurrent or subtext renders them ambiguous or disturbing to the contemporary viewer. In *Sage-femme*, when given a choice, the couple purchasing an infant

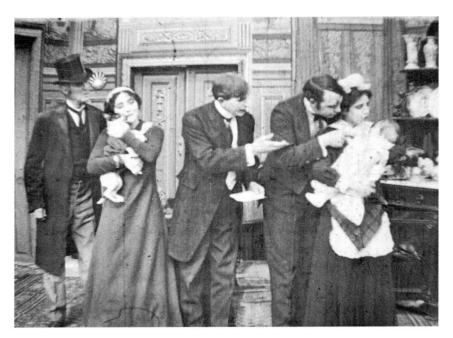

FIGURE 6.2. Denouement of Alice Guy's *Mixed Pets* (USA, 1911)
(Credit George Willemen)

FIGURE 6.3. The midwife picks out a baby to sell the young couple in
Sage-femme de première classe (1902) (Credit Colorlab Corporation, Md.)

from the cabbage fairy blatantly rejects first a black infant, then an Indian baby (identified by a single feather headdress). In both instances, these infants, unlike the others, are actually dolls. In a clear, if unconscious, racist indication, the wife covers her eyes when she is shown the black doll. In *Mixed Pets*, the cross-class dog/baby equation raises questions about class, traditional marriage, and child rearing. Guy's films recall vaudeville skits with their "tongue-in-cheek" associations, use of gags and props, as well as their literalistic punning titles: "canned harmony," "his double," and "mixed pets." As a form of play, they address serious underlying social, class, race and gender issues.

Conclusion

Throughout these and other short films, Guy uses a simple story line as base for a series of stylistic devices—be it disguises, shooting into mirrors and reflections, split screens, and close-up diegetic inserts (notes, newspaper ads, and letters)—as a form of play with the range of possibilities offered by cinema. If these devices appear awkward—(for example, too-lengthy close-ups of a clock in *Matrimony's Speed Limit* [1913] to designate passing time) or narratively inefficient—they are fascinating in their establishment of a space in cinema for representing the life and atmosphere of the bourgeois home, courtship, heterosexual marriage, and children, articulated through play. Thus the transcontinental shift in Guy's personal life and career and her films' mixing European filmmaking traditions with an emerging, American, "classical" style can be understood within the larger context of social, economic, and cultural changes occurring internationally in cinema during the transitional era. And we may investigate how a woman like Guy was both successful and unsuccessful at adapting to those changes.

Notes

1. Moreover, many pioneers exaggerated their accomplishments or simply confused dates and facts.

2. Guy's parents immigrated to Chile, where her father founded the first bookshops in Valparaiso and Santiago. As an infant, she was raised by her grandmother in Carouge, a Geneva suburb.

3. When old enough, Alice joined her siblings at the Convent of the Sacred Heart at Viry on the Swiss border. Guy's religious education and conservative family background were typical of the French petit-bourgeois class.

4. Deeds for the New Jersey Studio Company reveal that the Bergen County Commissioner of Deeds required a clause for a married woman, stating that "she signed sealed and delivered the same as her voluntary act and deed freely without any fear of threats or compulsion of her said husband" (Koszarski 2011, 2).

5. McMahan (2002) writes that Guy's children visited the studio regularly and that her daughter Simone appeared in several films.

6. Williams (1992) describes Guy's resourcefulness in locating and later reusing materials for props and sets in different films in order to economize.

7. Referring to Solax as "American" was obviously a marketing decision to differentiate Solax's product from that of other independent foreign producers, especially considering the Motion Picture Patent Company's barrier to entry of foreign products, particularly French films (see Abel [1999 and 2006] and below, pp. 10–11). French films were particularly targeted for their depictions of crime, an accusation Guy responds to in Levine's article quoted below, pp. 11–12.

8. To my knowledge, Guy did not engage women as metteurs-en-scène, scriptwriters, cameramen, or set designers, thereby restricting their roles to acting.

9. Koszarski suggests that Herbert may deliberately have kept a low profile when Solax moved to Fort Lee since he was still tied to Gaumont, and that he allowed the *Moving Picture World* to report that Madame, "the presiding genius of Solax," planned the studio and the factory (2011, 2).

10. Rather, it was largely the result of Solax's reliance on selling its product outright to distributors, its inability to compete with barriers imposed by the MPPC's vertical and horizontal oligopoly, and the increased demand for financial resources imposed by the advent of more elaborate feature productions.

11. Guy continued, "I have a daughter who detests the film industry." She added, "As I now live with my daughter, I contain myself" (Bachy 1985, 34).

References

Abel, Richard. 1999. *The Red Rooster Scare: Making Cinema American 1910–1914*. Berkeley: University of California Press.

———. 2006. *Americanizing the Movies and "Movie-Mad" Audiences, 1910–1914*. Berkeley: University of California Press.

Bachy, Victor. 1985. "Conversations with Alice Guy." Translated by Lois Grjebine. Reprinted from *Les Premiers ans du cinéma Français: Proceedings of the Fifth International Colloquium of the Institute Jean Vigo*, 31–42. Perpignan: Institut Jean Vigo.

Gaines, Jane. 2007. "Are They Us? Women's Work on Women's Work in the Silent International Film Industries." Paper presented at *Non Solo Dive* conference, Bologna, Italy (December).

Gates, Harvey H. 1912. "Alice Blaché. A Dominant Figure in Pictures." *New York Dramatic Mirror* 58 (November 6): 28. Reprinted in Guy Blaché 1996, 131.

Gianati, Maurice. 2012. "Alice Guy a-t-elle existé?" Paper delivered at La Cinémathèque Française (October 29). Available at www.cinémathèque.française (accessed June 2013).

Guy Blaché, Alice. 1996. *The Memoirs of Alice Guy Blaché*. Edited by Anthony Slide. Translated by Roberta and Simone Blaché. 2nd ed. Lanham, Md.: Scarecrow.

Harrison, Louis Reeves. 1912. "Studio Saunterings." *Moving Picture World* 12 (11): 1007–11. Reprinted in Guy Blaché 1996, 117.

Levine, H. Z. 1912. "Madame Alice Blaché." *Photoplay* 11 (2): 37–38. Reprinted in Guy Blaché 1996, 115.

Koszarski Richard. 2011. "A Note on Alice Guy Blaché and Fort Lee." Unpublished essay.

———. 2004. *Fort Lee, the Film Town*. Rome: Libbey.

McMahan, Alison. 2002. *Alice Guy Blaché: Lost Visionary of the Cinema*. New York: Continuum.

Musser, Charles. 1996. "Pre-Classical American Cinema: Its Changing Modes of Production." In *Silent Film*, edited by Richard Abel, 85–108. New Brunswick, N.J.: Rutgers University Press.

Schlüpmann, Heide. 2008. "An Alliance between Film History and Film Theory." Unpublished paper presented at Women and Silent Screen conference, Bologna, Italy (June).

Slide, Anthony. 2012. "Early Women Filmmakers: The Real Numbers." *Film History* 24 (1): 114–21.

Staiger, Janet. 1985. "The Division and Order of Production: the Subdivision of the Work from the First Years through the 1920s." In *The Classical Hollywood Cinema: Film Style & Mode of Production to 1960*, by David Bordwell, Janet Staiger, and Kristin Thompson, 142–54. New York: Columbia University Press.

Williams, Alan. 1992. *Republic of Images: A History of French Filmmaking*. Cambridge: Harvard University Press.

CHAPTER 7

A Major Contribution to Feminist Film History

Maria Klonaris and Katerina Thomadaki's
Cinéma corporel (*Cinema of the Body*)

CÉCILE CHICH

In November 2012 the Bibliothèque Nationale de France (BnF), together with the Archives Françaises du Film/CNC (Centre National de la Cinématographie), dedicated a special event to the artistic duo Maria Klonaris and Katerina Thomadaki. This was the launch of the Klonaris/Thomadaki Archive, established at the prestigious National Library of France in collaboration with the artists. Lodged within the Audiovisual Department, the archive is dedicated to the (so far) four decades of a collaborative practice that encompasses films, photographic, digital and audio works, multimedia performances, and projection environments. It also includes video documents on the artists' performances and installations, as well as their written texts and a wealth of essays, catalogs, and articles published on their work.

To the outer eye, it may seem paradoxical that filmmakers should find such recognition within a *library*. Yet to whomever knows these inspiring and endearing artists, who challenge both aesthetic and institutional frontiers, this does not seem a paradox but one of the many breakthroughs that define their path. Equally, their multimedia work defies the assumed distinction between cinema and the fine arts, as well as the association of film with 35mm. Thus, a decade earlier they had gained state recognition as major filmmakers when the French National Film Archives/CNC undertook, under their supervision, the restoration of a selection of their Super 8 films on 35mm. This, according to Eric Le Roy, president of the International Federation of Film Archives, constituted a world premiere in film archiving history.[1] In both cases Klonaris/Thomadaki opened new doors in what is a burning issue for many independent filmmakers: the preservation of their work.

What defines Klonaris/Thomadaki's strategy is their conscious choice to work at the intersection of art territories. Over four decades they have authored more than a hundred different pieces in various media accompanied by substantial theoretical work.[2] If unfamiliar to general Anglophone audiences, those interested in avant-garde, feminist, or queer cinema know Klonaris/Thomadaki's work, not through mainstream film exhibition venues but through art gallery, museum, and experimental media circuits—they have been showcased, among others, at the Millenium, the legendary experimental film venue in New York, as well as at MoMA, at the National Gallery of Art and the Museum for Women in the Arts in Washington. In Europe they are well known in the experimental film scene since launching their *Cinéma corporel* (*Cinema of the Body*)[3] in 1976 in Paris, and also in London, where from 1979 on they showed their films and expanded cinema projections at the London Filmmakers' Co-op, Lux, the BFI, and Tate Modern. In France, when the Pompidou Center presented the first Klonaris/Thomadaki retrospective in 1980, the two artists became known as pioneers in interdisciplinary arts. Since then, rare for French experimental filmmakers, their reputation has reached many countries, and many international festivals and museums have commissioned their multimedia performances and installations. "Among the best known avant-garde artists working in France" (Pirnat-Spahić 2002, 10), they have been celebrated as "major figures of experimental and expanded cinema, innovators in photography, pioneers in media intermix and projection environments" (Gattinoni 2002, 37).

Maria Klonaris and Katerina Thomadaki, then, have received considerable and, for women experimental filmmakers, rare recognition by critics, philosophers and scientists, as well as feminist and art enthusiasts. Yet their work remains largely unknown to Anglo-American film historians and theorists. This apparent anomaly points toward the problematic lack of visibility of women experimental filmmakers in film history, where avant-garde work is marginalized in separate chapters or volumes as if disconnected from the development of film history proper—and in any case is largely identified with the iconoclastic male artist. A second problem is that foreign artists are poorly represented in Anglophone histories of the "avant-garde." Moreover, since Klonaris and Thomadaki come from hybrid national-cultural backgrounds, their work cannot be assigned to a particular national history. Third, multimedia practice such as theirs, which transcends traditional categories of "art" and "film," challenges not only the systems for cinema distribution and exhibition—thereby reducing the visibility of such work to film historical re-search—but also the formal definitions of cinema on which film historiography is traditionally based. Thus, in the interests of developing an inclusive history of women artists' interventions in film and media, this chapter seeks to demonstrate the centrality of the work of Klonaris and Thomadaki to the project of writing a feminist women's film history. To this end I focus on the aesthetic and concep-tual choices they made and on their thought-provoking contributions to feminist film practice. In the process this chapter illustrates the kind of challenges to film historiography posed by work that fits neither the accepted categories of feminist theory nor those of a history based on the specificity of film or on national and cultural homogeneity.

Outside the Canon

In *Women's Experimental Cinema: Critical Frameworks*, Robin Blaetz notes: "[Women experimental filmmakers] have fallen through the cracks of both the history of the avant-garde and feminist scholarship" (2007, 5). On the one hand, avant-garde cinema has been written as a primarily masculine field. On the other hand, feminist scholarship has focused on narrative cinema. Yet, she adds, women experimental filmmakers have the ability to "expand the canon of [both]" (2007, 5). This analysis is echoed by Petrolle and Wexman: "Many critics tend to ignore or undervalue this work in part because women's experimental films frequently revise the very paradigms within which this cinema has traditionally been con-sidered" (2005, 1). In other words, by positing themselves outside the politics and aesthetics of a largely male preserve, outside the canons of both avant-garde and mainstream cinema, women experimental filmmakers have fallen outside historical discourse, have been marginalized or plainly ignored. In fact, it could be said that they form what Lauren Rabinovitz calls "points of resistance" (1991).

Maria Klonaris and Katerina Thomadaki's *Cinéma corporel* is such a "point of resistance." Beginning in 1976, theirs is a practice that challenges many assumptions about film, art, authorial, and spectatorial experiences. If *Cinéma corporel* shares with experimental cinema its independence from the mainstream and interest in formal exploration, it offers neither media-specific formalism nor deconstructive intervention. If it shares with feminist cinema concerns about women's represen-tation, it is neither narrative nor documentary. And if it pioneered in France the question of gender, it also precedes queer cinema by a decade. *Cinéma corporel* is singular in at least two important aspects: it intermixes media forms and cul-tural references, generating conceptual and formal innovations. And it is based on double authorship: both artists share all aspects of production and theory, assuming a double signature, which "overthrows the profoundly rooted idea of the One and all powerful male director as the only legitimate *auteur*" (Klonaris/ Thomadaki in Gržinić 2011, 193).

As this chapter aims to demonstrate—Klonaris and Thomadaki's *Cinéma corporel* represents, for women's cinema, *a strategy of dissidence*. In form, content, concept, and approach, it calls for a revisitation of "film" outside the canon established in traditional film history. In any case, it highlights the need to "heighten the visibility of women's contributions to traditions of formal innovation and explore how formal innovation enables women to enlarge discourses about women's subjectivity" and art (Petrolle and Wexman 2005, 3).

A Cinema of Rupture

The question of strategy has long been discussed among feminist scholars and filmmakers in the English-speaking world. In the 1970s, feminist film theory emerged in Britain, analyzing mainstream cinema as charged with sexual and social power relations of dominant patriarchal ideology. Woman, it argued, is the Other. Based on this analysis, discussions thrived on the question of strategy: How to figure "women as women" or construct the female point of view? How to circumvent the centrality of the male gaze, and with what implications for narrative forms? How to create positive forms of identification for female viewers? Should a feminist cinema be inside or outside the mainstream? Or should it function as a "counter-cinema" deploying "negative aesthetics," as advocated by the two major theorists Claire Johnston and Laura Mulvey?

Likewise, Klonaris and Thomadaki analyzed mainstream cinema as a paradigm of male domination; however, they did not choose "counter-aesthetics." Their strategy adopts neither disnarrativity [*dysnarrativité*] (as does, say, Chantal Akerman or Marguerite Duras) nor "negative aesthetics" in response to Hollywood canons—in fact, they have little interest in Hollywood. A film genealogy would, rather, trace their cinematic inspiration to European cinema (Bergman, Antonioni, Paradjanov), as well as to the historical avant-garde of the 1920s and to the New American Cinema (in particular to Maya Deren, Gregory Markopoulos, Stan Vanderbeek). Rather than engaging in negative strategies, which would ultimately become sterile, they prefer an affirmative position: "We rather strive to create alternative languages. [...] The universe we propose is not subjected to predefined codes. It emerges from some other, non pre-existing place which it makes visible" (Klonaris/Thomadaki in Brenez 2002, 93).

Having chosen experimental cinema—and the low-budget Super 8 format to achieve full independence of conception, production and distribution[4]—Klonaris and Thomadaki's second principle was equality and interchangeability of roles, whereby the two artists would alone shoot, edit, and project their films, as well as star in them (sometimes with a guest performer)—an appropriation of technics seen as a feminist act in itself, but also as a way to entirely redefine the cinematic apparatus. Third, their cinema was opened up—*décloisonné*—encompassing different media as well as live performance.

In her 1975 ground-breaking article, Laura Mulvey expresses her wish for a feminist avant-garde, a "new language of desire" that would include rupture and reflexivity and would reinvent visual pleasure by "free[ing] the look of the camera into its materiality of time and space and the look of the audience into dialectic, passionate detachment" (18). Klonaris and Thomadaki's *Cinéma corporel* seems to fulfill this wish. Yet as they created their first co-signed film, *Double Labyrinth* (1975–76), within the privacy of their studio, the artists were unfamiliar with the debates among English scholars. Freshly exiled from a patriarchal Greece traumatized by dictatorship into a post-1968 Paris, they had thrown themselves into an intense film, performance, and photography practice in order to pursue the experiments they had started in Athens with their *Théâtre corporel*.[5] This practice had emerged as a matter of urgency—in their own words, an "absolute need" to define themselves anew in a different sociocultural landscape, to invent a thoroughly personal language, aims which transpire in their late-1970s manifestoes, such as their 1977 *Manifesto for a Radical Femininity, for an Other Cinema*:

PASSION FOR RADICAL CREATION: THIS OTHER CINEMA

Insubordination. Independence. Rupture. Autonomy [. . .]
A Radical Femininity can only flourish within a radical creation.
I create my own images.
I invent my vision, neither "natural" nor "normal" nor "objective," but *real*
since it emerges from desire
and understandable if one forgets
what one has been taught to understand.
I unleash my introspection.
I expose my roots and my sufferings: childhood, desire, rebellion, oppression,
       torture, old age, death.
I expose my social and archetypal colors: red, black, white, pink, gold and
       silver.
I perform my own mental structures and geometries.
My body image imprints the film.
I open myself to you through my own sentient and sensitive body.
My body of woman/subject.

I offer you the rituals of my identity.
Haemorrhage of identity not mediated by someone else, but asserted by
    myself
before you.
I am looking at you.
I am questioning you.
I give birth to an OTHER cinema.
(2003, 8–9, my translation)

As invoked in this manifesto, the *Cinéma corporel* directly invests the question of gendered self-representation within a radical film practice, with female body-identity at the center of artistic query—a proposition unique in France at the time. It forms the core of Klonaris/Thomadaki's art, which, throughout the years, would develop into different cycles of works: *The Body Tetralogy* (1975–79) reinvents the representation of the female body and subjectivity through concepts such as *body action, actante, intercorporeality*, and *corporalized projection*, while *The Cycle of the Unheimlich* (1977–82) explores the female as *uncanny*. Thereafter, their work departed from self-representation to investigate and subvert gender through intersex bodies in *The Cycle of Hermaphrodites* (1982–90) and *The Angel Cycle* (1985–present). To this must be added the *Portrait Series* (1979–2000), and works on mythical or "monstrous" figures, *Electra's Dream* (1983–90), *Persephone* (1993), *Sublime Disasters: The Twins* (1995–2000). Today, Klonaris/Thomadaki's work is moving further into the relations between subjectivity and cosmology. All these cycles have in common the aim to represent what the artists call "dissident bodies" (see Gržinić and Pirnat-Spahić 2002) and "dissident subjectivities" (see Gržinić 2011).

Reinventing Gendered Subjectivity: Self-Representation and *Intercorporeality*

Centered on the *woman/subject*[6] and conceived as a *double-mirror, Double Labyrinth*, the first film of *The Body Tetralogy*, establishes the principles of *Cinéma corporel* (see figure 7.1). Its twice six actions (in the first half, Katerina performs and is filmed by Maria; in the second, Maria performs and is filmed by Katerina) show the *actante*[7] acting out the intimate forces of her identity while inventing a silent body language that breaks away from sexual, social, and cultural definitions of "womanhood." Facing her, the *filmante* invents a subjective filmic inscription. The dynamics between *actante* and *filmante* through the *camera-mirror*, including the interaction of gazes, are central to the film, adding tension and complexity to the

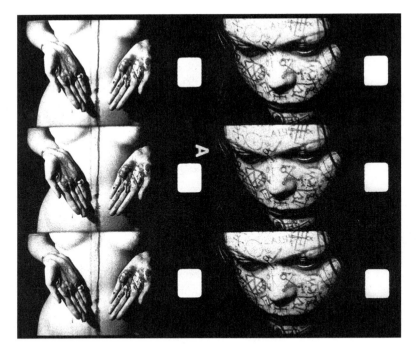

FIGURE 7.1. Katerina Thomadaki and Maria Klonaris in *Double Labyrinth* (1975–76), Klonaris/Thomadaki—Super 8, color, silent, 50 minutes, transferred onto 16mm, National Museum of Modern Art, Pompidou Center Film Collections (Photo by and courtesy of Klonaris/Thomadaki)

already-dense performance taking place within an abstract space-time. The symmetrical structure of the film highlights the cinematic moment as an encounter of two female subjectivities, two female body-psyches, staged within a very personal camera obscura—what the artists call an *intercorporeal apparatus*. Aesthetically, the film deploys centrality and frontality, constant black background and dramatic chiaroscuros; colors are carefully selected, and so are camera movements and editing rhythms; silence becomes a dimension in itself.

Evidently, *Double Labyrinth* breaches film conventions and subverts the traditional roles of subject and object of the gaze. This leads to a redefinition of "femininity" itself: unlike the actress, the *actante* is not a looked-at object, and "femininity" is neither an essence nor just a socially defined concept. It is in fact the very object of inquiry by the self-reflexive subject who creates her own disruptive visual language. Thus, "self" as "woman" is the female subject who reinvents her own power and freedom at the very moment of cinematic inscription. Correlatively, film is redefined as a subjective territory of resistance, a process that owes nothing to fiction but everything to an authentic *secret dialogue* between two women artists.

If in the late-1970s these politics (based upon "the personal is political") met the concerns of other contemporary women artists, as well as a generation of feminist activists, Maria Klonaris and Katerina Thomadaki were not originally driven by feminist analyses but inspired by their own theatrical practice developed in Athens between 1967 and 1974. The experimental group they had then created favored *drasis* (action) over traditional acting, and they worked on physical presence and interpersonal dynamics rather than the spoken word. Their language of symbolic gestures derived possibly from their Greek and Egyptian cultural heritage, where timeless rituals were, at the time of their youth, still surviving.[8] But their *Cinéma corporel* also met contemporary Western art practice: Body Art was thriving in Paris in the 1970s, thanks to artists Gina Pane and Michel Journiac. Inscribed within a post-1968 generation's concern with body politics, feminism, and gay liberation, and drawing on Foucault's analysis of power structures and sexuality, French body artists viewed their own bodies as the primary matter of their art, performing "actions" to reveal social determinisms inscribed within physical existence. *Art corporel* saw itself as a radical criticism of society (and part of *Art sociologique*), as "an existential discourse from the depths of being" (Pluchart 1983, 260) and an "epistemological rupture" within art (Journiac 1987, 12). This resonated strongly with Klonaris/Thomadaki, who also defined the body as a site of opposition to sociocultural pressure and viewed "action" as a body language disclosing an unsubmissive force emerging out of trauma or desire. They named their *Cinéma corporel* after their *Théâtre corporel* and *Art corporel*. Their work, however, was distinct from Body Art because it was based on an interpersonal process. Furthermore, Klonaris/Thomadaki were preoccupied with image and re-presentation, as well as with technological mediation and projection mechanisms:

> The body is the first material *screen* where we project the rituals of our desire. It is in that other *camera obscura*, the cinema hall, that the screen becomes a precise object, and projection a physical act. By handling the projectors ourselves, we create a mirror effect between projecting and projected bodies. By our presence in the room, we give a physical quality to the cinematic apparatus. (1981, 26)

Projection is *corporalized*. In relocating *body action* in film, Klonaris/Thomadaki define the performer as both projected and projecting body, and the *woman/subject* as a self-defining artist taking into her own hands the means of representation. Simultaneously an imaginary and demystified apparatus, the *Cinéma corporel* makes of film a projective art for women's empowerment—an empowerment worked from *within*, as an uncanny female power emerges right in front of the camera. Their 1978 *Manifesto for a Cinema of the Body* clearly makes the connection body-action-film and declares it an artistic/political act:

Because   the meaning of the body is violent
Because   my body is danger of life and death
Because   my body is of woman-subject
Because   my images are born out of all the bodies of my body
Because   my images are blood made visible . . .
(2003, 10–11, my translation)

The *Cinéma corporel* in Relation to Experimental Cinema

In the mid-1970s, the Parisian scene of experimental cinema was, just as in the United States, the United Kingdom, and Germany, dominated by structuralism. Focus was on the formal specificities of film; the human form was strongly rejected. Two freshly arrived young women disrupted the status quo: they filmed the female body, claimed both subjectivity and unconventional artistic authorship, introduced intercultural imagery, and fought for media hybridity. Altogether profound, sensual, and sensitive, their *Cinéma corporel* was also rigorously conceived and formally inventive; it created images at once figurative, abstract, and fascinating; it showed masterful rhythmic editing and an innovative *écriture filmique*; it was intellectual yet beyond *logos*, requesting other modes of perception yet accessible to all. With two *auteures* committed to technical perfection, it surprised more than one that Super 8 could achieve such aesthetic quality.

The *Cinéma corporel* was also a counterproposition to another male trend in experimental film, inspired by the American Underground and focused on representing sexual fantasies. In these films, the (generally male) body is constructed as object, and the viewer has no choice but to witness the filmmaker's homoerotic voyeurism and fetishism. Contrariwise, Klonaris and Thomadaki's conceptualized femaleness and interrogation of the viewer's positioning offered clear challenges: the *actante's auto-mise-en-scène*, and her direct gazes to the camera, circumvent voyeurism, while the *filmante's* subjective camera disrupts the possibility of conventional identification. The films also convey recurring *mises-en-abyme* through a series of mirror effects, both inside the frame and within the cinema space, where the two artists stage themselves as live performing-projecting bodies. Therefore, the viewer is given a reflection of his-her own gaze and needs to find new modalities of engagement with the film. He-she becomes fully aware of the here-and-now of screening and is confronted by disturbing questions about identity, psychic forces, and the vulnerability of embodiment. Simultaneously, he-she awakens to film as construct, pondering cinematic language, as he-she discovers visions drawn out of a subjectivity not only unwilling to conform but also in the very process of reinventing language itself.

The *Cinéma corporel* naturally found responsive audiences within feminist circles (women's film festivals were thriving across Europe in the 1970s and 1980s). However, so unexpected were Klonaris/Thomadaki's choices that the filmmakers provided their audiences with screening notes, personal introductions, and open debates. Interaction with the public became part of their practice, as did their regular theoretical writings, and engagement with different forms of cultural activism, such as experimental film workshops. At the same time, Klonaris/Thomadaki partly met the concerns of other feminist artists and filmmakers, mostly outside France. For example, Robin Blaetz (2007, 5) sees the female American avant-garde as the "counter-cinema" that Claire Johnston called for. Although rooted in more varied aesthetic practices and political positions than simple opposition to Hollywood, filmmakers such as Marjorie Keller, Barbara Rubin, Gunvor Nelson, or Barbara Hammer were all engaged in reinventing audiovisual language. Among these, a number addressed the particularly thorny issue of the representation of the female body: Amy Greenfield and Yvonne Rainer were interested in the dancing body, while Carolee Schneemann and also the Austrian Valie Export blurred the boundaries between cinema and performance.

Like Klonaris/Thomadaki, both of these latter performer-filmmakers worked on self-portraiture and promulgated new interpretations of female sexuality. All took the risk of intimate self-exposure and, to transpose Marsha Meskimmon's comment on women painters, "all question[ed] the boundaries of acceptability in the representation of women in our culture" (1996, 165). In the case of Klonaris/Thomadaki, their work deploys, over the span of four decades, interiorized visions of the female subject's body-mind, their reinvented cinematic language of interiority becoming a strategy of subversion. However, more radically than their American counterparts, they have penetrated the core of the cinematic unconscious and established an imagery that emerges intimately from the film apparatus itself. In so doing, they have interrogated the unconscious of our culture.

Revisiting Myths, Deploying Figures of Female Power

In the late-1970s, Maria Klonaris and Katerina Thomadaki pioneered a reflection on the uncanny in experimental film. Dedicated to the Freudian concept (Unheimlich—the familiar become strange), *The Cycle of the Unheimlich* (1977–82) is a series of feature-length (and mostly silent) films in which the artists' language is at

FIGURE 7.2. Katerina Thomadaki in *Unheimlich I: Secret Dialogue* (1977–79) by Klonaris/Thomadaki—Super 8, color, silent, 70 minutes, restored in 35mm by the French Film Archives under Maria Klonaris and Katerina Thomadaki's supervision, with additional support by the J. F. Costopoulos Foundation, Athens (French Film Archives/CNC Film Collections) (Photo by and courtesy of Klonaris/Thomadaki)

its most radical and, for the viewer, most unsettling (see figure 7.2). Here, "body" is flesh, psyche, memory, image, desire, language, symbol, icon, *Eros, Thanatos, mythos*. . . . Silence, darkness, and mystery define this world. The (all female) *actantes* appear costumed and masked, facing the camera in enigmatic postures, creating constant tensions between movement and stasis. Through the effects of intensely rhythmic editing, these figures appear and disappear in the dark, slip, slide, and flit, enacting a realm of the hidden, the invisible, the inarticulable—what the artists call "The Ungraspable" (1990, 48). Here, film becomes a visionary medium, which has, as the Surrealists saw, great affinity with dreaming.

The accompanying notes for *Unheimlich I: Secret Dialogue* (1977–79) cite Schelling's definition (as quoted by Freud in his 1919 essay): "The *uncanny* is everything that ought to have remained secret and hidden, but comes to light." For Klonaris/Thomadaki, the *uncanny* becomes "the unconscious emerging onto the surface of the film." They explain: "The body is the raw material of our cinema"; through the body "the mental image becomes spatialized thought. It is a *philosophical state of matter*, whereby the unconscious clothes itself in the appearance of the body. The *I/within* reveals itself as *I/outside*, and the language of the body materializes the language of the unconscious" (1981, 25 [emphasis in original]). In these films, as in later installations, they revisit archetypal figures of pre-patriarchal Mediterranean cultures, hidden in "the closed chamber of the mind, the silent matrix of dreams." *The Cycle of the Unheimlich* is a full immersion into "hypnoid states, intermediate, dream-like consciousness, when the mind lets open a world of suspended images" (Klonaris/Thomadaki in Brenez 2002, 103).

Klonaris and Thomadaki associated the uncanny with "the feminine," which in their films appears as a theater of personae—forms of masquerade and sometimes excess. Far from representing an essentialist (and necessarily heteronormative) "feminine," *The Cycle of the Unheimlich* activates deeply ingrained and vivid cultural memories. Evocations of baroque figures, Byzantine icons, Egyptian paintings, Cretan frescoes, Noh actors, Fayum portraits . . . abound. The films seem to display the *actantes'* inner labyrinthine museum.

This strategy is central to the feminist problematic: how to overcome the sexual and social coding of "woman" and develop new forms of identification. In this respect, *The Cycle of the Unheimlich* contributes significantly in several ways to discourses on identity, whether sexual or cultural. One is through its deep entry into the Symbolic, disturbing the dominant order that governs sexuality. Another is the artists' claim for hybrid cultural identity rooted in complex contemporary forms of identification and displacement. Thus, their aesthetics produce a clash of cultures and eras, challenging the practices of Western and even feminist art.

In "Film, Gender and Anthropology," Klonaris/Thomadaki explain their defiance of Western cultural hegemony. According to them, it leads to an impoverishment of human expression:

Our concern for surviving ancient or non-European rites comes not only from our cultural origins, but also from our conviction that "outsiders" unveil the

FIGURE 7.3. Maria Klonaris in *Pulsar* (2001) by Klonaris/Thomadaki—
digital video, color, original music by Spiros Faros, 14 minutes
(Photo by and courtesy of Klonaris/Thomadaki)

lacks and failures of Western cultures. [. . .] Symptoms of hierarchization of cultures are present everywhere. . . . Dynamics of oppression create exclusions which tend to destroy peripheral cultures, but equally, they simultaneously dry out and flatten central cultures. [. . .] By rejecting mythical thought as a block, Western civilisation has placed itself once more at the top of its own hierarchical pyramid. The dominant currents in contemporary art, supported by the art market, display the symptoms of an anthropological mutation of the mind: from now on, the only legitimate imagination seems to be the one constructed by media or by the techno-establishment. (2008, 71)

This argument is highlighted by philosopher Marie-José Mondzain in her reading of *Pulsar* (see figure 7.3), a digital video that echoes, in 2001, the uncanny "hypnoid states" of the earlier *Unheimlich I: Secret Dialogue*. Mondzain demonstrates how Klonaris/Thomadaki continue to shift representations as they rework Western foundation myths through a disturbing *mise-en-crise* (unsettlement) of the viewer's position:

Pulsar entranced me . . . astonished me . . . [it] is simultaneously pulse, impulse and repulse. There is a very powerful dynamic of Maria Klonaris' body and face in relation to the viewer, constantly set as far away as possible and as near as possible, caught in some sort of organic beat, in a pulsing and light circulation. . . . This produces a surprising inversion of another apparatus: the apparatus of the Creation, as painted by Michelangelo. . . . In *Pulsar*, this classical, well-accepted, religious and aesthetic order is replaced by a completely different rhetoric. Suddenly, here is set a new Genesis, in which a body of both darkness and light, a kind of biological presence to which I was immediately receptive, pushes me back, gives birth to me, attracts me and holds me captive in its power. It offers me limitless likeness in complete unlikeness. This cosmogonic presence is a woman. (2002, 53)

Subverting Gender: *Intersex* and *Intermedia*

From the early 1980s, Maria Klonaris and Katerina Thomadaki started representing bodies outside the binary gender system and inside the hybrid and fluid. In *The Cycle of the Hermaphrodites* (1982–1990) and the ongoing *Angel Cycle* (1985–present), the artists continue to venture through technologies and body images, destabilizing gender norms through pioneering multimedia projection environments. While the first cycle explores the doubly-sexed archetype represented by the Louvre's Hellenistic statue "The Sleeping Hermaphrodite," *The Angel Cycle* reflects the "collapse of gender" stated in their 1995 manifesto, "Intersexuality and Intermedia." The image-matrix of *The Angel Cycle* is the photograph of an intersex person found in Maria's father's medical archives. Through both the subject's inherent sexual hybridity and various multimedia forms, Klonaris and Thomadaki develop the notion of *mosaic identity*. Already, the *radical feminine* in their 1977 manifesto was defined as "a symbiosis of female and male energies" (2003, 8). In this sense, all their female, androgynous, hermaphrodite, angelic, and twin figurations are *dissident bodies*. As Slovenian artist and theorist Marina Gržinić summarizes, their art addresses "the question of the dissident body as a counter-subjectivity, of the body that thinks and acts, rebels and disrupts, but also *disfigures*" (2011, 189).

Like the emblematic Angel of their œuvre, Klonaris/Thomadaki's images are all posited between flesh and abstraction, the incarnate and the projected, the sensible and the invisible, the mythical and the real. As such, they define identity as both *mosaic* and *ungraspable*, raising a core question: *What is an image?* With the technological and intellectual tools of our age, Maria Klonaris and Katerina Thomadaki question the image—not only as a reflection of our bodies, not only as metaphor and allegory for our minds, and not only as a means of challenging social understandings, but in order to reinvent its profound, inherently symbolic power for women—in all its political, philosophical, and metaphysical dimensions.

■ ■ ■

During the course of this chapter, we observed three main reasons why Maria Klonaris and Katerina Thomadaki's *Cinéma corporel* has been overlooked by Anglo-American film scholars: its inscription within women's avant-garde cinema, its intercultural visual imagination, and its intermixing of media—all of which challenge the organizational categories—genre; media; nationality—by which historiographic scholarship and publishing houses operate. We have demonstrated how it both belongs to and transcends feminist cinema through its singular "dissident" strategies. As such, it has its full place within women's film historiography, but a historiography that encompasses a widened definition of film language and experience. Klonaris/Thomadaki have created subversive representations of women, which both address and further push feminist questions about film. They have also invented cinematic forms which demand "film" be rethought, especially if the cinematic is to survive during the digital age. Finally, they have opened new territories of film reception, proving that feminist art can profoundly transform viewers' experience and impact on the wider cultural landscape. Such transformation of film practice equally demands transformation of the categories by which we approach archival preservation, historiographic research, and history writing. The CNC restorations and the BnF Klonaris/Thomadaki Archive, we hope, will not only preserve but ensure an increased exposure of this remarkable work—not only for our pleasure but because it helps us to become richer, resisting humans.

This text is dedicated to Maria Klonaris,
who passed away peacefully on January 13, 2014.

Notes

1. "These restorations are both unique and exemplary for our institution, as the very form of these films required a non-traditional restoration procedure, making use of highly performative techniques which do not correspond to the usual archiving criteria. This exceptional work finds no equivalent in the world of the International Federation of Film Archives, the organization having no record of acknowledging experimental film as part of film history. This work is now admired by many foreign archives and cinematheques" (Le Roy 2006, 12).

2. For the full list of their works, see: http://www.klonaris-thomadaki.net. In the 1990s they advocated a "media ecology" when they founded the Quadriennale Rencontres Internationales Art Cinéma/Vidéo/Ordinateur, the first event in France to bring together film, video and digital arts. For these events, they promoted other independent audiovisual artists, with women constituting more than half the participants.

3. The artists coined the term *Le Cinéma corporel* in the mid-1970s, publishing their English usage as *Cinema of the Body* in 1981. The recent term "French Cinema of the Body" used by

Anglo-American critics about new auteurs working within the film industry is not related to their concept.

4. In the 1970s and 1980s, experimental film was not recognized and therefore not funded by the French state. The Centre National de la Cinématographie was (and still is) preoccupied with narrative and documentary film, while the Culture Ministry supported (and still does) the "arts plastiques." Consequently, Klonaris/Thomadaki's Super 8 films were self-funded. However, their multimedia installations or site-specific environments continue to be commissioned and funded by institutions (museums, art centres, festivals, and the like). In 1985 the artists created their own distribution structure, A.S.T.A.R.T.I., and some of their films and videos appear in the catalogs of French experimental film and video distributors.

5. Their adaptations of Jean Genet's *The Maids* (1968) and Oscar Wilde's *Salomé* (1969) were particularly praised by critics.

6. From here on, italicized terms indicate the artists' concepts.

7. "To shatter ossified roles, to abolish power relations, to remain *subject* on both sides of the camera . . . we introduced the term *actante*, as opposed to actress, to denote our function in front of the camera" (Klonaris/Thomadaki 1990, 57).

8. Their early years made the two artists perfectly trilingual and gave them a profound intercultural identity. Klonaris was born in Cairo, Egypt, as part of the Greek diaspora. She spent her childhood in Alexandria and was educated at the English Girl's College before moving to Athens as an adolescent. Thomadaki was born and raised in Athens. There, both studied at the Hellenic-American College before entering university, and they acquired an intimate knowledge of French at the French Institute. They continued their studies at Paris Sorbonne, where Thomadaki today is adjunct professor in Media Studies and Experimental Film.

References

Blaetz, Robin, ed. 2007. *Women's Experimental Cinema: Critical Frameworks*. Durham, N.C.: Duke University Press.

Brenez, Nicole. 2002. "Entretien avec Maria Klonaris et Katerina Thomadaki: Rites de l'intelligence et filmscultes." In Gržinić and Pirnat-Spahić, *Klonaris/Thomadaki*, 89–104.

Chich, Cécile, ed. 2006. *Klonaris/Thomadaki: Le Cinéma corporel—Corps sublimes/ Intersexe et Intermédia*. Paris: L'Harmattan.

Gattinoni, Christian. 2002. "Klonaris/Thomadaki: Le destin politique des anges." *Art Press* 275 (January): 36–41.

Gržinić, Marina. 2011. "Dissident Subjectivities: The Filmmakers as a Double Author; A Conversation with Maria Klonaris and Katerina Thomadaki." In *Subjectivity*, edited by Dominique Chateau, 189–205. Amsterdam: Amsterdam University Press.

Gržinić, Marina, and Nina Pirnat-Spahić, eds. 2002. *Klonaris/Thomadaki: Stranger than Angel; Disidentska telesa/Corps dissidents/Dissident Bodies*. Ljubljana: Cankarjev Dom.

Johnston, Claire. 1973. "Women's Cinema as Counter-Cinema." In *Notes on Women's Cinema*, edited by Claire Johnston, 24–31. London: SEFT.

Journiac, Michel, ed. 1987. *L'Enjeu de la représentation: Le corps*. Paris: Institut d'Esthétique de l'Université Panthéon-Sorbonne.

Klonaris, Maria, and Katerina Thomadaki. 1981. "Cinema of the Body." *Undercut* 2 (August): 22–26.

———. 1990. "L'Insaisissable/The Ungraspable." *Performance* 62 (November): 48–71.

———. 1999. http://www.klonaris-thomadaki.net.

———. 2000. "Intersexuality and Intermedia: A Manifesto." In *Maska: Women's Strategies in Media*, edited by Marina Gržinić, 20–24. Ljubljana: Maska.

———. 2003. *Manifestes 1976–2002*. Paris: Cahiers Paris Expérimental.

———. 2008. "Film, Gender and Anthropology: A Letter from the 'First World.'" In *New Feminism: Worlds of Feminism, Queer and Networking Conditions*, edited by Marina Gržinić and Rosa Reitsamer, 65–72. Vienna: Löcker.

Le Roy, Eric. 2006. "A propos de la restauration des films *Selva* de Maria Klonaris et *Chutes. Désert. Syn* de Katerina Thomadaki par les Archives françaises du film." *Journal of Film Preservation* 72 (November): 35–36.

Meskimmon, Marsha. 1996. *The Art of Reflection: Women Artists' Self-Portraiture in the Twentieth Century*. London: Scarlet.

Mondzain, Marie-José. 2002. "Figures of Otherness and Difference in the Work of Maria Klonaris and Katerina Thomadaki." In Gržinić and Pirnat-Spahić, *Klonaris/Thomadaki*, 45–55.

Mulvey, Laura. 1975. "Visual Pleasure and Narrative Cinema." *Screen* 16 (3): 6–18.

Petrolle, Jean, and Virginia Wright Wexman, eds. 2005. "Introduction: Experimental Filmmaking and Women's Subjectivity." In *Women and Experimental Filmmaking*, 1–17. Urbana: University of Illinois Press.

Pirnat-Spahić, Nina. 2002. "Preface." In Gržinić and Pirnat-Spahić, *Klonaris/Thomadaki*, 10–11.

Pluchart, François. 1983. *L'Art Corporel*. Paris: Limage2.

Rabinovitz, Lauren. 1991. *Points of Resistance: Women, Power and Politics in the New York Avant-Garde Cinema, 1943–71*. Urbana: University of Illinois Press.

CHAPTER 8

Feminism and Women's Film History in 1980s Turkey

EYLEM ATAKAV

This chapter focuses on the relationship between feminism and women's film history in the context of 1980s Turkey.[1] I take women's film history to include not only the history of women filmmakers and the films they have made but also (important here) the relationship between the history of Turkey's film industry and feminism. Central to this chapter is the proposition that the enforced depoliticization introduced in Turkey after the 1980 coup opened up a space for feminist concerns to be expressed within commercial cinema. In the ensuing decade the feminist movement was able to flourish precisely because it was not perceived as political or politically significant, while at the same time there was an increased tendency for films to focus on women's issues and lives in order to avoid overtly political content. However, while the political context gave rise to the newly humanized, more independent heroine that characterized Turkish cinema in this period, the films were nevertheless made largely within the structures of a patriarchal commercial cinema. This chapter begins with a historical overview of the feminist movement in Turkey and then explores its visible traces in film texts produced during the 1980s in order to argue that those films can be most productively understood as explorations of gendered power relations.

The Women's Movement

In the 1970s Turkey witnessed a period of increased and violent political polarization between the Left and Right, during which each side attacked the other.

Following this initial political unrest, both sides joined in attacking the institutions of the state, provoking its retaliation in turn. Traditionally perceived to be the guardian of the Turkish state and constitution, the army intervened to put an end to what appeared to be incipient civil war. The military coup of September 12, 1980, crushed all political parties—particularly leftist organizations—and temporarily suspended democracy, thereby bringing normal political life to a halt. The coup attempted a systematic depoliticization of the masses. In the ensuing atmosphere of repression, the first social movement that demonstrated the courage to voice any opposition and to articulate its demands was the women's movement. Attempts to identify how feminism operated in this depoliticized space as a political movement have led to considerable debate. Did the movement seek merely to appear nonpolitical? Or did it intend to be nonpolitical? Or was it simply not perceived as political? On the one hand, scholars like Şirin Tekeli (1995), Ramazan Gülendam (2001), and Aysu Gelgeç-Gürpınar (2006) claim that feminism could only have come to the forefront after the 1980 military coup. They argue that if the leftist movement had not been hit so severely by the coup, women would not have been able to question the hegemony of the male leaders. On the other hand, some maintain that even if the left-wing organizations had not been crushed, the women involved in them would still have discovered women's oppression just as Western feminists did.

Following the establishment of the Turkish Republic in 1923 under the leadership of Mustafa Kemal Atatürk, the vision of a Westernized—namely liberal, democratic, and secular—Turkey had been promoted via a series of reforms. Under these so-called Kemalist reforms women had been given certain basic rights by the state through what is often termed state feminism. Indeed, women's equality became a matter of national policy, and women were encouraged to enter universities, pursue professions, and even run for parliament. Yet Turkey remained a male-dominated state and culture, with deeply entrenched patriarchal values.

As already noted, political polarization and radicalization in Turkey during the 1970s led to a social and political milieu that resembled civil war. The two main groupings involved, on the one side, numerous paramilitary rightist groups and organizations and, on the other, radical extraparliamentary leftist groups and organizations who had been influenced by the spread of Marxism and the student revolt of 1968 (Gülendam, 2001). As Tekeli (1995) points out, in the 1970s left-wing political groups became effective in defining the political agenda of the country, introducing concepts of economic underdevelopment, imperialism, economic and social injustice, inequality, and class exploitation. Since women's exploitation and oppression were also issues of inequality and injustice, the Turkish Left additionally started focusing on women's rights as part of a systemic social transformation, and women were included in the leftist movements as comrades.[2] It is possible to argue, in this context, that the very idea of feminism became intertwined with the milieu of political polarization and radicalization. Women involved in this process began to realize, however, that women's oppression was based on an inherent patriarchal structure that would not simply be overthrown by a socialist revolution.

Thus it is only in the 1980s, following the coup, that women, for the first time, raised their own independent voices, precipitating the emergence of an influential and democratic women's movement. In the context of the military regime, women occupied a privileged position in that while other groups—including workers, students, civil servants, and political parties—were suppressed, women were able to engage in political activity. Whether it was because women's groups and their activism were thought to be insignificant or because the general concept of women's rights could root its legitimacy in the earlier Kemalist reforms, women were able to raise their voices. As Yeşim Arat (1994) expresses it, during a period when political activity was severely curtailed, women were able to exercise their political will (107). By doing so, they underlined the importance of becoming politicized; as a consequence, they directly contributed to a process of re-democratization. However, this movement of women was careful to remain independent of political parties. Decentralization was its basic principle, and different groups were free to decide on their specific mode of organization and actions: ad hoc committees, topic-based campaigns, associations, and journals provided opportunities for events like protest walks and petitions. Despite its small number of activists, such initiatives were able to mobilize a broad women's movement in Turkey.

As Aksu Bora and Asena Günal (2002) explain, the movement commenced with the emergence of small, informal consciousness-raising groups in which women talked about issues such as domestic violence, abortion, and careers (12). These discussion groups were followed by publications and involvement with the media. In 1982, the nonfeminist, nonprofit-oriented publishing company YAZKO offered women their first opportunity to produce specialized publications by and about women. Moreover, women writing in the weekly literary journal *Somut* were able to encourage other women to address salient concerns including abortion, domestic violence, and Turkish women's customary roles. These activities, together with the foundation of institutions like the Women's Library and Information Center, defined the contours of the women's movement in Turkey. Those involved in the movement followed feminist activism abroad and developed feminist perspectives on women's issues in Turkey. In 1983 some of these women organized a publishing service and consultancy called Kadın Çevresi (Women's Circle), located in Istanbul and aimed at "upholding women's labour within or outside the household" (Arat 1994, 103). In addition, a book club was formed, which translated feminist classics from other countries into Turkish and functioned as a forum for discussing such work as well as feminist issues. The same year, abortion was legalized in Turkey, while later, in 1986, a campaign took place to spur implementation of the 1985 UN Convention on the Elimination of All Forms of Discrimination against Women. With this campaign, women's groups from both Istanbul and Ankara initiated collective public activism for the first time. The year 1987 witnessed the launch of an extensive campaign against domestic violence, and a number of women's shelters were opened. Women also started a campaign against sexual harassment in both the public and private spheres (Müftüler-Bac 1999, 311).

Turkish women began to organize these initiatives when it was illegal in Turkey to organize politically in any form. They were able to do so because, as noted above, the women's movement did not align its political activity with any of the organized political parties. Like the Western women's movement, feminists in Turkey maintained that the state had to respect the private sphere and women's own decisions while at the same time protecting them from abuse and violence. These women were important because they ventured into the political arena to seek legitimacy for women as individuals in their own right, irrespective of social class, ethnic origin, level of education, or profession. Thus the women's movement voiced its opposition to the state, arguing that it had remained largely authoritarian, protesting against its restriction of women's civil rights and liberties, and thereby challenging both state tradition and the patriarchal system. Consequently, rather than expecting the state to liberate women, the movement's major activities were directed against state policies, laws, and the regime itself.

However, even when the movement was at its peak in terms of activism and publications, it was not perceived as political. This is illustrated by the "Dayağa Karşı Dayanışma Kampanyası" (Campaign for Solidarity against Beating) of May 10, 1987. Bora and Günal (2002) describe this event as follows:

> On Mother's Day, we planned to sell flowers and badges which said "Do not beat mothers." Unluckily, it poured with rain that day. We could not get organized no matter how much we tried. Only a few of us women gathered in front of the Cultural Centre of Altındağ Municipality. We gave out badges to those walking past, we waved our placards. The media was there, but we were not happy with our meeting, because we could not reach women. (24)[3]

The media's response to the event was disappointing, employing satire and ridicule with such newspaper headlines as "Yağmurda Yedi Güzel" (Seven Beauties under the Rain). The popular newspaper *Hürriyet*'s coverage was typical in the way it ridiculed the women's attempt to protest against domestic violence. On May 11, 1987, in a short paragraph their reporter wrote:

Six feminist women gave a briefing to *eight* members of the press, arguing that "the media, mosques, courts, customs, etc., they all protect men who beat [women]." ... The feminists of Ankara gave away badges to people while declaring "we do not want to live with the threat of being beaten," and "domestic violence turns violence into an ideology." They said there were quite a number of feminists in Ankara, but they intentionally organized individually rather than founding organizations. Among these women only one of them is married, the others said they did not think of marriage as yet. (cited in Bora and Günal 2002, 24–25, emphasis added)

It is obvious from the very first line that the women activists were being ridiculed, while in the last sentence the reporter implicitly questions how these mostly unmarried women could understand domestic violence and motherhood. In addition to such ridicule, the activities of the movement were frequently either given little coverage—resulting in underrepresentation—or simply misrepresented. Nevertheless, those activities successfully provided opportunities for individuals as well as groups to stand up for and promote women's interests and issues.

Women's Films and Turkish Cinema

During the 1970s, there had been a significant strand of social-realist films in Turkish film production. Within this strand, a number of films overtly dealt with and critiqued the negative effect of strict social traditions, especially in rural Turkey, on both men and women. Among these social-realist films are: Türkan Soray's *Dönüs* (The Return) (1972); Ömer Lüfi Akad's trilogy *Gelin* (The Bride) (1973), *Düğün* (The Wedding) (1973), and *Diyet* (Blood Money) (1974); Ömer Kavur's *Yatık Emine* (Leaning Emine) (1974); Yılmaz Güney's *Arkadas* (Friend) (1974); Süreyya Duru's *Bedrana* (Bedrana) (1974); Atıf Yılmaz's *Selvi Boylum Al Yazmalım* (The Girl with the Red Scarf) (1978); and Zeki Ökten's *Sürü* (The Herd) (1978). However, the plots of these films—in various ways and for a variety of reasons—end with women abandoning their own needs and desires, their problems narrowly conceived as resolvable by male "rescue from peril," by marriage, or—when neither is possible—by suicide.

In the immediate aftermath of the 1980 coup, such social-realist films were censored, banned, or destroyed as a result of the enforced depoliticization. At the same time, the film industry itself was undergoing a period of change. Even before the coup, the commercial film industry, known as Yeşilçam (Green Pine)—so named after the street in Istanbul where many actors, directors, and studios were based—had been struggling financially. The arrival of television in 1968 and the high cost of producing color films, combined with the political unrest, had resulted in a decline in both cinema audiences and film production. As a result, it had become common practice by 1980 to release popular genre films—such as action, adventure, comedy, erotic, horror, and sci-fi—on VHS in advance of any theatrical release in order to target the home-viewing market, while cinemas in urban centers tended to screen less-mainstream Yeşilçam and art-house films, which had enjoyed critical success at national and international film festivals. According to Savas Arslan, the number of Yeşilçam films produced annually during the first years of military rule bottomed out to approximately seventy. However, while cinema audiences remained in decline, during the second half of the 1980s the number of films produced annually started to increase, peaking at nearly two hundred in 1986 and 1987 (2011, 201).

Thus, many Yeşilçam filmmakers were able to continue working during the 1980s, but as a result of the depoliticization ushered in by the coup, they were unable to articulate directly political viewpoints and positions. In order to avoid overtly political content, they tended to focus on individuals' stories and particularly those of women. While such films could be read as subtly critiquing the wider social-political context, this focus on the individual opened up the possibility of far more multidimensional characters. Although the 1970s social-realist films had overtly critiqued Turkish society, they had nevertheless simplistically delineated female characters as either "good women" who served the male and conformed to the traditional roles assigned to them, or "bad women," femme fatales who could kiss, have sex, and commit adultery on screen. In the post-coup films, female characters were freed from this simple binary opposition, allowing narratives to develop a greater degree of depth and complexity.

In this context, and in parallel with the rise of feminism in Turkey, the 1980s witnessed a substantial number of "women's films" focusing on female characters engaged in a search for identity and independence within patriarchal society. These films tended to circulate on video first but were also screened on the film festival circuit, with some winning prizes. Just as the feminist movement made gender-related and women's rights issues more visible in wider society, recurring themes in films were female desire and sexuality; career women; sexual harassment; domestic violence and rape; motherhood; widowhood; and the concept of "honor" and what it meant for Turkish women. More fully rounded and believable characters appeared in these films, with the actresses who played them coming to be seen as agents of change as their onscreen roles started to evolve. For instance, the actress Müjde Ar had played the "good woman" in most—if not all—of her 1970s roles. She presented the image of a "virtuous" woman as defined by conformity to traditional roles within patriarchal structures. However, with the construction of more psychologically developed characters in her 1980s films,

Ar began to represent a different kind of woman, one who was independent and sophisticated. As illustrated by her roles in *Delikan* (The Juvenile) (Atıf Yılmaz, 1981), *Ah Güzel İstanbul* (Oh, Beautiful Istanbul) (Ömer Kavur, 1981), and *Göl* (The Lake) (Ömer Kavur, 1982), Ar's characters demonstrated that following one's own desires, kissing, having sex, and expressing sexuality freely did not make one a "bad woman." Equally, Türkan Şoray's characters in *Mine* (Atıf Yılmaz, 1982) and *Seni Seviyorum* (I Love You) (Atıf Yılmaz, 1983) reinforced the idea that a woman can experience sexuality without losing her integrity. Consequently—and echoing the public activism of the women's movement—what was previously considered *mahrem* (private) and had not been dealt with at all in films, or had been dealt with only covertly, was now being depicted overtly. As Atilla Dorsay writes in the early 1980s:

> A new woman character is appearing on the screens; one who not only senses her own sexuality but is also not afraid to actually follow her own desires freely and fearlessly. . . . Those women who did not have the opportunity to experience sexuality and their femininity, and who were not previously considered as equals to men on the screen, are now being represented as independent women in new films (which deal with sexuality and gender from a new perspective). I believe this new type of independent woman is one of the biggest changes in our cinema. (1984, 58)

Yet for the most part these films were made by (male) Yeşilçam directors, and despite what were quite profound shifts in narrative and character construction, the overall cinematic style, codes, and conventions remained largely those of traditional commercial cinema. Although the films introduced a more sophisticated and "human woman," they also continued to engage in the objectification of women, presenting them as having a range of choices necessarily limited within patriarchal society. As a result these 1980s women's films, although centered on female characters and their search for identity and independence, can also be viewed as expressing an ambivalence about whether women are ultimately capable of exercising independent agency.

The "Human" Woman in Turkish Cinema

This tension surrounding women's agency is very evident in the 1982 film, *Mine*, which has been described as "the pioneering film dealing with women's search for independence" (Scognamillo 2003, 212). It explores the relationship between women and society and their search for freedom from the oppressive conditions imposed by strict patriarchal traditions. The film seeks to represent the experience of a woman, the eponymous central character, caught in gendered power relations in a sexist environment. Through the film's foregrounding of this experience and its resulting challenge to the conventional dichotomy of good/bad woman, Mine (Türkan Şoray) becomes the pioneer "human woman" character of Turkish cinema.

Mine has been forced into an arranged marriage. She is not loved by her husband and does not love him, yet performs her "duties" as a housewife. They live in a small village with a tiny population, where Mine's husband works as the manager of the train station. The villagers tend to gossip, and the men in the village—young and old alike, and including the mayor, the engineer, and the builder—all have a crush on the beautiful Mine. Mine, however, is highly uncomfortable with their attentions. Throughout the film she is constantly "looked at," and in order to avoid these looks and the resulting harassment, she tends to stay at home. But whenever she is in the public sphere, her every move seems self-conscious. The film's visual style exaggerates this theme of being looked at, in the process making possible a critical reading of the objectification of female bodies while also highlighting Mine's mental and physical suffering. This is very evident in the film's two rape scenes. In one of these Mine is raped by her husband, whose violent access to his wife's body confirms that rape is not impossible in marriage. The scene is disturbing—as is any rape scene—shown via a montage of close-ups, with the camera frequently positioned at a low angle, following the movements of the husband's body, to convey a sense of brutality and disturbance. The camera's horizontal movement during the rape scene suggests mortification and subjection. Shots from Mine's point of view are also intercut with close-ups of the two bodies: while the husband is shown thrashing relentlessly on top of Mine on the floor, the camera moves along his body to her agonized face. The camera movement during this scene is shaky. What is significant here is that the audience is left with a sense of Mine's brutalization, rather than the husband's pleasure, which helps the viewer to identify with Mine and her suffering. When she subsequently leaves her husband to be with a man she does love, Mine can be viewed as winning her independence.

As a result, Mine can be seen as one of the most thought-provoking representations of the new, independent woman—she not only protests against her oppression but also asserts her own desire. However, it is also possible to argue that she goes from one man to another without becoming truly independent, that she instead simply transfers her needs from a man with whom she cannot share her desires to another with whom she feels she can. For this reason, the film can be interpreted as simultaneously opening up a feminist discourse while still reinforcing the norms of patriarchy.

Many of these 1980s women's films, however, focus on working women. *Dünden Sonra Yarından Önce* (After Yesterday, before Tomorrow) (Nisan Akman, 1987), for instance, focuses on the story of Gül (Zuhal Olcay), a successful filmmaker who struggles to achieve a balance between her career and marriage. In the course of the film she puts her career on hold because her husband Bulent (Eris Akman) asks her to consider giving up work so that she can fulfill the housewifely duties he expects of her. However, the more Gül dedicates herself to her life at home, the more depressed she becomes. She senses also that her husband's assistant Pelin (Sedef Ecer) is interested in Bulent, that Pelin tries to flirt with him at every opportunity. Although there are no scenes in the film that suggest Bulent is having an affair with Pelin, the more time he spends at work, the more reason Gül has to believe that he is. After a period in which she experiences a loss of self-confidence, attacks of jealousy, and increasing unhappiness, interspersed with fights with her husband, Gül decides to leave Bulent and resume her career by making a film about violence against women in working-class communities. Although Bulent has not been interested in Pelin, after Gül's return to work, he starts to spend his free time at Pelin's house. Thus Gül chooses to continue her life as a single, independent woman and let another woman "win" her husband, exchanging him for her freedom and career.

What makes this film significant is that it does not endorse the notion of women leaving their jobs to save their marriages. Instead, the focus is on patterns of negotiation in an urban, upper-class marriage where the wife is in love with her husband but has a demanding job and therefore does not devote herself entirely to him and her home. In addition, there is an exploration not only of how power dynamics are constructed, negotiated, and maintained in an urban marriage, but also of how they can be challenged. In the final scene, Gül is shown in long shot walking alone at night along a street. A high camera angle underlines her singleness as well as her independence. As Ruken Öztürk points out, this film offers an unconventional ending: "[It] does not result in the heroine being punished for choosing her career over marriage and losing her husband to another woman" (2004, 175). This is highlighted in the film's final dialogue between Gül and Pelin. Gül takes her husband's suitcase to Pelin's house, thinking that he is likely to be spending his time there, and Pelin asks: "Have I won?" Gül answers: "You have won, indeed. But what exactly have you won?" While the conflict between marriage and career still exists at the end of the film, this response nevertheless gives expression to the idea of an autonomous woman, one who can exercise freedom of choice and determine her own identity.

Other 1980s films deal with women who are caught in the clutches of strict customs and patriarchal traditions. One such is Şerif Gören's 1985 film *Kurbağalar* (The Frogs), which focuses on widowhood in rural Turkey. It is set in a small village in Western Turkey, where the villagers are low-paid factory workers or laborers. Men in the village collect frogs at night from the nearby river to sell to the local factory, which makes use of the frog skins in its production process. After the death of her husband, Elmas (Hulya Kocyigit) has to take on traditionally masculine jobs (like cultivating the land and collecting frogs) in order to support herself and her child. Ali (Talat Bulut), who returns to the village after serving a prison sentence, has had feelings for Elmas since before her marriage. After a night together, however, Ali leaves Elmas—although it is not clear why he makes this decision. Within this narrative the film focuses on the kinds of pressures that shape women's identity and sexuality in rural Turkey. Indeed, Elmas not only suffers from the difficult conditions of widowhood—including in this instance Ali's decision not to stay with her—but also from the unwelcome (sexual) attention she receives after being widowed. Although the narrative constructs her as a strong woman, willing to break with custom by taking on traditionally masculine jobs in order to retain her independence, in visual terms she remains for the most part objectified, frequently looked at (and indeed spoken about) by the male characters.

As in *Mine*, however, the film exaggerates the objectification of Elmas, similarly opening up the possibility of a critical reading. The film's construction of a male point of view reaches its most visible when erotic pleasure and sexual "violence" merge in a pivotal scene. When Elmas is working by the river one day, a (married) man hides in some bushes and, while lying down, gazes at Elmas's silhouette. Cutting between the two of them, the film shows the man sexually stimulating himself while gazing at Elmas. The pace of the editing quickens, staying aligned with the man's moving body, to create a sense of tension. The very eroticism of this scene suggests a form of sexual violence: Elmas's image is effectively raped, without her even knowing. The film foregrounds this act of violence by making the male gaze visible and presenting it from the point of view of the male character. This overemphasis on the fetishization of her image (body) suggests that any degree of independent agency she achieves provokes a backlash within the narrative—in this instance, as suggested, the "rape" of her image. While the film explores a woman's experiences and survival strategies as a widow—and allows Elmas a degree of independence—it simultaneously recognizes that village life is ruled by strict patriarchal values, which continue to determine the forms of resistance and struggle open to such women. In dealing with the conditions women in rural Turkey face, Elmas provides a moving example of the "human woman" in 1980s cinema.

Conclusion: Women on a Contested Screen

The three films briefly discussed here are representative of the corpus of 1980s Yeşilçam films dealing with the "new woman character." As illustrated by the discussion of the films and the historical, social, and political contexts within which the films were produced, there are inherent tensions and contradictions between gender practices and ideologies. On the one hand, women's issues were made visible not only by the women's movement but also in cinema, through the emergence of the "human woman" character in all her complexity, with the accompanying motif of an independent woman who is freer to express her desires and sexuality. But, on the other, these profound shifts in the representation of female characters and their narrative trajectories could at times be undercut by a visual style and filmic conventions that create an ambivalence about women's ability to exercise independent agency. Therefore, these 1980s women's films can be viewed as sites of power relations and political processes through which gender hierarchies are both re-created and contested. Turkish cinema thus functions both to oppose and to reinforce manifestations of male dominance in different narratives and contexts. Within these complex frameworks, gender asymmetry in Turkish society is produced, represented, and reproduced through film texts. It is ironic that the feminist ideas expressed in this group of 1980s films could become visible only as a result of the Turkish establishment's broader cultural disregard for feminism and the feminist movement's political significance.

Notes

All translations of Turkish language sources are my own.

1. For a detailed discussion of the films and issues discussed in this chapter, see: Eylem Atakav. 2012. *Women and Turkish Cinema: Gender Politics, Cultural Identity and Representation.* London and New York: Routledge.

2. It is relevant to note that at the time, women, working side by side with men, were called "bacı," which means "sister." This term eliminated the implication of sexuality, thereby countering the Islamic argument that women constituted a threat to public order.

3. Aksu Bora, a feminist activist and academic who took part in the 1980s movement, writes about this event in 1988, in *Sosyalist Feminist Kaktüs* (Socialist Feminist Cactus), a journal set up the same year by those women who had worked together in Women's Circle and in Solidarity against Beating.

References

Abisel, Nilgün. 1994. *Türk Sineması Üzerine Yazılar.* Ankara: Imge Yayınevi.

Adanır, Oğuz. 1994. *Sinemada Anlam ve Anlatım.* Izmir: Kitle Yayınları.

Algan, Necla. 1996. "80 Sonrasında Türk Sinemasında Estetik ve İdeoloji." *25.Kare* 16: 5–8.

Arat, Yeşim. 1994. "Women's Movement of the 1980s in Turkey: Radical Outcome of Liberal Kemalism?" In *Reconstructing Gender in the Middle East: Tradition, Identity and Power,* edited by Fatma Müge Göcek and Shiva Balaghi, 100–113. New York: Columbia University Press.

Arslan, Savas. 2011. *Cinema in Turkey: A New Critical History*. Oxford: Oxford University Press.

Bora, Aksu, and Asena Günal. 2002. *90'larda Türkiye'de Feminizm*. Istabul: Iletisim Yayınları.

Dorsay, Atilla. 1984. "Sinemamızda Yeni Cinsellik ve Özgür Kadın Tipi." *Gösteri* 49: 58–60.

Gelgeç-Gürpınar, Aysu. 2006. "Women in the Twentieth Century: Modernity, Feminism and Islam in Turkey." Unpublished master's thesis. Retrieved from http://dspace.uta.edu/bitstream/10106/37/1/umi-uta-1316.pdf (accessed February 19, 2014).

Gülendam, Ramazan. 2001. "The Development of a Feminist Discourse and Feminist Writing in Turkey: 1970–1990." *Kadın* 2 (1): 93–116.

Müftüler-Bac, Meltem. 1999. "Turkish Women's Predicament." *Women's Studies International Forum* 2 (3): 303–15.

Öztürk, Ruken. 2004. *Sinemanin Dişil Yüzü: Türkiye'de Kadın Yönetmenler*. Istanbul: Om Yayınevi.

Scognamillo, Giovanni. 2003. *Türk Sinema Tarihi*. İstanbul: Kabalcı Yayınevi.

Tekeli, Şirin. 1995. "Women in Turkey in the 1980s." In *Women in Modern Turkish Society: A Reader*, edited by Şirin Tekeli, 93–116. London: Zed.

CHAPTER 9

Traveling Memories

Women's Reminiscences of Displaced Childhood in Chilean Postdictatorship Documentary

ELIZABETH RAMÍREZ SOTO

In Lucía Salinas's 1990 film *Canto a la vida* (Song to Life), a documentary dealing with several women's return to Chile after having been exiled, the narrator asks: "Can the years we never lived be recalled?"[1] By doing so, the director, an exile herself, poses a fundamental question: How can a past that was not experienced directly, a past from which one has been expelled, be re-appropriated? This question, articulated at the threshold of Chile's first civilian government after seventeen years of the brutal military dictatorship led by General Augusto Pinochet (1973–1990), would be reformulated more than a decade later by a new generation of documentarians. These directors set out to explore the (im)possibilities of recalling a past that was only indirectly experienced, or perhaps not fully understood or remembered, because they were so young. In this postdictatorship generation, women have played a prominent part (see Mouesca 2005, 131–36), continuing the leading role assumed by the female relatives of victims and human rights activists in the memory struggles concerning the country's violent past and its legacies.

In fact, women filmmakers have long been involved in creative and distinctive ways in Chile's political struggles, as evident in the pioneering work of Marilú Mallet, Valeria Sarmiento, and Angelina Vázquez, who were only beginning their careers when they were forced into exile by the 1973 coup d'état. As Zuzana M.

Pick (1993) suggests, from the 1970s onward the public struggles of Latin American women have clearly nurtured the audio-visual production of female directors who have created "formally innovative approaches to documentary and fiction . . . [to give] a new form to the daily struggles of women [and] their will to speak up against oppression and break the silence that has marginalized them" (68). During the 1980s in Chile, a significant contingent of female documentarians, video artists, and photographers actively engaged in the struggle against dictatorship.

This chapter, through a discussion of *En algún lugar del cielo* (Somewhere in Heaven) (Alejandra Carmona, 2003), *El edificio de los chilenos* (The Chilean Building) (Macarena Aguiló, co-directed by Susana Foxley, 2010), and *El eco de las canciones* (The Echo of Songs) (Antonia Rossi, 2010), focuses on first-person documentaries by women who were born or grew up in exile. It focuses on these directors' cinematic construction of childhood memories, which are deeply entangled with the experience of growing up in an environment marked by political displacement. These directors' memories of displaced childhood are of a deeply affective nature and are often conveyed through the deployment of abundant archival materials (family pictures, home movies, letters, and drawings), the significant use of the traveling shot, as well as the elaboration of sophisticated reenactment sequences. The latter are mobilized not just as illustrative or evidentiary material but, as Bill Nichols (2008) has argued in his study of reenactment, as "an artistic interpretation" of the past that aims to fulfill, above all, an "affective function" (88).

In these works memories of the recent past assume a deeply sensuous quality, as they largely draw upon what Laura U. Marks calls "sense memories" (see Marks 2000, esp. 110–14, 194–242). Concerned with "the fabric of everyday experience that tends to elude verbal or visual records" (130), these directors turn to their sensorial memories of childhood, notably by privileging haptic images. Marks describes haptic images as those that invite the spectator to linger on the screen's surface before she realizes, if at all, what she is looking at (162–63). She also argues that despite their medium-specific differences, video and film (both of which are used by the documentaries under analysis in this chapter) share prohaptic features such as "changes in focus, graininess (achieved differently in each medium), and effects of under- and overexposure" (172). The works analyzed here seek to recreate aesthetically and in varying degrees the fragmented and irruptive nature of memories through different mechanisms in a collage-like style that combines heterogeneous materials including Super 8 or 16mm, video footage, home movies, family pictures, letters, drawings or animations, and reenacted sequences. The directors use the juxtaposition of these different elements, together with the traveling shot, to create deeply haptic sequences that make one feel "as though one were touching a film with one's eyes" (Marks 2000, xi).

Situating Second-Generation Documentaries

The directors Alejandra Carmona, Macarena Aguiló, and Antonia Rossi are part of what could be called a "literal" second generation in that they are the children of individuals "directly affected" by state repression. However, their backgrounds differ in important ways. Carmona was eight years old when she and her mother fled to East Germany. Her journalist father was one of the leaders of the *Movimiento de Izquierda Revolucionaria* (MIR), a revolutionary left-wing movement that was violently persecuted under Pinochet's dictatorship. He stayed in the country and went underground but was subsequently murdered in 1977 by agents of the regime. Aguiló's father was also an MIR leader, and in an attempt to find him the secret police kidnapped the director when she was still a small child. This made her one of the youngest victims of state repression and, as Aguiló relates in her documentary, she retains only some "vague memories" of that experience. After being set free, she was sent to Paris at age four and, after multiple displacements (including time in Belgium), grew up in Cuba. Both of her parents survived. Rossi was born in Italy in 1978 after her parents had already gone into exile, and she went to Chile ten years later. The significant differences in the life histories of these directors have shaped their personal documentary responses to the military coup in different ways. Yet their productions also share a number of features, notably: the disclosure of a familial bond with the past through the use of a first-person narrator (Rossi creates a fictional character, while Carmona and Aguiló perform the role of narrator themselves); an intricate connection between the personal and the collective; temporal digressions and disruptions, with past and present often merging with each other; and the experience of uprootedness during childhood.

These affective documentaries position themselves as deeply personal, subjective, and domestic narratives while remaining intricately woven with Chile's contemporary history. In this respect, they share many of the traits seen in the earlier works of exilic Chilean directors who began filming their homecomings in the 1980s, such as the seminal returns of Raúl Ruiz in *Lettre d'un cinéaste ou Le retour d'un amateur de bibliothèques* (Letter from a Filmmaker or The Return of a Library Lover) (1983) and Angelina Vázquez in *Fragmentos de un diario inacabado/Otteita Keskenjääneestä Päiväkirjasta* (Fragments from an Unfinished Diary) (1983). Elsewhere, I have termed these works "*desexilio* documentaries" (Ramírez Soto 2014). The concept of *desexilio* is an influential neologism created by Uruguayan writer Mario Benedetti (1984, 39–42), which means literally to return from exile, but the term strongly implies also that such an experience never ceases. I argue that although largely overlooked, these earlier homecoming documentaries anticipate recurring characteristics in a number of postdictatorship productions, such as the use of a first-person narrator and the foregrounding of performativity, as well as a fragmented construction and the cinematic exploration of the texture of the past. Furthermore, I believe it is possible to see the documentaries of Carmona, Aguiló, and Rossi as recent examples of "*desexilio* documentaries," in that they also foreground exile as an experience that never truly comes to an end. However, these more recent productions differ significantly from earlier cinematic returns, as they are infused with the generational bafflement of their younger directors and present less-straightforward homecoming journeys. These younger documentarians make explicit the gap between their own experiences and those of their parents, inscribing in their works—not only verbally but also aesthetically—a sense of confusion and perplexity. In these documentaries, as in the literary works of child survivors of the Holocaust, one can clearly see "both the child's helplessness and the adult's attempt to render that helplessness, retrospectively, in language" (Suleiman 2002, 292).

It is helpful here to draw on the ideas of Ana Amado and her discussion of the artistic memory practices of the sons and daughters of Argentine victims of the Dirty War. She describes these as artistic works that (often privileging the use of images) are "conceived as homage to and actualization of the genealogical bond [. . . but] present, however, a desire for distance and generational affirmation rather than an unconditional affective or ideological support" (Amado 2009, 157). Similarly, the productions of the Chilean directors discussed here create sophisticated mise-en-scènes that aim to actualize the parental bond (especially when severed or lost), while at the same time seeking to inscribe a distance from the epic discourses of their parents' generation. Most evidently, as seen in the cases of Carmona and Aguiló, they do so by including emotional onscreen testimonies that offer contested visions of the past from—to paraphrase Amado's terms—the perspective of, on the one hand, the parents and, on the other, the sons and daughters (145–203).

These children's homecomings seem less straightforward than those of the preceding generation, who, even when their actual journeys were interrupted or never completed, nonetheless inscribed in their films their desire to return from exile to their homeland, Chile. Yet where is home for these daughters of exile? Germany, Italy, France, Cuba? Chile? For Rossi, it seems as though it is an idea, or perhaps a set of reverberations from Chile felt in Italy; for Carmona, home appears to be the rigid communist Germany where she grew up as a rebel teenager; and for Aguiló, a community center in Cuba.

Traveling Women, Traveling Memories

Since the three documentaries discussed here deal with memories of uprootedness, I use the notion of "traveling memories" to consider their directors' concrete experiences of exile. Such a concept points to the distinctive use of traveling shots in these documentaries and acknowledges the transcultural dimension of these women's memories. Astrid Erll's definition of "traveling memory" articulates the itinerant aspects of memory, which she conceives of "as the incessant wandering of carriers, media, contents, forms, and practices of memory, their continual 'travels' and ongoing transformations through time and space, across social, linguistic and political borders" (Erll 2011, 11). I draw on this mobile understanding of memory to emphasize how these directors deal with and create memories that circulate and are in permanent motion. These documentaries can be considered itinerant in various ways; they foreground the fact that accounts of the recent past vary remarkably (and are reworked) from generation to generation, which is perhaps most strikingly evident in Rossi's experimental work that compiles a wide range of materials, including home movies, archival images from previous documentaries, and excerpts of old animation films, as well as animations created specifically for her production. These works also reverberate within, or reference, other Chilean documentaries. For example, while the seminal contemporaneous homecoming documentary *Calle Santa Fe* (Santa Fe Street) (Carmen Castillo, 2007) includes images from *The Chilean Building* when it was a work in progress, Aguiló's documentary, in turn, incorporates footage from *Éramos una vez* (Once We Were) (1979) by exilic director Leonardo de la Barra. They also "travel" from one country to another; these productions have circulated in international film festivals as well as alternative circuits abroad. Nonetheless—and this is crucial— they remain historically and politically grounded, creating memories that are at once strongly local and transnational.

I argue that in these documentaries affect and movement are intricately woven together. In these women's literal and metaphorical journeys to the "home" country and to its past, the fact that motion produces emotion and "that, correlatively, emotion contains a movement" (Bruno 2007, 6) becomes explicit in the traveling shot, which leads me to the more specific and material sense in which I use the idea of traveling, that of the moving image itself. These younger exiled directors' displacements are often inscribed in what Hamid Naficy has called "transitional and transnational sites" such as cars, trains, or boats (Naficy 2001, 154). Naficy theorizes such temporal and spatial figures of journeying as "thirdspace chronotopes," defined as a "slipzone" between homeland and exile, characteristic of the exilic condition (212). These "thirdspace chronotopes" are significantly "not just visual but also, and more important, synaesthetic, involving the entire human sensorium and memory" (153). It is perhaps in the form of the traveling shot that these "thirdspace chronotopes" materialize most clearly in these documentaries.

The uses of the tracking shot and its connection to the elaboration of complex temporalities that seek to collapse or blend past and present have a long tradition in the depiction of historical atrocities, which can been traced back to *Nuit et brouillard* (Night and Fog) (Alain Resnais, 1955) (see Hirsch 2004, 48–62). Like the exilic filmmakers who began returning to Chile more than two decades ago, the three directors under discussion here also draw upon this strategy to inscribe their (dis)encounters with the homeland or their adoptive countries as well as to reveal the presentness of the past, as will be seen shortly. In the following section, I examine specific sequences from the documentaries in question that articulate these directors' affective journeys, focusing on how they audiovisually convey a childlike imagery.

Staging the Past

In *Somewhere in Heaven*, Alejandra Carmona returns to Chile from her exile in Berlin, motivated by the desire to reconstruct the figure of her father. She makes explicit her act of return both discursively and formally, using several "thirdspace chronotopes" to inscribe her dislocation: she includes geographical displacements in various cars, as well as images of airports and railways stations (figure 9.1). The director acknowledges verbally the (im)possibility of accessing a past that was not directly experienced: "I begin to collect other people's images and memories that I make my own with the eagerness to get closer to my father." The director's return to Chile makes evident what Marianne Hirsch has suggested in her important discussion of postmemory in relation to the memories of the children of Holocaust survivors: Carmona's desire seems to be "not just to feel and know, but also to re-member, to re-build, to re-incarnate, to re-place, and to repair" (Hirsch 1997, 243).

The very opening shot is a reenactment sequence that immerses the spectator in the director's "memory of pain," as she calls it. It begins with a long take with a handheld camera that moves in slow motion inside the dark entrance of a building, presumably that of the flat in Berlin where Carmona lived as a child. The camera is positioned at the eye-level of a child, suggesting that this is the viewpoint of the director when she was twelve years old. The camera's shaky movement, presented in slow motion, seeks to mimic the child's state of anguish that anticipated the news of her father's death, a premonitory anguish that is also emphasized by the director's commentary. Carmona returns to this initial reenacted scene later in the documentary to illustrate her mother's own offscreen account of this tragic moment and how she delivered the news to her daughter. However, immediately after the mother recalls the very moment when she delivered the terrible news to Carmona—with the mother shown briefly rendering her emotional testimony in a conventional "talking head"—the quite simple illustrative reenactment that has been accompanying her account up until that point changes radically. What had

FIGURE 9.1. The car as "thirdspace chronotope" signifying geographic dislocation in Alejandra Carmona's *Somewhere in Heaven* (2003) (Courtesy of Carmona)

been a literal recreation of the girl's viewpoint (arriving at her flat) is displaced by a highly stylized reenactment of the affective impact that such a shattering event provoked in the director. Through a dissolve from her mother's interview, the spectator is now placed in a long, dim, basement-like tunnel. At the end of the tunnel, out of focus, there is a figure who is barely distinguishable. The camera moves rapidly toward the back of the tunnel through a tracking shot that ends, after an imperceptible cut, in an extreme close-up of the director's eye (as one can now distinguish, the figure was hers), and this dissolves into a photograph of her father, who is smiling. The sequence is accompanied by a soundtrack that builds up tension, particularly through the use of a ticking clock that fuses with that of heartbeats (Her father's? Hers?). Through a combination of blurry images, use of fast and slow camera movements, and rapid changes of focus, the director accomplishes in a few seconds a deeply affective sequence.

Macarena Aguiló's *The Chilean Building* deals with the memories of children of MIR militants as they recall their experiences of growing up in the "Project Home" in the late 1970s in Cuba. This project was a community center that sheltered around sixty children who were left in the care of twenty "social parents," while their own biological parents returned to Chile to fight underground against the military dictatorship. Aguiló was one of these children, and she begins her documentary with newsreel footage taken from a local television broadcast in which she was interviewed as one of the youngest victims of repression. The director, however, emphasizes a distance from this "official" discourse by shooting, from the intimacy of her home, the television monitor that shows her being interviewed onscreen. She chooses to evoke her twenty days in captivity by inscribing both visually and verbally her perceptions of the time: a slow panning shot of autumn leaves in Santiago from the present day is paired with memories she has of that autumn in the city: the dry air, the unbearable heat under her woollen clothes. And, rather than dwelling on that episode, she goes on to narrate the story of the "Chilean building"—as the "Project Home" was also known in Cuba.

Shortly after this opening sequence, the director narrates in voiceover an encounter with her mother in exile in Paris before Aguiló went to live in Cuba. While doing so she crafts an exceptional reenactment sequence that is profoundly haptic in quality and features both fictional elements and nonfictional archive materials. Paris is seen through the window of a train, a city that Aguiló filmed especially for the documentary in 16mm with a Bolex camera,[2] formally conveying the texture of those brief moments shared with her mother during her childhood (evoking even the taste of these memories through the visualization of colorful cupcakes as seen through a shop window, for example).

Soon after a series of brief shots taken from the train, in which Aguiló inscribes her temporal and spatial dislocation, the director exposes the generational gap between herself and her parents while developing a poignant critique of their privileging of revolutionary ideals—a choice that led to her childhood separation from them. The spectator is positioned now within a domestic space, looking onto an exterior urban landscape, as images filmed with a handheld 16mm camera pointing out from a window of a building in Paris (apparently her flat) are shown. The director's voiceover locates the spectator: "I went to school and she [her mother] worked. I went along to her meetings, where they smoked a lot, and sometimes I would understand something." The images of the city landscape as seen through the window are juxtaposed with the voiceover of a man talking about military tactics and revolutionary strategies: "What is the 'Popular War Strategy'? It doesn't mean we have to be shooting all the time . . ." His voice is interrupted by that of the director's, recorded when she was five years old: "And me? Oh! I want to pee!" Here, Aguiló conveys her confusion as a child and her limited understanding of the world of adults, making evident the difficulties of relating to their past political experiences while also questioning the boundaries between fiction and nonfiction.

This sequence produces a powerful temporal collapse; while the recording of the girl's voice dates back to the director's childhood years, the recording of the man's voice is recent. In fact, the voice belongs to Andrés Pascal, one of the historical leaders of the MIR, and dates from a speech he made at a gathering in 2004, which was held to commemorate the thirtieth anniversary of the death of the legendary leader of the party, Miguel Enríquez.[2] Through the inclusion of Pascal's speech, the voices of the parents and their fellow militants are thus replaced "with the voice of the authority of the political group, with hierarchy, the party's order," as Catalina Donoso (2012) asserts in her own reading of Aguiló's documentary (27). This is a remarkable sequence in which the use of fictional and nonfictional sources as well as the temporal collapse produced by their encounter poignantly highlight that "memory is the work [*oeuvre*] of fiction" (Rancière 2006, 158, translation in the original).

Emphasizing even further the point made by Rancière, Antonia Rossi's *The Echo of Songs*, located indeed on the brink of fiction, re-collects and interweaves in a poetic and unruly way documentary and fictional images, as well as animated sequences (some of which, as mentioned above, were made for the film, while others are lifted from old animated productions such as, tellingly, David Fleischer's 1939 film *Gulliver's Travels*). These images are woven together by the commentary of a fictive female narrator who speaks in the first person. Rossi's fictive character is constructed from numerous testimonies gathered from second-generation accounts of people who, like her, grew up or were born in exile, listening to their parents' songs and stories. The questions she posed to her interviewees were concerned with affect, as she was interested in capturing the perceptions, dreams, and smells they recalled, moving her interviewees away from the realm of reason.[3] The construction of a fictional character through different testimonial accounts was similarly sought at the visual level, as evidenced by extracts from home movies collected from various families, to which the director added other archival materials, such as footage of the 1980s protests against the dictatorship, captured by independent cameramen. The testimonies she gathered, together with the home movies she re-collected from those families, merge with Rossi's own personal material and are edited together in such a way that the image track creates a sense of the complex ways personal memories interweave with history. Through the editing of this recovered material, the director is able to construct both beautifully and wittily the process of growing up (from childbirth via the inclusion of home movies taken in hospital rooms to footage of graduation parties), effectively constructing an allegory of the displaced individual.

One might say that Rossi stages the reverberations of a history heard only through other people's voices. Her narrator embodies the collective experience of exile; the fact that she is nameless adds to such an allegorical function. Unlike the documentaries of Aguiló and Carmona discussed above, Rossi's aim is not to re-construct into a coherent narrative the scattered glimpses of childhood she has gathered. Aguiló and Carmona both seem to seek a certain wholeness in their documentaries, as each provides some kind of closure: Aguiló returns to her parents, as a gift, the letters they sent to her during her childhood, which she had typed up; Carmona visits her father's grave with her own young daughter. Rossi, however, seeks to clearly expose the fragments she re-collected as remnants, as she is interested in foregrounding their status as images discarded by history.[4] The director is indeed concerned in very complex ways with a formal reflection on the "prosthetic" character of memories, a notion theorized by Alison Landsberg (2004). That is, she engages in a cinematic exploration of the fact that (as Landsberg argues, along similar lines as Erll) memories circulate and are not necessarily grounded in lived experience; rather, different people in different contexts may also incorporate them, these other people's memories becoming therefore a constitutive part of their own identity in the present. Rossi stages through the material operations at stake in her work the fact that, as Landsberg asserts, "Cultural memories no longer have exclusive owners; they do not 'naturally' belong to anyone" (18).

For example, Rossi returns twice to an extreme and shaky close-up of the intense gaze of a girl, who may or may not be Rossi's older sister (figure 9.2). The girl in the home movie footage looks directly into the handheld camera, while the narrator says, on the first occasion: "Even today, I see the sign in her eyes of the time I didn't exist. The trip. The conviction. The sternness. All of our parents' reasons." The narrator continues: "Like a plague, we, as well as thousands of children, were born and raised on that same piece of borrowed land." The narrator/Rossi's "borrowed piece of land" is Italy (she hints at her family's trajectory from Santiago to Rome at the very beginning of her documentary through a map drawn by hand); yet this "borrowed land" could be any of the countries in which exiled children from Chile were born or raised. In fact, this commentary is accompanied by a montage of home-movie footage of children of different ages filmed in various locations: they are seen playing on the grass or in the snow, sitting on top of a car wearing short-sleeves or looking out from a balcony in winter clothes. So, whether the eyes of the girl are those of Rossi's sister or not doesn't really matter. Her eyes are the eyes of all those children forced to wander through the world. Rossi is not interested in singling out her own experience as the daughter of Chilean exiles as such but rather in creating a more radical polyphonic quilt in which many stories, her own and those of other children like herself, intertwine or merge.

Although Carmona, Aguiló, and Rossi are profoundly concerned with situating their own personal journeys in a wider cultural experience, it is Rossi in particular who engages most forcefully in the audio-visual exploration of the question that opened this chapter: How does one deal with a past that was not directly experienced? As such, I see her documentary as a sort of "hinge" that links the work of what I am calling here (in the absence of better terms) a "literal" second generation with the work of a "broader" second generation of directors—that is, with directors who may not present or reveal in their productions an explicit familial bond with a direct victim of state violence but who have nonetheless also engaged

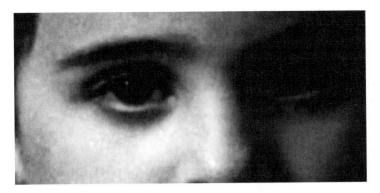

FIGURE 9.2. The close-up of the intense gaze of a girl, who
may or may not be the director's older sister, in Antonia
Rossi's *The Echo of Songs* (2010) (Courtesy of Rossi)

in deeply affective and sensuous ways of recalling the country's turbulent recent past. This is perhaps clearer when comparing Rossi's work with that of Tiziana Panizza (from this "broader" second generation), particularly with Panizza's short film *Remitente: Una carta visual* (Postage: A Visual Letter) (2008) (see Ramírez Soto 2010, 57–62). Both directors enact the same gesture toward the past: they both literally and materially borrow other people's images and make them their own (specifically, Super 8 home-movie footage in Panizza's case, which she rescued from oblivion in a flea market). I read this move as a political and aesthetic gesture: by including other people's domestic footage these two directors suggest that it is possible to incorporate other people's memories. By doing so, they avow that memories are not necessarily anchored to a subject, that there is no possible exclusive "ownership" of the past. They emphasize through their audio-visual strategies that "authenticity is no longer considered a necessary element of memory. Where memories come from matters less than how they enable a person to live in the present" (Landsberg 2004, 42).

The three documentaries analyzed in this chapter reflect, to varying degrees, on the fact that the memories as well as the legacies of Chile's dictatorial past extend well beyond those who have been "directly affected" by state terrorism, even beyond their children. They therefore help us move away from a restrictive view of postdictatorship nonfiction productions as responses that have emerged solely from those directly affected by state repression. Such a view is clearly inadequate when dealing with the broad scope of state violence, the radical transformation of Chilean society that occurred under the military dictatorship, and the heterogeneous documentary responses that have been prompted in the context of postdictatorial Chile.

Notes

1. All English translations of original sources in Spanish are mine, except for the documentaries that have original subtitles.

2. Aguiló, personal communication, March 18, 2011.

3. Aguiló, personal communication, April 22, 2011.

4. Rossi, personal communication, July 13, 2011.

5. Ibid.

References

Amado, Ana. 2009. *La Imagen Justa: Cine Argentino y Política (1980–2007)*. Buenos Aires: Colihue.

Benedetti, Mario. 1984. *El Desexilio y Otras Conjeturas*. Madrid: El País.

Bruno, Guiliana. 2007. *Atlas of Emotion: Journeys in Art, Architecture and Film*. 2nd edition. New York: Verso.

Donoso, Catalina. 2012. "Sobre Algunas Estrategias Fílmicas para una Propuesta de Primera Persona Documental." *Comunicación y Medios* 26:23–30.

Erll, Astrid. 2011. "Travelling Memory." *Parallax* 17 (4): 4–18. Available at http://dx.doi.org/10.1080/13534645.2011.605570 (accessed February 28, 2010).

Hirsch, Joshua. 2004. *Afterimage: Film, Trauma, and the Holocaust*. Philadelphia: Temple University Press.

Hirsch, Marianne. 1997. *Family Frames: Photography, Narrative, and Postmemory*. Cambridge, Mass.: Harvard University Press.

Landsberg, Alison. 2004. *Prosthetic Memory: The Transformation of American Remembrance in the Age of Mass Culture*. New York: Columbia University Press.

Marks, Laura U. 2000. *The Skin of the Film: Intercultural Cinema, Embodiment, and the Senses*. Durham, N.C.: Duke University Press.

Mouesca, Jacqueline. 2005. *El Documental Chileno*. Santiago: LOM.

Naficy, Hamid. 2001. *An Accented Cinema: Exilic and Diasporic Filmmaking*. Princeton, N.J.: Princeton University Press.

Nichols, Bill. 2008. "Documentary Reenactment and the Fantasmatic Subject." *Critical Inquiry* 35 (1):72–89. Available at http://www.jstor.org/stable/10.1086/595629 (accessed March 20, 2011).

Pick, Zuzana M. 1993. *The New Latin American Cinema: A Continental Project*. Austin: University of Texas Press.

Ramírez Soto, Elizabeth. 2010. "Estrategias Para (No) Olvidar: Notas Sobre Dos Documentales Chilenos de la Post-dictadura." *Aisthesis* 47:45–63. Available at http://dx.doi.org/10.4067/S0718-71812010000100004 (accessed November 3, 2013).

———. 2014. "Journeys of *Desexilio*: The Bridge between the Past and the Present." *Rethinking History: The Journal of Theory and Practice* 18 (3). Available at http://dx.doi.org/10.1080/13642529.2014.898421 (accessed March 31, 2014).

Rancière, Jacques. 2006. *Film Fables*. Translated by Emiliano Battista. Oxford: Berg.

Suleiman, Susan Rubin. 2002. "The 1.5 Generation: Thinking About Child Survivors and the Holocaust." *American Imago* 59 (3): 277–95.

CHAPTER 10

Revising the Colonial Past, Undoing "National" Histories

Women Filmmakers in Kannada, Marathi, and Bengali Cinemas

RASHMI SAWHNEY

Out of the 1,255 films produced in India in 2011, 206 were in Hindi (the national language), and the remaining 1,049 films were made in fifteen regional languages (mainly in Tamil, Telugu, Kannada, Bangla, and Marathi). Despite this, scholarship on Indian cinema is generally framed within singular linguistic and production contexts attached to regional industries, or, when placed within the logic of "national cinema," refers mainly to Hindi or Bombay cinema. Literature on regional cinemas, which is often published in local languages, is rarely translated, limiting the scope for transregional or transnational comparison, although several important volumes on regional film cultures have been published in English in recent years.[1] I argue here that the multiplicity of linguistic, production, and cultural histories of Indian cinemas demand pluralistic approaches to film historiography and that the absence of these, in turn, has serious consequences for understanding Indian women's cinema.[2] Leveraging a particular moment in Indian film history—the emergence in the 1980s of a women's cinema—and reflecting on the cinematic construction of gender debates in colonial India through its films, I attempt to chart the challenges they pose to establishing "national" narratives of gender or film history.

Despite a growing body of international literature, anthologies on women's cinema seldom represent India in more than customary entries on Deepa Mehta, Gurinder Chadha, and Mira Nair (all of whom are diasporic filmmakers producing films in Hindustani and English). However, in order to understand women's cinema in India, it is imperative to look beyond Hindustani or Bombay cinema and rearticulate this history via the multiple flows between region and nation, including questions of language and regional cultures.

The problem of invisibility and absence in archives and "national" histories has vexed many speaking from the margins of grand narratives and canons, and it remains an important task of historical reconstruction to attend to these voices. Rather than "reintroducing women into an untransformed history as yet another series of facts to be assimilated into a pre-existing chronology" (Johnston [1975] 2000, 140), the necessary task is the recalibration of our historical lens, and I attempt this via a discussion of three films made in Kannada (*Phaniyamma*, Prema Karanth, 1983), Marathi (*Rao Saheb*, Vijaya Mehta, 1986), and Bangla (*Sati*, Aparna Sen, 1989). All three films are about gender and reform in late-nineteenth and early-twentieth-century colonial India and together present a constellation that supports the development of a feminist historiography of Indian cinema.

The Historical Present: Cinema as Agent of Cultural Translation

Until the 1980s, women's filmmaking in India remained dispersed across regional languages, and it is only since then that women's cinema begins to emerge as an identifiable trope. By the 1980s, if the New Wave cinema experiment was on the decline, a crop of women directors, writers, editors, and producers like Sai Paranjpye, Prema Karanth, Aparna Sen, Kalpana Lajmi, Aruna Raje, Vijaya Mehta, and others were beginning to make films addressing sensitive social issues, including those centered on questions of gender and of cinematic form. Despite their emergence and the fact that their films were usually either produced by the National Film Development Corporation or by independent producers working outside the logics of the commercial film industry, none of these women figures in popular accounts of the new wave, which is constituted largely as an exclusive "boys club." It is not my intention here to argue for their inclusion within the New Wave fold or to prove the aesthetic or social merit of the films; I aim merely to point out that, while this group of women were making films that appeared to be saying interesting things, they did not fit into established classifications of film history.

It is worth noting that the 1980s represents an extremely violent decade with Operation Bluestar and the 1984 massacre of thousands of Sikhs marking bloody episodes in modern Indian history. This was also the decade that witnessed a tremendous increase in the appeal of violence in cinema, both through the character of "the angry young man" and the "vigilante women films" glorifying corporeal revenge. Tasked with bridging the transition from Nehruvian socialism to capitalism-based liberalization in India, the 1980s have been generally condemned as a confused aberration in modern Indian history. This perception holds true in historical accounts of Indian cinema too, where the 1980s have been deemed the lost decade by filmmakers and film scholars alike. The important contributions made by women filmmakers have been sidelined by this grand narrative, and the consequence is the failure to take note of the genesis of women's cinema in India, especially since it has never been consciously positioned as a "movement." The films produced by these directors did not abide by common aesthetic or thematic concerns but instead were dispersed across a wide gamut of New Wave or commercial forms, ranging from comedy and satire to historical films. However, through the 1980s a clear foundation for women's cinema had been established, offering a locus for critiquing the established national history of Indian cinema.

By the 1980s, the women's movement had gathered force, and intense debates on legal rights, marriage and inheritance laws, dowry and dowry deaths, education, employment, health, sexuality, and domestic violence had become a dominant part of public discourse. These debates laid grounds for urgently revisiting the gender and reform questions of the colonial period, allowing the three films I will discuss here to straddle the distance between past and present with some intimacy. These historical films, therefore, do not just render the past visible but become interlocuters between history and the present. Much like exiles, they are characterized by liminality, functioning in the "here and now" of their production as bearers of another reality; interpreting and representing for their immediate audiences some distant—other—time, place, people. Thus, willy-nilly, they are landed with the complicated role of cultural translation taking on meaning in the context of historical as well as contemporary discourses.

The central narrative of Indian history throughout the colonial period is a gendered discourse. Three broad strokes to this narrative can be outlined as follows: the colonizer-colonized relationship is established through patriarchal power structures; Indian men are deemed effeminate by the colonialists, resulting in some nationalist responses—including many women's—glorifying martial qualities; and the moral right to imperial domination is justified by highlighting the "degraded position" of women in Indian society. A combination of regressive British imperialism along with the highly oppressive practices of Indian patriarchy, invoked intense responses from both sides. What became popularly alluded to as "the women's question" emerged as the central symbolic issue in determining whether Indians were fit to govern themselves or not. The nuances of this debate were many, but broadly speaking, the search was on to fashion a new modern identity for the women of India in order to justify self-rule. It is not surprising that the "problems" that first caught the attention of the British as well as the Indian reformists were visibly repressive practices such as sati and widowhood rituals. The Hindu Widow's Remarriage Act (1856), the Age of Consent Act (1891), and the Abolishment of Sati Act (1829) all had a direct or indirect bearing on the status of widows.[3] Along with a new charter for women's education, codes of dress, and norms of public engagement, the project of crafting the modern-yet-modest new Indian woman was in full swing. A large number of films made in the pre-independence era, generically referred to as "socials," testify to this "national" imaginary of the Indian woman, who was expected to play the multiple roles of dutiful wife, nurturing mother, faithful companion, sacrificing nationalist, and upholder of tradition.[4]

However, what was construed as a "national" discourse on gender and reform often took on different inflections and urgencies in regional contexts. This regional diversity has been all but sacrificed in much of Hindi cinema—arguably, even a film like Deepa Mehta's *Water* (2005) settles for a re-construction of the ghats of Benaras, which is exactly the site on which colonial attention too was focused. Although widowhood rituals and customs differed by region and caste, the visibility given to practices such as sati—which were localized mainly to Bengal and Rajasthan—often gave them the appearance of a "national issue." On the other hand, in what loosely constitutes the South, including Karnataka, Tamilnadu, and Orissa, the key reformist question revolved around the status of *devdasis*, who were temple dancers, ritually married off in service to to the temple deity but permitted to have a sexual life and bear children by choice. These were lower-caste women, unlike the upper-caste suttees of the North. Thus, the forcefields of reformist discourse and the bodies upon which they acted or toward which they were directed were not uniform across the country.

Nonetheless, a dominant narrative about the reform movement and its relationship with gender and nation has been established through influential scholarship that has addressed mainly the specificities of Bengal.[5] Recognizable snapshots of this discourse include the figure of the *bhadramahila* (the respectable middle-class woman) and the division between *andarooni/baharooni* (inner and outer sanctums, architecturally, physically, and metaphorically).[6] Partha Chatterjee (1989) also draws upon this framework in explaining that the women's question disappears from national public debate by the early twentieth century because by then the "modern Indian woman" had been cast as an allegory of nation and left to nurture "tradition" in the so-called inner sphere. Contrary to Chatterjee's reading, the three films discussed here highlight interpretations suggesting women used the metaphorical inner space, and most significantly their own bodies, to enact participation in wider public debates on gender and reform. However, rather than a question of truth value—did this really happen in the nineteenth and twentieth centuries?—the more important question to ask is how a 1980s imagining of Indian women's lives in the colonial era contributes to the development of a feminist practice in our contemporary moment.

Location, Context, and Regional Cinema

Valentina Vitali's (2008) incisive essay on Indian film historiography makes an argument against Hollywood-inspired linearity and emphasizes instead a Jamesonian (1991) approach attentive to the relationship between co-existing, multiple modes of production, and film forms. I take Vitali's argument beyond "national cinema" to suggest that the multiple production centers in India,[7] each catering to one or more linguistic contexts, drawing upon particular production infrastructures, and representing distinct cultural and political histories, are critical to a film history that recognizes the joins and ruptures between region and nation. In what follows, I look at *Phaniyamma*, *Raosaheb*, and *Sati* as 1980s interpretations of the gender and reform debate in colonial India—assigning to them the work of "cultural/historical translation." In the process, while redrawing the lines of a national film history, I demonstrate how these films participate in a national "contemporary" as women's cinema.

Phaniyamma, the Kannada film, is an adaptation of M. K. Indira's 1976 novel of the same name based on the life story of Phaniyamma (1870–1952), who lived in the village of Hebbalige in the Malnad district of Karnataka.[8] Against the backdrop of Brahmin orthodoxy, the film portrays local history over a seventy-year period through the life of Phaniyamma (Sharda Rao). Phani is married at the young age of nine, as was common practice in the nineteenth century, and is widowed soon after.[9] She then has to undergo the rituals of widowhood, crop her hair, and take up an austere life. The film documents changes in village life—especially the slow decline of Brahmin orthodoxy—through Phani's point of view, transcribed through a reflective, biographical aesthetic. The fact that national independence is attained at some point in the narrative is unmarked, and so, largely, is the wider political ferment across the country. Instead, the film foregrounds the immediate repercussions of oppressive social customs, rituals, and taboos for women. Social transformation is marked through and upon Phani's body: from birth to death, her body becomes a repository of changes taking place in her immediate society, including improving social circumstances for women.

The film opens with an introduction to the village, highlighting first its natural ecology, then the postmaster's (Phani's father's) house, starting from public and work spaces, moving inward to the living and kitchen spaces, and finally into the inner courtyard, the culturally rich women's space where mythological stories are shared. This careful spatial framing indicating local power dynamics is set up through Madhu Ambat's cinematography. The historicity of the narrative is established as the film unfolds through Phani's reflections on her own life, on Brahmin orthodoxy and rituals, broken every now and then by scenes of the "present," where Phani becomes a participant in social transformation. Instead of locking history into a completed past, this temporal juxtaposition suggests the fluidity of historical processes at work. Spatial framing captures the passing of time when Phani introduces us to a small dark room in the house where she lived as a young widow, observing her younger self in the room. Editing, cinematography, and mise-en-scène construct a mode of beckoning, or subject positioning, for contemporary audiences by foregrounding desire (both its restriction and its realization) as the link between past, present, and future. The enunciation of desire bridges the regional and national, drawing upon local performative traditions such as *yaksha-gana*,[10] which juxtapose luscious sounds, landscapes, and colors with the restraint on women's desires demanded by orthodox traditions and the nationalist project.

The 1970s and 1980s marked a high point in Kannada cinema. A new realist tradition, Nayva, had developed in Kannada literature during this period, to include filmmakers and writers like Girish Karnad, U. R. Ananthamurthy, Pattabhirama Reddy, and B. V. Karanth. Prema Karanth, too, belonged to this group and was closely involved with Beneka, the theater group B. V. Karanth had set up in Bangalore. The writers, theater directors, actors, and filmmakers who were part of the Navya movement were interested in exposing social hypocrisies and the oppression of caste, tradition, and patriarchy. *Phaniyamma* belongs to this new wave of Kannada cinema. There are several noteworthy names associated with the film: Chandrashekar Kambar wrote lyrics for the film; Aruna Vikas (Raje), director of films like *Rihaee* (1988) and one of the earliest female graduates of the Film and Television Institute of India, edited the film; and Prema Karanth's husband, B. V. Karanth, a reputed theater director and music composer known for his modern experimentations with *yakshagana*, composed its music. Gender, caste, and language became the cornerstones for the Kannada New Wave, which referenced, on the one hand, the long trajectory of anticaste movements starting with the twelfth-century poet-saint Basavanna, and on the other, Karnataka's establishment in 1973 as a separate state, thereby focusing linguistic identity (it earlier existed as the State of Mysore). As a consequence of this creative context, *Phaniyamma* is among one of the most striking films to explore a cinematic aesthetic deeply anchored in local idioms of performance, landscape, rhythm and cultural history.

A couple of years prior to the release of *Phaniyamma*, Aparna Sen had made *36 Chowringhee Lane* (1981), which addressed the postcolonial situation of the

FIGURE 10.1. Phaniyamma (Sharda Rao) gazing into the dark room where she lived as a young widow in *Phaniyamma* (1983)

FIGURE 10.2. Phani looking upon a vision of her childhood in the postmaster's house

Anglo-Indian community in Calcutta, and Sai Paranjpye had made *Sparsh* (1980), *Chashme Buddoor* (1981), and *Katha* (1983). There suddenly seemed to be a body of films by women, which were being screened in film festivals in India and outside; the idea of an Indian women's cinema began to gather force. By the time Vijaya Mehta made *Raosaheb* in 1986, women's cinema was increasingly recognized, particularly for documentary. In a 1981 interview at the First International Conference on Women's Film and Video held in Amsterdam, the Bangalore-based documentary filmmaker Deepa Dhanraj spoke about a collaborative project, "Yugantar: 1981–82, Outline of Work," which aimed to situate film within a wider repertoire for use by women's activist groups. By 1985 the first all-women film collective, Mediastorm, had been set up in Delhi by Shohini Ghosh, Sabina Kidwai, Shikha Jhingan, Ranjani Mazumdar, Sabina Gadihoke, and Charu Gargi during the controversial lead-up to the Muslim Women's (Protection of Rights on Divorce) Bill

(1986).[11] Mediastorm produced *In Secular India* (1986), about the implications of the Bill, and later, *From the Burning Embers* (1988), about prevalent practices of sati; there was also *Kiska Dharam, Kiska Desh* ("Whose Country Is It, Anyway?" 1991), tracking the rise of the Hindu right-wing following the Ram Janmabhoomi movement. Through these and other efforts, a trans-state alignment was established between feminist activism, anticommunal politics, workers' and union movements, and film. Many women working with the fictional, feature-length format were also situated within this wider ecology of progressive thought, creativity, and activism. Vijaya Mehta is one such, whose films bear the influence of her theater background and middle-class Maharashtrain upbringing in Bombay.

Raosaheb is based on Jaywant Dalvi's play *Barrister* (1977) and exposes the hypocritical attitudes of Anglicized Indian reformists in the early twentieth century.[12] Radhakka (Neelu Phule), a provincial working-class woman and her husband, live as house helps with Raosaheb (Anupam Kher), an England-educated, Anglicized, upper-class barrister, who shares an opulent mansion with his old aunt or Maushi (Vijaya Mehta). In a mode akin to George Bernard Shaw's Henry Higgins, Raosaheb finds in Radhakka an ideal subject to educate and reform. Their mutual curiosity is stimulated by the vastly different worlds each one belongs to. Although the characters were originally created by Dalvi, Mehta had long contemplated the nature of "difference" and often spoken about how an encounter with the "other"—the physical and metaphorical "stepping out" of one's familiar context—is crucial to finding one's own identity and location.[13]

The drama begins when Radhakka's husband dies and her father-in-law expects her to shave her head and follow an austere lifestyle. Raosaheb is outraged and vehemently opposes this. The Widow Remarriage Act had been passed some fifty years prior to the historical setting of this film, and Maushi suggests that Raosaheb marry Radahakka. But he remains indecisive, unable to follow through on his progressive ideas. Frustrated by the situation, Radhakka shaves her hair and takes up a widow's life to mark her protest, centering her identity on terms she negotiates.

By the 1900s, a century of "reform" had generated among women skepticism about its radical potential, and as an act of historical translation, *Raosaheb* connects the dissatisfaction of the 1980s with that at the turn of the century. Vijaya Mehta, who was born in 1934, belongs to a generation that has literally witnessed modern Indian history unfold. Her mother and grandmothers belonged to the period and cultural milieu depicted in *Raosaheb*. In making Dalvi's characters come alive onscreen, Mehta infuses them with traces of characters from her own life. In her essay "Abode of Colours" (2005) she mentions the two most influential figures from

FIGURE 10.3. Front cover of the publicity booklet for *Raosaheb* (1986): Raddhakka (Neelu Phule), Maushi (Vijaya Mehta), and Raosaheb (Anupam Kher)

her pre-theater life: her mother, a strong-willed, religious-minded matriarch who had perfected the act of looking after the diverse needs of a large household; and her progressive humanist uncle, V. B. Karnik, in whose house she for the most part grew up and from whom she inherited her atheistic outlook. As an active contributor to Marathi theater in the 1960s, introducing a modernist Brechtian style and founding the experimental group Rangayana, Mehta states that her theater career allowed her to resolve the contradictions between the strong feminism and regressive ritualism she witnessed simultaneously as she grew up with her mother and paternal grandmother:

The women whose roles I played in theatre became a part of my real world. Through them I discovered my mother and grandmothers. My friends from the West argued with me, saying that women of the early 20th century found compensation because they had no choices. . . . With the forces of globalisation and progress, we do have more choices, but the strength, wisdom and endurance with which my mother and grandmothers coped with life make them perhaps stronger than us modern women. They were governed by their social norms and ethical codes of conduct as we are by ours. They found an identity, distinct and centred, something that we also strive for. (Mehta 2005, 201)

Mehta's observations on her family members clearly influenced her construction of her characters, as is seen in Maushi, who bears striking resemblance to descriptions of her own grandmother. Her questioning of what "progress" and "feminism" mean for Indian women resonates with Padma Anagol's compelling formulation of women's agency within a larger structural framework:

... a conception of female agency that centres on uncovering the intentions and experiences of Indian women as they asserted their rights, addressed social inequalities and rejected or adapted tradition in an engagement with the world around them. ... In doing so it moves beyond the rather limited configurations of agency based on issues of "consent" or "coercion," "transgression" or "subversion," or which reduce autonomy to mere resistance essentially reactive to the interventions of the colonial state or Indian men. ... [F]emale agency originates where other forms of agency are present, coexisting and competing with them. (Anagol 2005,10)

In the project of feminist historiography, therefore, we must place Vijaya Mehta and her theater and film work within a continuum that contains the ideas of women like the Marathi writer, Lakshmibai Tilak (1868–1936), whose autobiography, *Smruti Chitre*, has deeply influenced Mehta's feminism, as well as the two women's rights activists, Ramabai Ranade (1862–1924) and Pandita Ramabai (1858–1922), each of whom played a critical part in shaping a feminist ideology in Maharashtra. This feminism was in conversation with the history of caste consciousness and women's education, established through the work of men like Jotirao Phule and Bhimrao Ambedkar. These linkages situate responses to gender and reform questions within a bifurcated structure, producing joins and cleavages vis-à-vis the "national." *Raosaheb*'s ridicule of the Anglicized reformist and his incapacity to act echoes that of Maharashtrian men and women who in the late nineteenth and early twentieth centuries challenged oppressive social norms without adopting Anglicized mannerisms. In a 1980s film, this history regains meaning through Mehta's own journey of shaping a feminism for herself.

This brings me to the final film I will discuss here, Aparna Sen's *Sati*, as a limit case for the politics of gender, rendering its central protagonist, Uma (Shabana Azmi), as a mute girl. The film is set in 1828 (a year before sati was abolished) in the heyday of reformist activism in Bengal. Uma, who is orphaned at birth, is raised by her mother's brother and his wife and is considered a liability. The wretched girl is cursed with a horoscope that promises widowhood; nobody is prepared to marry her, and her horoscope hinders even a younger sister's marriage. A village priest advises she be wedded to a peepul tree—a ritual, he claims, sanctioned by the vedas—so the family finds one that she is particularly fond of. Soon after, she is seduced by the village teacher, becomes pregnant, refuses to identify the father, and is thrown out to live in the cowshed. On a stormy night, the cowshed is washed away. Uma seeks shelter under the peepul tree, which gets uprooted in the storm, crashes, and kills her. The villagers declare her a sati and the film ends with a ceremony extolling Uma's virtues in her death. The film critiques Brahmin orthodoxy, exposing marriage and death as rituals symbolic of a wider economy

FIGURE 10.4. Uma (Shabana Azmi) being married to the peepul tree in *Sati* (1989)

(for Bengal's Kulin Brahmins who practiced polygamy, each new marriage brought a new bride price, and thus more income for the household).

Sati was made two years after Roop Kanwar had been burnt alive on her husband's funeral pyre in Deorala district of Rajasthan. This incident had attracted great media attention and public debate and had further mobilized the feminist movement. A number of arguments—not yet faded from public memory in 1989—had been put forward both against and in support of the practice of sati. Ironically, these arguments were not too dissimilar to those in circulation in the early nineteenth century before sati was banned.[14] Thus the film entered into an already existing discursive context that was not just historical and distant but also contemporary.

Aparna Sen's representation of Uma as a mute character has been described by Shoma Chatterji (2002) as symbolizing abjectness. On the contrary, I would argue that Uma's muteness represents not only despair but a desperate reclaiming of the self, and that this combination has been the longstay of feminist politics. For example, while in the Mahabharata epic, Draupadi swears not to oil or tie her long hair until it has been washed in the blood of her oppressors, Mahasveta Devi's Santhal incarnation of the character in her short story as Dopdi Mehjen[15] refuses to wash or clothe herself after she has been raped during a police interrogation about her Naxalite activities.[16] These tactics are not simply a matter of fiction or

161

theory: they recall numerous incidents, most notably the 2004 protest following the rape and killing of Thanglam Manorama by the Assam Rifles in Manipur, when a group of women marched naked holding a large banner demanding "Indian Army: Rape Us."[17] Internationally, too, women artists like Marina Abramovic have reclaimed their space and prerogative by making their bodies their canvas, giving rise to "performance art" as a radical practice. In fact, one cannot help but wonder if Uma's muteness is a performative nod toward the "silencing" of many vernacular tongues and knowledge systems across India, following the Bengali reformist Raja Ram Mohun Roy's spirited advocacy for "English education" in the nineteenth century. *Sati* highlights the tragedy and economic basis of the practice in its historical context and brings this to bear on the 1980s as a farcical reenactment of a turbid nationalism built on an abusive idea of tradition.

The three films together work to open out the unique possibilities of a pluralistic film historiography, compelling us to be attentive to the regional differences and transregional collaborations that have been a pervasive part of Indian cinema since its very beginnings. Women's cinema in the 1980s takes an oppositional stance to the idea of the national while simultaneously being marked by it. In conclusion, I wish to draw attention to the fact that even as some of these films signal the evolutionary process of history, film historiography itself gets destabilized in the way that films engage the contemporary moment of writing or analysis. This peculiarity of cinema, in its materiality as celluloid, or its ephemerality in digital form, constitutes an archive of the present, translating the past, while being in conversation with a projected future. Thus, a critical film historiography involves a conversation between multiple contemporaneities: in this case, the contemporaneity of reformist discourse in colonial India; the contemporaneity of 1980s cinema; and the contemporaneity of early twenty-first-century India, where this writing is situated. At the same time, each of these junctures involves a real or metaphorical spatial struggle against the hegemonies of the time, which threaten to reduce the multiplicities of language, culture, representation, and identity, and where a critical historiography working through cinema, literature, or theory seeks the companionship of the past in moving forward.

Notes

1. See for example, S. V. Srinivas's *Megastar: Chiranjeevi and Telgu Cinema after N.T. Rama Rao* (2009) and *Politics as Performance: A Social History of the Telugu Cinema* (2013); M. Madhava Prasad's *Cine-Politics: Film Stars and Political Existence in South India* (2014); Sara Dickey's *Cinema and the Urban Poor in South India* (2007); Anand Pandian's edited volume *Subramaniyapuram: The Tamil Film in English Translation* (2014); Swarnavel Eswaran Pillai's

Madras Studios: Narrative, Genre, and Ideology in Tamil Cinema (2015); Sharmistha Gooptu's *Bengali Cinema: An Other Nation* (2010).

2. Although the term "woman's cinema" has multiple meanings, ranging from films for a female audience, films representing strong female characters or a feminist narrative, or films produced by an all-woman crew (see Butler 2002), I here mean films by women directors—not to close off the term's wider meanings, but for the sake of focus.

3. The Portuguese banned sati in Goa around 1515; the first formal British ban in 1798 was restricted to Calcutta; after the Indian reformer Raja Rammohun Roy started his anti-sati campaign in 1812, the practice was formally banned in the Bengal Presidency in 1829 by Governor General William Bentick; the practice continued to remain legal in some princely states after 1829 and was banned in Jaipur only in 1846.

4. I use the term "national" here in its imaginary capacities as a prefiguration of the geographical and political nation-state.

5. This indicates a disjuncture between the "national" in political-social history and cinema history. Feminist film historiography, therefore, contributes to recalibrating both histories.

6. The inside/outside binary is poignantly depicted in all its complexity in Tagore's novel (1916) and Satyajit Ray's film, *Ghare Baire* (1984).

7. In addition to the Bombay film industry, which produces the country's Hindi films, there are large film industries located in Hyderabad and Chennai for films in Telegu, Tamil, Kannada, and Malyalam; Marathi films are produced in Bombay and Pune; Bengali films in Kolkata; Bhojpuri films in Ranchi and Patna; and increasingly in the last two decades, smaller but vibrant industries have emerged in places like Ladakh, Manipur, Malegaon (only 280 kilometers from Mumbai), which function as community-driven, small-scale units where films are directed, acted in, produced, exhibited, and watched by local residents.

8. The English translation of the novel published by Kaali for Women in 1989 won Tejaswini Niranjana a Sahitya Academy Award. The film won the National Award for "best Kannada film" and a FIPRESCI (International Federation of Film Critics) award in 1983.

9. "Amma" literally means "mother" and is appended as a mode of address to women's names, especially for older women in South India.

10. *Yakshagana* is a form of folk theater that combines dance, music, dialogue, costume, makeup, and stage techniques. It is believed to have originated from preclassical music and theater during the Bhakti movement (tenth to sixteenth centuries A.D.) in the Malnad district of Karnataka, but in the past two centuries it has spread across Karnataka.

11. In 1986, sixty-two-year-old Shah Bano appealed to the supreme court for the right to alimony, since she had no financial means to raise her children. After seven years and several sittings, the court ordered her ex-husband to pay up to a maximum of Rs 500 per month. Although the courts had given such orders before, their statements about the Quran generated opposition from the Muslim orthodoxy, which made the congress government at the time reject the judgement and opt instead for the less progressive Muslim Women's Bill.

12. Dalvi's play is itself adapted from his Marathi novel, *Andharachya Parambya*, and Vijaya Mehta also directed the play in its original run.

13. A particularly interesting interview with Mehta in Marathi where she discusses the idea of "difference" can be viewed here: http://www.youtube.com/watch?v=xSMa0xSec6M (accessed October 2, 2013).

14. For a critique of the literature on sati, see Ania Loomba's "Dead Women Tell No Tales" (1993).

15. The Santhals are the largest tribal community in India, living predominantly in the states of Jharkhand, West Bengal, Odisha, Assam, and Bihar. The Santhal revolt of 1855 is an important landmark in Indian and subaltern history, marking one of the earliest large-scale protests against the British colonizers, as well as Bengali landlords and moneylenders. Several stories by the Bangla writer and tribal rights activist Mahasveta Devi are based on Santhal history.

16. Naxalites are members of various extreme left Maoist groups operating across Jharkhand, Chattisgarh, West Bengal, and Odisha in northeastern India, often involved in violent confrontations with the state, police, and army. The term references the origin of the movement in the Naxalbari district of Bengal in the late 1960s.

17. Manorama had been accused of belonging to the banned People's Liberation Army (PLA).

References

Anagol, Padma. 2005. *The Emergence of Feminism in India, 1850–1920*. Hampshire: Ashgate.

Butler, Alison. 2002. *Women's Cinema: The Contested Screen*. London: Wallflower.

Chatterjee, Partha. 1989. "The Nationalist Resolution of the Women's Question." In *Recasting Women: Essays in Indian Colonial History*, edited by Kumkum Sangari and Sudesh Vaid, 233–53. New Delhi: Kali for Women.

Chatterji, Shoma. 2002. *Parama and Other Outsiders: The Films of Aparna Sen*. Calcutta: Parumita.

Devi, Mahasveta. 1997. *Breast Stories*. Translated by Gayatri Chakraverty Spivak. Calcutta: Seagull.

Dickey, Sara. 2007. *Cinema and the Urban Poor in South India*. Cambridge: Cambridge University Press.

Ghosh, Shohini et al. 2012. "Mediastorm: Memories of a Collective." In *Making News, Breaking News, Her Own Way: Stories by the Winners of the Chameli Devi Jain Award for Outstanding Women Mediapersons*, edited by Latika Padgaonkar and Shubha Singh, 105–114. New Delhi. Tranquebar.

Gooptu, Sharmistha. 2010. *Bengali Cinema: An Other Nation*. New Delhi: Roli.

Jameson, Fredric. 1991. *Postmodernism; or, The Cultural Logic of Late Capitalism*. Durham, N.C.: Duke University Press.

Johnston, Claire. [1975] 2000. "Dorothy Arzner: Critical Strategies." In *Feminism and Film*, edited by E. Ann Kaplan, 139–48. Oxford: Oxford University Press.

Lesage Julia. 1986. "Interview with Deepa Dhanraj." *Jump Cut: A Review of Contemporary Media* 31 (March): 40–42. Available at http://www.ejumpcut.org/archive/onlinessays/JC31folder/DhanrajInt.html (accessed October 2, 2013).

Loomba, Ania. 1993. "Dead Women Tell No Tales: Issues of Female Subjectivity, Subaltern Agency, and Tradition in Colonial and Post-Colonial Writings on Widow-Immolation in India." *History Workshop Journal* 36:209–27.

Mehta, Vijaya. 2005. "Abode of Colours." In *A Space of Her Own*, edited by Jasodhara Bagchi and Leela Gulati, 181–202. New Delhi: Sage.

Pandian, Anand. 2014. *Subramaniyapuram: The Tamil Film in English Translation*. Chennai: Blaft.

Pillai, Swarnavel Eswaran. 2015. *Madras Studios: Narrative, Genre, and Ideology in Tamil Cinema*. London: Sage.

Prasad, Madhava. 2014. *Cine-Politics: Film Stars and Political Existence in South India*. New Delhi: Orient Blackswan.

Srinivas, S. V. 2009. *Megastar: Chiranjeevi and Telgu Cinema after N.T. Rama Rao*. New Delhi: Oxford University Press.

———. 2013. *Politics as Performance: A Social History of the Telugu Cinema*. Ranikhet: Permanent Black.

Vitali, Valentina. 2008. "Not a Biography of the 'Indian Cinema': Historiography and the Question of National Cinema in India." In *Theorising National Cinema*, edited by Valentina Vitali and Paul Willemen, 262–73. London: British Film Institute.

CHAPTER 11

Hollywood Transgressor or Hollywood Transvestite?

The Reception of Kathryn Bigelow's *The Hurt Locker*

KATARZYNA PASZKIEWICZ

Kathryn Bigelow at the Oscars

Presenting the 2010 Best Director Academy Award, actress and filmmaker Barbara Streisand told the audience at the Kodak Theater: "From among the five gifted nominees tonight, the winner could be, for the first time, a woman." As she checked the name in the envelope, she proudly announced: "Well, the time has come." And after a dramatic pause she declared Kathryn Bigelow the winner. Although her gender was clearly underscored in this short but powerful statement, Bigelow herself did not address this issue in her acceptance speech. Instead, she praised her fellow nominees and emphasized the collaborative nature of her achievement, thanking the cast and crew who helped her make *The Hurt Locker* (2008). While many commentators in the mainstream press celebrated her triumph as a female director in a predominantly male industry, the event also provoked a considerable number of hostile responses that emanated mainly, and perhaps perplexingly, from feminist circles. In her critical piece titled "Kathryn Bigelow: The Absentee Feminist," Susan G. Cole accused the filmmaker of making no reference to the significance of her accomplishment for feminism and expressed her deepest regret that some "feminist bashers . . . cheer her on for remaining resolutely gender neutral. They love the fact that she won her prize for a war movie that blows up, for being one of the boys, for telling feminists to get off her cloud" (2010).

Bigelow's acceptance speech and critical responses to it should not surprise if we consider Christina Lane's (2000) observation that "her connections to feminism, as represented in public discourse, have always been ambiguous. She seems quite conscious of feminist politics and willing to engage with feminism, but she remains ambivalent about labeling her films in terms of gender politics" (101). Not only does Bigelow reject the "feminist" tag, she has also consistently resisted any attempt to categorize her as a "female" director—whether in relation to her films, her position in the industry, or audiences. At the same time, the repeated insistence on Bigelow's seeming gender neutrality has been closely intertwined with public discourses characterizing her filmmaking as "muscular," since she usually works within presumed "masculinist" genres (see Jermyn 2003).

Bigelow is therefore an uneasy figure for feminist historiography, as her work puts into tension the conjunction of women's filmmaking, gender, film genre, and feminism, something palpably dramatized by her nomination for the Best Director Oscar for *The Hurt Locker*. She remained routinely silent on the issue of gender and refused to talk about being a feminist touchstone—a gesture *New York Times* film critic Manohla Dargis (2010) considered a "quiet yet profound form of rebellion" against "nosy interviewers" who insist on designating her as a *female* director. Yet her femininity is still a crucial trope, which has been central not only in the textual analyses of her films but also in the popular and critical debates around her status as an auteur. It is significant that, following Bigelow's win, Sigourney Weaver—who starred in James Cameron's *Avatar* (2009), the sci-fi picture by Bigelow's former husband that competed with *The Hurt Locker* in several Oscar categories—allegedly attributed Cameron's "defeat" in the Best Director category to the fact that he "didn't have breasts," claiming that the Academy wanted to make history by naming its first ever female Best Director. As Rona Murray (2011) remarks in connection with these kinds of comments, "resistance is futile, even disingenuous, since Bigelow's femininity in a man's world has consistently been the brand signifier to sell her movies. . . . Going forward, faced with a slew of commentary in respect of her historic win, this has no prospect of changing since she will (ironically) be forever associated with being the woman who broke the glass ceiling" (7).

The success of *The Hurt Locker* and the varied responses provoked by Bigelow's receipt of the Best Director Oscar has certainly renewed scholarly and critical interest in women's filmmaking and the position of female directors within the Hollywood industry. My aim is to contribute to these debates by highlighting the problematic relationship between women's filmmaking, gender, and feminism as it plays out in the context of reception. The chapter offers a reception history of *The Hurt Locker* by exploring some of the critical discourses that circulated around this film, as well as raising methodological questions about the role of critical response in the discursive circulation and reception of women's films.

In order to approach the multiple responses to *The Hurt Locker*, I adopt the context-activated reception theory proposed by Janet Staiger (2000), which focuses on the historically constructed interpretative strategies and tactics that spectators bring to the cinema. Staiger insists that every period in the history of cinema witnesses several modes of reception and that "any individual viewer may engage *even within the same theatergoing experience* in these various modes of reception" (43, emphasis in original). While Staiger does not distinguish professional critics from fans or from general film-going audiences, the latter will not be addressed here. Instead, I employ her approach to identify the interpretative assumptions that gave *The Hurt Locker* meaning for a specific range of audiences—that is, professional critics, nonprofessional film enthusiasts, and scholars—in order to locate its reception in a given historical moment.

The reviews and commentaries surveyed in this chapter arguably appeal to four key intertextual discourses: the (anti)feminist credentials of Bigelow and her films, the verisimilitude of the Iraq War film, the construction of Bigelow's authorship, and the presumed self-conscious play with gender and genre in *The Hurt Locker*. With regard to the first of these, I look at the accusations leveled at and hostile reactions to both *The Hurt Locker* and Bigelow's receipt of the Best Director Oscar, arguing that they operate within the "mass culture paradigm" and thereby assume a specific form of feminist cultural politics in terms of women's cinema. To explore the discursive themes of verisimilitude, authorship, and self-conscious play, I go on to consider other interpretative frames of reference—realist, modernist, and postmodernist—within which different types of critics approached Bigelow's work.

The extent of critical and scholarly responses to the film renders uncovering everything written about the film to be outside this chapter's scope. However, a sample of reviews and commentaries from a variety of sources—major UK and U.S. national papers, academic journals, blogs (written by professionals and nonprofessionals) and the most popular review Web sites (which include fan reviews—such as Rotten Tomatoes and Metacritic)—are available and useful for our discussion. I will correlate this material (which I accessed from November 2010 to March 2011) with the wider discursive fields within which they operate to map the interpretative frameworks structuring the quoted responses to the film. Rather than endeavoring to exhaust all the factors involved in encounters between *The Hurt Locker* and the above range of reviewers and commentators, this chapter aims to place the movie within polymorphous historical frameworks to achieve a "*Rashomon*-like effect," whereby, as Barbara Klinger (1997) puts it, "the researcher uncovers different historical 'truths' about a film as she/he analyses how it has been deployed within past social relations" (110). Therefore, instead of attempting to identify a fixed historical meaning, I am interested in pointing up "discontinuities and differences characterizing the uses of a particular film within and beyond its initial appearance" (112).

Transgressor vs. Transvestite: Mass Culture Framework

As a way of probing the discourse around Bigelow's feminist or nonfeminist credentials, it is worth turning to Luke Collins (2012), who notes in his discussion of *Point Break* (1991) that there are marked discrepancies in the scholarly criticism of Bigelow, "from avant-garde auteur to artistic bankruptcy" (56). His observation remains relevant, since her practice as a director is still being constructed around what will be defined here as a "Hollywood transgressor"/"Hollywood transvestite" dichotomy. This reflects two different ways of conceptualizing popular culture, as theorized by Stuart Hall: the positive "popular culture" framework, which emphasizes the potential for resistance and transgression already present in the production and use of mass-produced commodities, and the negative "mass culture" framework within which commercially produced culture is debased (see Hollows 2000, 26). The first term in the proposed dichotomy, that of "Hollywood transgressor," is derived from the subtitle of the scholarly monograph *The Cinema of Kathryn Bigelow* (Jermyn and Redmond 2003), while "Hollywood transvestite" makes reference to a frequently quoted *salon.com* review of *The Hurt Locker*, written by academic-turned-fulltime-media-critic Martha Nochimson (2010) and provocatively titled "Kathryn Bigelow: Feminist Pioneer or Tough Guy in Drag?" This opposition draws on two different discourses: scholarly, represented by Jermyn and Redmond, and informal news journalism, exemplified by Nochimson.[1] Yet the "Hollywood transgressor"/"Hollywood transvestite" opposition, which stems from these discursive practices, seems to define Bigelow's career, since on the one hand she is often classified as "a European-inspired auteur working within the Hollywood cinema machine" who breaks gender roles and genre traditions (Jermyn and Redmond 2003, 2–3), and on the other she is perceived as a mainstream "action director" disguised as a man to earn the respect of the cinematic industry (Nochimson 2010).

Even though Bigelow's status has been negotiated in various ways, it is the "tough guy in drag" tag that pervades in the negative responses provoked by Bigelow's receipt of the Oscar for Best Director. Nochimson and various journalists writing with the major newspapers, such as Kate Muir from the *Times* and Richard Adams, who blogs on politics and culture for *The Guardian*, read *The Hurt Locker* as "anti-feminist" or "anti-women," using arguments that reveal certain assumptions about women's filmmaking and the types of films female directors make (or should make). First, it was frequently argued that Bigelow betrayed women, for she "masquerade[d] as a hyper-macho bad boy" (Nochimson 2010) and sold out to join the "big boys' club" (Muir 2010). Second, the film was criticized for its lack of (positive) images of women. For instance, Adams (2010) wrote that "there's a small irony that Bigelow is lauded for being the first woman to win 'best director' for a movie that has scarcely any speaking roles for women. *The Hurt Locker* is a very 'male' movie in that sense." Finally, Nochimson (2010) regretted the cultural marginalization of genres traditionally codified as "feminine"—that conventionally target female audiences and that women directors tend to work in. In particular, she noted that the differences between how *The Hurt Locker* has been lauded and how women directors such as Nancy Meyers and Nora Ephron have endured "summary dismissal" reveal that Hollywood overtly privileges "muscular filmmaking" and "the military landscape" over "the domestic landscape" present in genres typically directed by women, such as the "organic, life-affirming" romantic comedy.

There seem to be different but overlapping issues operating in the responses cited above. The complex questions about gender that these comments raise cannot be addressed in detail here, but it is worth pointing to how they operate within the "mass culture" framework as described by Hall and later discussed by Joanne Hollows (2000) in relation to women's work within popular culture and particular forms of feminist cultural politics. According to Hall (in Hollows 2000), this conception of popular culture claims that it is something imposed from *outside* on the passive masses who live in a permanent state of "false consciousness" (26). Therefore, within this framework commercially produced popular culture is usually degraded. Drawing on these remarks, Hollows observes that in some forms of feminism a distinction is frequently made between a "bad" patriarchal mass culture and feminist avant-garde culture. Such a distinction can be observed, according to Hollows (who quotes cultural theorist Judith Williamson), within that strand of feminist film criticism that creates "an opposition between avant-garde, feminist 'non-narrative, difficult, even boring, oppositional cinema' and its degraded 'other', popular, patriarchal 'realist, narrative, mainstream cinema'" (2000, 28).[2]

Bigelow, most of whose films cannot be classified as either mainstream or oppositional (or, in Jermyn and Redmond's terms, as either Hollywood or art-house), does not easily fit into those categories. Nevertheless, in many reviews *The Hurt Locker* was identified as "mainstream," in spite of the fact that the film was made on a relatively low budget financed by non-Hollywood companies (although a film's financing arrangements do not necessarily correlate exactly to its aesthetics). While the boundaries between mainstream and avant-garde (or "indie cinema") are breaking down in both postmodernist practice and theoretical thinking, they frequently persist in journalism. And what is interesting here, is that Bigelow's apparent abandonment of her earlier experimental work for mainstream narrative fiction was understood as an inevitable elision of feminist politics, an attitude that fits with the "mass culture" paradigm discussed by Hollows.

Another issue raised by the reviews framed within the "(anti-)feminist" discourse is the question of images of women and, subsequently, of gendered spectatorial address. In addition to reprimanding Bigelow for supposedly "selling out" to join the Hollywood male elite, the reviews mentioned above criticized her for not representing women in her film. Although it is true that Bigelow ignored the development of women characters in *The Hurt Locker*, emphatically decentering them in the narrative, this can be explained by the generic conventions of war films, which were overlooked in the rush to gendered judgment. The search for "positive" female characterization in Bigelow's movie recalls the longstanding debate over the "images of women" initiated in the 1970s, when feminists working in the social sciences addressed how women were represented in the "content" of media production, and when it was postulated that female stereotypes should be replaced by "positive" images of women. As some scholars observed, placing this type of expectation on women directors is not only reductive, since it risks underestimating various individual and institutional factors involved in the filmmaking process, but it also presents theoretical difficulties, such as the subjective and mutable notion of a "positive image" (Jermyn 2003, 139).

When claiming that Hollywood dismisses women's genres, Nochimson seems to take for granted that being a man or a woman is simple, self-evident, and invariable, and that film genres employ a single gender address. A war film, which features central male protagonists and secondary female characters, is perceived thus in terms of the ubiquitous male spectator. This leads to the assertion, frequently questioned by a number of feminist film scholars, that spectators align themselves necessarily according to the binary opposition of gender and that filmic pleasures are gender specific.[3] As Pam Cook (2012) has shown, this assertion is closely interlinked with "the idea that certain genres are, or . . . have been, more 'suitable' for women as either viewers or as filmmakers," which relegates women to a separate space defined as "women's culture" (38).

This simplistic categorization of genres by gender and the supposed gender-to-gender identification does not allow for the nuances in Bigelow's film practice, nor does such categorization challenge the essentialist notions of "male" or "female" filmmaking. In order to transcend the transgressor/transvestite dichotomy and other binary oppositions underpinning the "mass culture" paradigm often activated to assess the subversive or regressive character of *The Hurt Locker*, it is helpful to account for other reading contexts. While the film's critical reception was dominated by the debate around Bigelow's femininity and (anti-)feminism, the tendency to focus solely on a gendered discourse might overshadow the importance of other interpretative strategies mobilized across a range of public discourses to interpret and write about the movie.

The Realist Framework

The analysis of the critical reception for *The Hurt Locker* in the major U.S. and UK media shows that the film was predominantly contextualized (and evaluated) within a realist frame of signification. Most reviewers in this discursive range tended to focus primarily on the plot and the characters, debating whether the film was plausible and raising the question of its verisimilitude. As professional film critic Roger Ebert (2009) stated, Bigelow "creates a convincing portrayal of the conditions a man like James faces." Apart from the accuracy of plot and characters, the critics (and Bigelow herself) foregrounded how the documentary-like style heightened the sensorial immersion of the audience, conveying the shattered nature of the experiences of individual soldiers, and how the film succeeded in capturing the "real" war. For instance, Lisa Schwarzbaum (2009), a film journalist writing in *Entertainment Weekly*, argued: "This ain't no war videogame, no flashy, cinematic art piece; there's nothing virtual about this reality."

This reading strategy was also widely employed on film review Web sites, such as Metacritic and Rotten Tomatoes, which include posts by nonprofessional critics, and where the discourse of soldiers or veterans was highly visible. Although some of those posting found it highly realistic compared with other Hollywood war films, most of the soldiers rejected the film because of its *lack* of verisimilitude. Some left-wing commentators blamed Bigelow for not providing a deep insight into the nature of the Iraq war—in their opinion, *The Hurt Locker* avoided the wider political context, focusing solely on the celebration of individual heroism in a Hollywood style. This was also the main argument of war photographer Michael Kamber (2010), writing for the *New York Times* photography blog. He perceived *The Hurt Locker* as not realistic enough, accusing Bigelow of glamorizing the war and the protagonist, who "appears to be fighting the war alone."

The predominance of this interpretative framework is not surprising, since in the war film, correspondence with reality has always been an important criterion of validity. It is noteworthy that the same reading strategy, based on detecting the realist aesthetics of *The Hurt Locker*, produced opposing evaluations of the film: on the one hand, the argument for its "documentary" style was intertwined with the film's supposedly apolitical stance, to which a number of the left-wing commentators negatively attributed its success; and on the other, it was seen as a way of providing a serious critique of the U.S. mission in Iraq.

The Modernist Framework

While the realist framework and its concern with correspondence to reality seems prevalent in the mainstream media and on popular internet review sites, we might also discern another strand of critical reception, called here modernist. This strand focuses specifically on Bigelow's aesthetic strategies in *The Hurt Locker*, which in turn help categorize her film as art-house cinema. In the readings operating within this discursive framework, the role of Bigelow as an auteur was emphasized and was accompanied by the frequent categorization of *The Hurt Locker* as an art film, distinct from Hollywood products in its "seriousness" and in having an inferred "message" from its creator. The attention to film authorship as a reading strategy was more persistent in academic journals and specialized magazines, although it was also present in some of the online reviews, both journalists' blogs and fan review sites. Critics highlighted, for instance, that the film refused to adopt a traditional narrative arc: they perceived the narrative as episodic, fragmented, and "difficult." Film critic Amy Taubin (2009) described *The Hurt Locker* as "a structuralist war movie" and applauded its "brilliant choreography" that combined multiple viewpoints and quick, nervous editing, while Anne Thompson (2009) from *Variety* wrote, "This movie is intellectually rigorous and stylishly crafted." In his scholarly analysis of *The Hurt Locker*, Douglas A. Cunningham (2010) focused on its "overall disruption—even explosion—of mainstream narrative drive" and highlighted the director's relation to the innovative narrative trends in the cinematic avant-garde and European art-house films of Antonioni, Bergman, Godard, and Resnais, which "heavily influenced Bigelow's own style and philosophy" (4). In a similar manner, but with a less academic tone, Metacritic Web site fan EtienneW dubbed the film "[a] masterclass, truly wonderful cinema" and dedicated it "to those that see and enjoy movies as high art" (January 27, 2010).

In reviews that focused on proving or undermining Bigelow's status as auteur, her biography was often mentioned: on the one hand her studies at the San Francisco Art Institute and her scholarship at the Whitney Museum of Art in New York City, as evidence of her training in "high art" and her intellectual background; on the other, her professional and personal relationship with James Cameron, which often provoked insinuations that she owed her success to him. A number of major media critics also produced a clear genre dichotomy between Cameron's *Avatar* and Bigelow's *The Hurt Locker*: a Hollywood 3-D megabudget sci-fi flick versus a presumed smaller-scale art-house war film. In the run-up to the Oscars this opposition was imbued with tabloid rivalrous (and sometimes overtly sexist) coverage: in *Forbes*, for instance, we could read, "This time, it's personal. Why wouldn't Bigelow want to best her ex, especially when he reportedly left her for his lead actress in *The Terminator*?" (Blakeley 2010). This association with Cameron proves tricky for Bigelow's status as an auteur, since it is frequently entwined with allegations that their past marriage benefited her career. On the other hand, in opposition to Cameron's more "mainstream" generic fiction, it could help situate her as an "art-house" director. It is clear, however, that the contraposition of Cameron's and Bigelow's respective films still draws on a "mass culture" paradigm, placing them at opposite ends of a high culture vs. low culture spectrum. The reviews by Taubin, Thompson, Cunningham, and EtienneW try to locate Bigelow within an auteurist concept of filmmaking and thus contradict those who claim that Bigelow "sold out." Nevertheless, while her "muscular filmmaking" might fit comfortably within "classical auteurism," which—as Angela Martin (2008) argues—is determined by values such as self-expression, violence, and virility (128–129), such a gesture might prove highly problematic for feminist film criticism, as it suggests women filmmakers can be considered auteurs only in *particular* ways.

The Postmodernist Framework

What the above responses arguably overlook is that despite its "modernist aesthetics," Bigelow's film contains a considerable number of explosions, characteristic of big-budget Hollywood filmmaking. These suggest her interest in spectacle as much as narrative and frame her work within the action genre format. In contrast to the "modernist" readings, the "postmodernist" responses to the film did notice Bigelow's fascination with (and sometimes revision of) popular genre cinema. In these reviews and film analyses, found mostly in journal articles and scholarly critiques, her oeuvre was often depicted as transcending the binary opposition between high and popular culture, or—in the words of Caetlin Benson-Allott (2010) in her article for *Film Quarterly*—as "neither simply subversive nor easily classifiable as commercial" (33). Writing for *Jump Cut*, Robert Alpert (2010) compared Bigelow with other "best of the old-school" U.S. genre directors, such as Sam Fuller, Anthony Mann, and Sam Peckinpah, to contextualize her as an action auteur who returns to the same personal themes and obsessions, demonstrating a distinct visual style while working *within* genre cinema.

Another feature emphasized by academic critics was Bigelow's self-conscious attitude toward her filmmaking that is also deeply informed by generic reconfiguration. As Alpert, for instance, argued: "Bigelow's movie is self-consciously about herself and the limits of her moviemaking. It is no coincidence that many of the film's scenes resemble the making of a movie" (2010). This reflexive attitude was often conceptualized as a rethinking of the war genre itself, in particular through her dialogical interactions with the western. Bigelow was praised in some reviews for engaging the heroic myth of the West and for rethinking the western's idealized masculinity. In their insightful scholarly analysis of the film and its reception Yvonne Tasker and Eylem Atakav (2010) argue that *The Hurt Locker* explores the nature of the masculinity long celebrated by Hollywood—the archetypal western hero who protects a community—and mention her other action-oriented "masculine" titles, such as *Point Break* (1991) or *K19: The Widowmaker* (2002), to demonstrate how Bigelow "[has] fairly consistently explored themes to do with men, violence and masculinity" (58). While this intertextual reading strategy, which suggests potential connections with Bigelow's earlier work, might serve to construct her as a *genre auteur*, at the same time it may also evidence her critical play with genre cinema and its gender conventions, particularly the western and its supposed conservative ideology. In this context the issue of Bigelow's gender comes to the fore again, since being a woman director who allegedly subverts Hollywood gender types and genres effectively mobilizes the discourse of "Hollywood transgressor": as Deborah Jermyn and Sean Redmond (2003) assert in their scholarly analysis, "[her] work partly falls within *and* partly infringes the parameters of Hollywood cinema" (3).

Yet as the hostile responses to *The Hurt Locker* might suggest, reviewers and commentators are more reticent now about drawing on such a postmodernist discourse. As Rona Murray (2011) has observed in her scholarly analysis of Bigelow's career, whereas working within genres perceived as "muscular" and depicting male subjects used to be seen by feminist scholars writing in the 1990s as Bigelow's transgression of gender and its sexual politics, in the context of *The Hurt Locker* it "remains too much of a betrayal for some female critics" (17). There has been a clear shift, she argues, "from a perception of a positive political power in the transgressive representations of the earlier films to a more negative assessment of the transgressive nature of Bigelow herself as a successful woman filmmaker in Hollywood" (2). While this certainly is not the first time that Bigelow has directed a film signified culturally as "masculine," it is the first time she has garnered this much attention. Her success at the Oscars ceremony—read by Nochimson as managing to be one of the boys, in institutional terms—seems to cement her "masculinity" in a negative way and therefore undercut the transgression discourse.

Conclusion

In the controversies around interpreting *The Hurt Locker*—which arise from the various classifications of Kathryn Bigelow as (anti-)feminist, female, masculinist, mainstream, and art-house director—it is clear that Bigelow's status is under continuous negotiation. Her recent success has renewed critical and scholarly interest in women filmmakers and women's authorship, but these prove to be intensely problematic categories, especially for those women directors who gain entrance into Hollywood (see Lane 2000). As illustrated at the beginning of this chapter, some reviewers did not feel comfortable with Bigelow's mobilizing of supposedly "masculine" genres, with her repeated refusal of both feminist and gendered identities, and with the fact that her latest genre movies are closer to mainstream, commercial narrative cinema than to conventionally understood feminist filmmaking.

Offering an overview of the multiple reading contexts that gave *The Hurt Locker* meaning for a variety of reviewers and commentators provides a basis from which to transcend the binary oppositions of the "mass culture" paradigm discussed by Hollows and helps us better understand the film's critical reception as an arena for public discussion and debate, revealing what is in play around questions of identity, gender, and women's filmmaking. Addressing the different critical frameworks within which women's filmmaking is discussed can redirect demands for a specifically feminist aesthetic or "woman's voice" to an examination of the multiple factors that come together in the negotiation and struggle over making sense of particular examples of women's work.

Notes

I would like to thank Christine Gledhill and Julia Knight for their generous feedback on an earlier version of this chapter.

1. It is also worth distinguishing between feminist academics and professional critics influenced by feminism, and noting the time lag that often exists in the circulation of ideas from academe to journalism.

2. In her discussion of this opposition, Hollows refers to a particular "realist" aesthetic, usually associated in film theory with the notion of classical Hollywood cinema (Bordwell, Staiger, and Thompson 1985). She does not take into consideration the practice of some feminist filmmakers (especially documentary makers) who utilize realism, nor does she mention nonmainstream, noncommercial cinema that is narrative driven. On the other hand, her view on "avant-gardist tendencies" marks a clear shift in the history of feminist film criticism that earlier would find avant-garde practice exhilaratingly destructive.

3. See for example Clover (1992) and her discussion of cross-identification in horror cinema.

References

Adams, Richard. 2010. "The Hurt Locker Is Empty." *Richard Adam's Blog. The Guardian*, March 9. Available at http://www.guardian.co.uk/commentisfree/cifamerica/2010/mar/09/oscars-kathryn-bigelow-hurt-locker-iraq (accessed January 11, 2011).

Alpert, Robert. 2010. "Kathryn Bigelow's *The Hurt Locker*: A Jack-in-the-Box Story." *Jump Cut: A Review of Contemporary Media* 52. Available at http://www.ejumpcut.org/currentissue/alpertHurtlocker/index.html (accessed December 15, 2010).

Benson-Allott, Caetlin. 2010. "Undoing Violence: Politics, Genre, and Duration in Kathryn Bigelow's Cinema." *Film Quarterly* 64 (2): 33–43.

Blakeley, Kiri. 2010. "Kathryn Bigelow vs. James Cameron: An Oscar-Themed Battle of the Exes." *Forbes*, February 2. Available at http://www.forbes.com/2010/02/02/james-cameron-avatar-kathryn-bigelow-hurt-locker-forbes-woman-time-oscar-nominations.html (accessed December 15, 2010).

Bordwell, David, Janet Staiger, and Kristin Thompson. 1985. *The Classical Hollywood Cinema—Film Style and Mode of Production to 1960*. London: Routledge.

Clover, Carol J. 1992. *Men, Women, and Chain Saws: Gender in the Modern Horror Film*. Princeton, N.J.: Princeton University Press.

Cole, Susan G. 2010. "Kathryn Bigelow. The Absentee Feminist." *Now Toronto*, March 11. Available at http://www.nowtoronto.com/daily/story.cfm?content=174034 (accessed May 15, 2010).

Collins, Luke. 2012. "100% Pure Adrenaline: Gender and Generic Surface in *Point Break*." In *Gender Meets Genre in Postwar Cinemas*, edited by Christine Gledhill, 54–67. Urbana: University of Illinois Press.

Cook, Pam. 2012. "No Fixed Address: The Women's Picture from *Outrage* to *Blue Steel*." In *Gender Meets Genre in Postwar Cinemas*, edited by Christine Gledhill, 29–40. Urbana: University of Illinois Press.

Cunningham, Douglas A. 2010. "Explosive Structure: Fragmenting the New Modernist War Narrative in *The Hurt Locker*." *Cineaction* 81: 2–10.

Dargis, Manohla. 2010. "How Oscar Found Ms. Right." *New York Times*, March 10. Available at http://www.nytimes.com/2010/03/14/movies/14dargis.html (accessed November 7, 2010).

Ebert, Roger. 2009. "The Best Films of the Decade." *Roger Ebert's Journal. Chicago Sun-Times*, December 30. Available at http://blogs.suntimes.com/ebert/2009/12/the_best_films_of_the_decade.html (accessed January 15, 2011).

Hollows, Joanne. 2000. *Feminism, Femininity, and Popular Culture*. Manchester: Manchester University Press.

Jermyn, Deborah. 2003. "Cherchez la Femme: *The Weight of Water* and the Search for Bigelow in a 'Bigelow Film.'" In Jermyn and Redmond, *Cinema of Kathryn Bigelow*, 125–44.

Jermyn, Deborah, and Sean Redmond. 2003. *The Cinema of Kathryn Bigelow: Hollywood Transgressor*. London: Wallflower.

Kamber, Michael. 2010. "How Not to Depict a War." *Lens* [blog]. *New York Times*, March 1. Available at http://lens.blogs.nytimes.com/2010/03/01/essay-15 (accessed November 20, 2010).

Klinger, Barbara. 1997. "Film History Terminable and Interminable: Recovering the Past in Reception Studies." *Screen* 38 (2): 107–28.

Lane, Christina. 2000. *Feminist Hollywood: From Born in Flames to Point Break*. Detroit: Wayne State University Press.

Martin, Angela. 2008. "Refocusing Authorship in Women's Filmmaking." In *Auteurs and Authorship: A Film Reader*, edited by Barry Keith Grant, 127–34. Malden, Mass.: Blackwell.

Muir, Kate. 2010. "Kathryn Bigelow's Great Leap Forward—Or Was It?" *Times*, March 12. Available at http://www.thetimes.co.uk/tto/arts/film/article2464415.ece (accessed January 11, 2011).

Murray, Rona. 2011. "Tough Guy in Drag? How the External, Critical Discourses Surrounding Kathryn Bigelow Demonstrate the Wider Problems of the Gender Question." *Networking Knowledge: Journal of the MeCCSA Postgraduate Network* 4 (1): 1–22.

Nochimson, Martha. 2010. "Kathryn Bigelow: Feminist Pioneer or Tough Guy in Drag?" *Salon.com*, February 24. Available at http://www.salon.com/2010/02/24/bigelow_3 (accessed January 15, 2011).

Schwarzbaum, Lisa. 2009. "The Hurt Locker." *Entertainment Weekly*, June 17. Available at http://www.ew.com/ew/article/0,20285519,00.html (accessed November 24, 2010).

Staiger, Janet. 2000. *Perverse Spectators: The Practices of Film Reception*. New York: New York University Press.

Tasker, Yvonne, and Eylem Atakav. 2010. "The Hurt Locker: Male Intimacy, Violence, and the Iraq War Movie." *Cine: Journal of Film Studies* 1 (2): 57–70.

Taubin, Amy. 2009. "Hard Wired: Kathryn Bigelow's *The Hurt Locker* Packs a Powerful Experiential Punch." *Film Society of Lincoln Center*, May/June. Available at http://filmlinccom.siteprotect.net/fcm/mj09/hurtlocker.htm (accessed December 2, 2010).

Thompson, Anne. 2009. "*Hurt Locker*, Other Award Pics Directed by Women." *Thomson on Hollywood. Variety*, June, 28. Available athttp://weblogs.variety.com/thompsonon hollywood/2009/06/hurt-locker-other-award-pics-directed-by-women.html (accessed December 12, 2010).

PART III

Women at Work

CHAPTER 12

Gossip, Labor, and Female Stardom in Pre-Independence Indian Cinema

The Case of Shanta Apte

NEEPA MAJUMDAR

On the evening of July 17, 1939, a crowd gathered outside the Prabhat Film Company in Pune, India, where the studio's famous singing star Shanta Apte sat and occasionally lay on a bench. Dressed in "trousers and a sports shirt," according to the *Mirror* magazine (July 25, 1939), she was staging a hunger strike in protest against the studio's withholding pay for the days in June that she had not come to work. Accompanied by her brother and lawyer, she remained on the bench for two nights and one day and drank only salted water. During this time a constable was called to control the crowd, and management tried to negotiate with her. Eventually her doctor and her brother succeeded in persuading her to return home. Reporting of the event in India varied: from the *Bombay Chronicle*'s daily coverage, through the *Mirror*'s extensive weekly reporting (including statements by both studio and star), to the best-known film magazine, *filmindia*, running a single, curt paragraph; it was also reported as far away as Australia.

Apte's hunger strike is one of those small events out of which the vaster network of women's film history is constituted. This chapter thinks through the various frameworks through which this event was, and may still be, read. It is worth noting first that, although Indian cinema had become well established by the mid-1920s, the task of seeking historical documentation even as late as 1939 is plagued by major gaps and absences. In later accounts, Apte's hunger strike, if mentioned at all, has taken on the frozen qualities of that single phrase—"Shanta Apte's hunger strike"—offering itself up as completely self-explanatory. Yet if we agree with Walter Benjamin (1968) that the past is to be seized up as images that flash up in the present (255), then it was precisely this ossified image that offered itself up to me as a strongly visualized moment, one that presented itself as eminently suited to be blasted "out of the continuum of history" rather than as a window into the past "as it really was" (261). This image from 1939 of a major female star, lying on a bench outside Prabhat studios dressed in men's clothing, poses precisely the question of how to do women's film history—first, because I understand "doing" history as a call to frame and interpret a set of contexts that open up the event as an unfolding rather than finished action, or again in Benjamin's words as "a present . . . in transition" (262). But second, because this event highlights the incomplete nature of doing history in the context of Indian cinema, where source materials are more arbitrarily available than in most Euro-American cinemas, foregrounding the greater degree to which imaginative speculation must play a role in film history. Nevertheless, I begin with some tentative details pertaining to this story's major players, as drawn from various sources.

Apte and Prabhat

In 1932, aged sixteen, Apte began work at Prabhat. Her first major role came in the 1934 film *Amrtimanthan* (The Churning), while her peak years there were 1936 to 1937. In 1936 Prabhat released two films that launched the two major aspects of Apte's star persona: *Amar Jyoti* (Eternal Flame) established her as a major singing star, and *Rajput Ramani* (Rajput Princess) revealed her onscreen fiery temperament. In both films, she played a secondary role to the main star. The following year, 1937, she made her most famous film, *Kunku* (The Unexpected), which was released in two languages (Marathi and Hindi). Here she played the resistant young bride of an old man, refusing to consummate the marriage, and earning for the film a place in the Indian film canon because of its reputation for progressive gender politics.

Clearly, Apte's hunger strike precipitated her break with Prabhat and her last film with the studio was *Gopal Krishna* in 1938, made one year earlier. After leaving Prabhat, she continued to work for other studios until her death in 1964. Some of her later films dovetailed nicely with what became her established image as an activist. In 1942, for instance, she made *Apna Ghar/Aple Ghar* (My House) at the rival studio New Theatres, playing a social reformer working with tribal people to try to unionize them against forest contractors, one of whom is her own husband. Her husband's change of heart at the film's conclusion echoes the narrative out-

FIGURE 12.1. Shanta Apte in her 1937 film, *Kunku* (The Unexpected), taken from the back cover of *filmindia*, October 1937

come of *Kunku*, where her much older husband realizes the injustice of his marriage and commits suicide to free his bride.

Apte's two-day hunger strike in 1939, which is all but forgotten today, arguably marked the beginning of the decline of a relatively short-lived acting career, if one considers her best work to have been with Prabhat studios. As this chapter suggests, Apte herself may have realized this at the time of her hunger strike, mainly because of the highly insecure terms of employment for actors on contract. Prabhat Film Company was established in 1929 in Kolhapur, but moved to Pune in 1933. It was one of the few vertically integrated studios in India in that it initially had long-term contracts with distributors, then took on distribution itself, and also owned theaters in Bombay, Pune, and Madras. The studio closed in 1953, which was also the year of Apte's final film. By that time, hindsight showed that both she and Prabhat had reached the height of their fame in the 1930s.

Stardom as Labor

The foregoing discussion casts the studio as exploiter and Apte as victim, but there may be reasons to complicate this picture. In May 1939 Prabhat became a limited company, and according to the *Mirror*:

> Miss Apte wrote a letter to the Company asking for a clarification of her position with the limited concern. The directors of the concern did not think [sic] worth their while to give any reply to her letter. As a result she did not go to the studio for over two weeks. The directors also resented certain reports that were given to the Press by her and her brother. (July 25, 1939)

Depending on whom you believe, Apte either used this as an excuse or was confused by this change, refusing to come to work for two weeks in June while seeking clarification about the status of her contract—essentially trying to see if the studio's new status effectively canceled the remaining year of her contract, which it did not. When she came to collect her monthly salary on July 7, according to the studio (*Bombay Chronicle*, July 21, 1939; *Mirror*, July 25, 1939), she was to have been paid in full but objected to signing a receipt for her pay that included a statement taking note of her two-week absence. The studio wanted her to take her pay and sign the document. She wanted them to remove the statement, apologize to her, and only then would she accept her full pay (*Mirror*, August 1, 1939). Quite transparently, she was trying to break her contract, accusing the studio of not paying her. But these details were not really the story's public face, and the relation between this labor dispute and its public face perfectly matches the relation between star image and the labor realities underlying it.

Shanta Apte's case, however, has some singularities. While disputes between stars and studios did occur, they were rarely covered in film magazines, though they did appear in regular newspapers if the disputes ended up in court. Another star, Ermeline, for example, went to court to try to break her contract, but there was no sign of this in any of the film magazines and only one small newspaper report whose headline did not even mention her name (*Times of India*, September 15, 1927). In contrast, Apte's *public* performance of her grievances against the studio clearly violated unspoken norms of propriety on many levels. There are two points of note about Apte's behavior on this occasion: that she was making herself at home on the bench normally occupied by the studio's gateman and that she was wearing "trousers and a sports shirt." While her attire was a violation of gender norms, her location violated class boundaries. Keen to point out the dramatic contrast afforded by the "idol of thousands" occupying the seat of a gateman, the *Mirror* (July 25, 1939) started its report of the event with a series of paradoxes: "Glamour and asceticism, beauty and a prolonged bickering, screen and a sense of highly developed self-respect, hunger-strike and salary, and stardom and *satyagrah* are things that have very rarely gone together."

The fact that this hunger strike appeared contradictory to stardom demonstrates the largely invisible substratum of labor behind any story of stardom. In her 1995 book *Negotiating Hollywood*, Danae Clark points out that star studies is itself implicated in "a capitalist perspective by structurally precluding any consideration of Hollywood's rank-and-file labor force. Scholarly interest is thus limited to those individual stars who have 'risen above' or transcended the ranks of ordinary craft workers . . . to produce something of artistic merit" (6). As she argues, stars themselves were also "encouraged to identify themselves as 'artists' rather than 'workers,'" a classification guaranteed to drive a wedge between stars and other actors

(6). With stars, because their labor appears transparently available for discussion via their screen performances, it becomes easy to ignore their actual status as salaried employees whose contracts might reveal their greater or lesser alignment with *other* actors and workers in the studio. By studying actual studio contracts, Jane Gaines (1991) was able to demonstrate how Hollywood stars added riders to studio contracts so as to assert some level of autonomy and control over their images. This is where the arbitrary and speculative nature of "doing" film history comes up in the case of Indian cinema, since contracts and studio business papers are virtually unavailable for scrutiny and their very existence comes as a matter of some surprise because of the overwhelmingly repeated narrative of the largely informal structures of the Indian film industry. To the contrary, Apte's strike offers us a brief glimpse, unusual in the Indian context, of the underlying tensions of labor relations marking the structures of film business. In the contemporaneous coverage of this event, these underlying structures remained shadowy and implicit despite the unusually detailed coverage in the *Mirror*. In the absence of additional sources of information, there is no way to ascertain the exact nature of Apte's contract or the details of the changes in the studio's business status that gave Apte the excuse she was looking for to try to break her contract.

Although none of the contemporaneous public accounts of this event explicitly commented on the relation between this strike and other strikes that dominated the headlines at that time, their responses implied that a star's hunger strike constituted nothing less than a trivialization of national and industrial politics. The *Mirror* (July 25, 1939), for instance, sarcastically noted her hunger strike as "further evidence of the rapid advance of the Indian film industry and its adoption of Western technique," going on to observe: "A hunger strike—that's a new idea, one which out-Hollywoods Hollywood . . . Western stars lack the requisite ascetic spirit. Sex appeal and *Satyagraha* are not often found together in the same person." It is helpful to keep in mind here that in the nearby Bombay cotton mills, workers' strikes were continuing on and off between 1937 and 1939. Newspaper headlines for July 25, 1939 were also dominated by news of a hundred political prisoners in Calcutta who were on hunger strike, with public appeals by Rajendra Prasad and Mahatma Gandhi for them to call off the strike. Hunger strikes and other forms of civil disobedience were generally in the air that year, as in March, for example, Gandhi had embarked on another of his own numerous hunger strikes, something that was reported as far away as the *Pittsburgh Post-Gazette*.

The view that Apte's strike trivialized hunger strikes as a form of resistance because it occurred in the arena of entertainment merely repeated and reinforced the assumption that stardom and labor belong in separate worlds. Other accounts trivializing the event included parodies in which other stars were reported as going on hunger strike for a variety of ridiculous reasons, all tied in some way to dominant traits of their star images (*Mirror*, August 1, 1939). Apte was clearly tapping into the most spectacular language available to her in contemporaneous political discourse: first by recognizing that a refusal to eat at home or inside the studio would not constitute a hunger strike, and that she needed to be visible in the public eye to be politically effective; and second, by her public violation of gender and class norms. That her act made spectators uncomfortable is indicated in the *Mirror*'s account (July 25, 1939), which reported that it was embarrassing to approach Apte to ask questions because she would be lying down on the bench even during the day.

A Breach of Etiquette

This event can be read in the discursive context of norms of female propriety pertaining to *public* displays of personhood. Both Apte's hunger strike and her autobiography, published the following year, elicited similarly negative responses. In August 1939, one fan, for instance, wrote, "Your jumping into news everyday betokens, if not an inborn eccentricity in you, an utter lack of mature understanding" and referred to the hunger strike as her "recent acrobatics" (*Mirror*, August 1, 1939). He tells her that she has "defiled" her own name by her recent stunt, asserting: "What a bad example you have set to your less fortunate colleagues to ventilate a grievance." This echoed a statement put out by Prabhat's directors that "discipline is as much a necessity with 'stars' as with 'extras'" (*Mirror*, July 25, 1939). Reviews of her autobiography, reminding readers of her hunger strike and other improper behavior, suggested that both constituted a breach of etiquette and a too-strident public airing of her grievances against her studio. As with other actresses who similarly aired their grievances in the public forum of autobiographies, Apte's book was received in a tone of disciplinary admonishment. Although an editorial in the *Mirror* (May 12, 1940) did note that "the spirited Poona girl and one of our foremost film stars has created another record by publishing her book *Jau Mee Cinemat* in eight regional languages," the piece was titled "Think, Shanta, Think!" and delivered an overall negative review of Apte's autobiography. According to the review, her book maintained that "there is a ghastly dark background to this apparently attractive profession," which sucks an artist's lifeblood and then throws her out on the streets. The public knows nothing about this dark side because "newspapers who ordinarily champion the cause of the oppressed connive at the glaring injustice in film studios because they are bribed to be blind to the faults of the industry and to be court-jesters to the producers." Taking exception to such "sweeping statements" the review dismisses her book as one-sided and prejudiced, saying that her account makes the proprietors of film studios seem like "modern midases" who have reached their position "by starving and generally exploiting the artistes." But, argues the reviewer, "nothing could be further from the truth" because producers are helplessly dependent on artistes once production is underway and treat them well because they depend on them for their own livelihood. Indeed, the review reports that no one else has claimed to have been exploited, while producers have gone out of business because they have had to pay prohibitively high salaries to stars. Yet, of course, as evidenced by newspaper reports, several stars did bring court cases against their studios. The reviewer's assertions also gloss over the hierarchies in the film acting profession, mentioning only the highest paid, and thus participates in the divisions that capitalism thrives on. The review ends by admonishing Apte: "Before you make sweeping allegations, Shanta, you should think, and not be carried away by your own haughtiness and prejudices."

The studio similarly reframed the labor dispute as a breach of decent behavior, claiming that Apte "hurled abusive language" at the directors, refused to accept their compromises or the refreshments they sent out to her, and insisted that she was taking her grievances to the public "in some strange manner" (*Bombay Chronicle*, July 21, 1939; *Mirror*, July 25, 1939). What is behind these claims is an ideological construction of the studio as family and of Apte as the wayward child who takes domestic disputes out into the public square. The event's brief coverage in *filmindia* (August 1939) also participated in this kind of admonishment by expressing surprise that Apte resorted to a hunger strike rather than "coming to an amicable settlement with her proprietors." Clark notes that in the studio era the family discourse "functioned according to a model of 'paternal tyranny'" (20) but also effectively masked the actual hierarchies of labor in the film industry. Both the idea of the star as artist and the studio as family work to deflect any recognition of the star as worker occupying a position of subordination in relation to the directors and of privilege in relation to other workers, including actors. Similarly, the *Mirror's* (July 25, 1939) coverage of Apte's hunger strike removes it from the realms of labor dispute and turns it into "adventure" by comparing it to Hollywood and Elstree stars' experiences of being threatened by kidnappers or having their jewels stolen.

Apte as Activist

Apte, for her part, responded to the studio's account of the dispute by resolutely returning the issue to its labor context. She consciously persists in using the Gandhian term "satyagraha" or agitation for truth, saying:

My satyagraha had no bearing upon the question of salary or my contract with the Company but as a protest against the most insulting and intimidating treatment meted out to me. It was an humble protest of a worker against the big bosses. The Directors, fearing exposure of their high-handed actions, have tried to twist the facts and attempted to show that my satyagraha was for the sake of a paltry sum of money. (*Mirror*, August 1, 1939)

Apte's self-conscious molding of her image in terms of activism was meant to align herself with the groundswell of labor agitation in both the film industry and elsewhere by insistently denying any difference between stars and other film workers. In response to the many strikes of the 1930s, the Indian Factories Act would eventually be passed in 1948 in order to put in place some basic worker rights. However, the act's provisions were not immediately applied to the film industry, as the studios argued that working conditions—specifically the question of overtime—were quite different in their industry compared to other industries. Film workers petitioned the Film Enquiry Committee of 1951 to get overtime employment recognized within the film industry and to complain about the absence of any form of job security. The committee ended up siding with the studios and exempting the film industry from the Factories Act, arguing that its provisions for overtime did not apply in an industry where work is irregular and times of intensive work may be followed by relatively low work loads (Patil, paragraph 237). But the committee did recommend that film workers establish an association or union to safeguard their interests (Patil, paragraph 211).

Although the issue of labor organization in the film industry was not formally recognized until 1951, it was—as Apte noted in her autobiography—a cause already much championed by the print media in the 1930s, though rarely on behalf of stars. Baburao Patel, editor at *filmindia*, was, for instance, a frequent advocate for film workers' rights. The June 1939 issue carried an editorial titled "Grinding the Theatre Workers." In it Patel attacked the outrageous cut in pay that cinema theater workers suffered for each day they failed to work, sometimes amounting to as much as 25 percent of their monthly salary for each day missed, and called for a theater workers' trade union.

In *filmindia*'s August 1939 issue K. A. Abbas, a highly regarded Prabhat screenwriter and left-wing journalist, wrote an article titled "Give Them a Square Deal." Although Abbas did not directly address Apte's dispute, unlike others who championed the rights of extras and other workers, his piece did address the labor conditions of stars. Focusing primarily on debunking the idea that stars live in luxury, he drew attention to the short span of their careers—the opposite of the argument the *Mirror* review used in May 1940 to dismiss the claims in Apte's autobiography, asserting that it is *directors* who can be ruined by stars' demands for high salaries. The rest of Abbas's article addressed the exploitation of stars using a language that identified the studios as capitalist organizations that are built on the "life-blood" of actors. He recommends that a Cine Artistes' Association be formed to "raise the question of decent wages for all artistes," saying that he is "sure that every conscientious journalist will support them" (27). Indeed, as a self-professed socialist, Abbas ended by arguing: "I don't see any reason why the studio proprietors should not be persuaded (if necessary, forced) to share their profits with the men and women whose hard work brings in the cash." Ironically, of course, this was published in the very same magazine that had admonished Apte for her inability to reach an amicable agreement with the studio.

Despite Abbas's observations, few journalists saw Apte's days away from work in the same terms and instead read her actions as the self-indulgent tantrum of a spoiled and ill-behaved actress. But outside the circle of film journalists, many viewers saw continuities between Apte's fiery onscreen image and her now fairly well-established offscreen activist image. In January 1940 she was invited to open a new talkie theater called RADIO in Belgaum. This suggests her popularity was undiminished, despite a decline in film roles, while the name of the theater she inaugurated would indicate that the primary source of her popularity was her singing voice. Indeed, a "mammoth crowd" of five thousand welcomed her when she arrived at Belgaum railway station, while one of the speeches at the event referred to her as "the skylark of our screen." Another speech by a woman who was a political activist in the Congress Party referred to Apte as a "girl of revolt" and encouraged other women to emulate her "fighting nature" (*Mirror*, February 4, 1940). The *Mirror's* report of this theater opening also provided the full text of Apte's speech, which initially seems aligned with what, by that time, were thoroughly conventional calls for the improvement of morality in the film profession, but she explains: "I will make myself clear. . . . I mean the business honesty of producers must attain a higher degree so that the workers in the Studios would feel a greater sense of security and will be able to devote more energy with great enthusiasm to the task allotted them." She notes two themes also addressed in her autobiography: that producers in general are corrupt and that journalists are rarely honest in their assessment of films and studios, being themselves in the pockets of studio bosses. She ends by saying that though she may currently be a "lone fighter" in this cause, she has no doubt others will join her. By initially casting her critique of the studio in terms of the familiar call for improved morality in the cinema, Apte is able to move on to reiterate her commitment to labor politics and improving working conditions in the industry.

Apte as "Fiery"

While one of the speeches noted above used the term "girl of revolt" and referred to her "fighting nature," the epithet "fiery" that was so often repeated positively about Apte's screen persona became a malleable term that could just as easily stand for "badly behaved" offscreen. In fact, whether she was considered badly behaved or fiery, the continuities between Apte's on- and offscreen image were repeatedly remarked upon and in one case directly linked to another episode in Apte's offscreen public life. The *Mirror*'s initial report (July 25, 1939) on the hunger strike notes that this was the second time in a few months that Apte had been in the public eye, reminding readers of their report "a few months ago" on "her sensational slashing of a film-journalist." The details of this event were fleshed out years later by gossip writer Saadat Hasan Manto. The film journalist was *filmindia*'s editor Baburao Patel, who had the power to make or break star careers through his journal's reviews. According to Manto (1998): "Babu Rao wrote such venomous pieces about her in *Filmindia* [sic] that being the true Marathi she was, she burst into Babu Rao's office one day, dressed in her riding gear and whipped him six or seven times with her riding crop" (191). This gave *filmindia*'s editor a personal axe to grind, so it was no surprise that the magazine accorded Apte's hunger strike only the briefest mention.

Many articles about Apte refer to her "fighting" image in only a very generalized way. But a closer look at specific moments in *Kunku* (1937) shows this image encompasses both the resistance to traditional gender roles so characteristic of Apte's film roles and the explicit resistance to class boundaries that marked her offscreen persona. *Kunku* constructs a family that was highly unconventional for the movies, not because of the young woman and her much older husband at its core, but because of the old man's two adult children and their contrasting relations with the young bride. The son is a lecherous fool who gets his comeuppance at the hands of Apte's character. In a scene where the young woman's husband reprimands his son for his sexualized innuendos toward his stepmother, his insulting rejoinder is that his father is the one who has violated norms of decency by marrying such a young wife. While the father stands there with head bowed in shame, Apte's character picks up a stick and beats the son, demanding he apologize to his father. Shot in one take, the scene is framed in long shot that allows us to see the full vigor with which Apte wields the stick against the cowering son in what is clearly not a merely symbolic gesture. This scene in her most famous film would surely have been recalled by many viewers when news circulated of Apte's "sensational slashing" of *filmindia*'s editor.

The stepson is contrasted with his sister, a social worker and feminist played by Shakuntala Paranjpye—herself a labor activist working with the International Labor Organization in Geneva in the 1930s. In the film, she is shown as someone Apte's character admires and so functions as Apte's mentor. When her stepdaughter visits her, Apte's character sings Henry Wadsworth Longfellow's poem "A Psalm of Life" in a scene that serves as a song sequence, but one that encapsulates their shared social engagement. With its entreaty to "Be not like dumb, driven cattle!/ Be a hero in the strife!/Let us, then, be up and doing/ . . . Still achieving, still pursuing/ . . . But to act, that each to-morrow/Find us farther than today," the song is strongly encoded as a feminist irruption, and its rendition in English serves to connect this domestic activist space to a larger international one of feminist and labor solidarity.

While Apte's opening of the new talkie theater in Belgaum in 1940 evidenced her continuing popularity, she had not been given the lead role in what became the most highly publicized film from Prabhat studios the previous year. Instead, the lead role in *Aadmi* (aka *Life is for Living*, 1939) went to the unknown actress Shanta Hublikar. As we know, Apte was trying to break her contract with Prabhat. But the studio wanted her to play a nonstarring role in the 1940 film *Sant Dnyaneshwar*, while the starring role would go to Gouri, a Prabhat employee who, despite no acting experience, had been cast—and met with unexpected success—as the cantankerous wife of Sant Tukaram in the eponymous 1936 film (Majumdar 2010). Thus Apte was supplanted by Shanta Hublikar in one film and by Gouri in another, decisions which were reported in *filmindia* in February 1939. From July through to December of that year, the magazine's pages were plastered with images from *Aadmi* and advertisements for *Sant Dnyaneshwar*.

These clear signs of the ongoing displacement of one star by others strongly suggest that Apte undertook her hunger strike at the very moment when her labor power was most at risk, at what may have seemed to be the end of her star career. What emerges here is that despite her highly successful performance in *Kunku* (1937) and second billing on *Gopal Krishna* (1938), she was still passed over for major roles, most likely because of her "fiery" reputation. She had only one year remaining on her contract with Prabhat, but even a few months off the cinematic screen and off the pages of film magazines could spell the end of a career. Since being in the public eye could not by itself sustain a star career, Apte's hunger strike should not be read merely as a publicity stunt but more as an attempt to break her contract so she could seek work elsewhere. The system whereby stars under contract were not given any work to do, even if their salary was paid, was actually a form of control that made it impossible for an actress to revive a flagging career by going elsewhere. If Apte's absence from primary roles at Prabhat in 1939–40 is a symptom of the mechanisms by which studios could discipline unruly stars, then her hunger strike was a way to resist such disciplining—though a cynical view might argue that her concern for actors' labor rights was merely an act masking a fairly mundane in-house dispute.

Conclusion

Implied in the contemporaneous responses to Apte's strike are a set of widely divergent interpretations of the event itself: Was it about her own contract or actors' rights in general? Was she behaving badly, or did she have legitimate grievances? Was it anxiety about her own career or injured self-respect? The question here is: How much labor are we to attach to this image from the past? In Indian cinema of this period, the dominant discourse of the moral and cultural labor of stardom called for an improved class of actors (Majumdar 2009). But in doing so it completely bypassed the legal discourse of stardom as material labor—even though the star was written into early cinema history as a salaried studio employee, rather than as someone with charisma or talent. Thus labor and work, in their many meanings, hover on the edges of the discourse of stardom but become a breach of etiquette with precisely the moral labor of decorum seeming to be violated when Shanta Apte went on hunger strike.

References

Benjamin, Walter. 1968. *Illuminations: Essays and Reflections*. Edited by Hannah Arendt. Translated by Harry Zohn. New York: Schocken.

Clark, Danae. 1995. *Negotiating Hollywood: The Cultural Politics of Actors' Labor*. Minneapolis: University of Minnesota Press.

Gaines, Jane M. 1991. *Contested Culture: The Image, the Voice, and the Law*. Chapel Hill: University of North Carolina Press.

Majumdar, Neepa. 2009. *Wanted Cultured Ladies Only! Female Stardom and Cinema in India, 1930s-1950s*. Urbana: University of Illinois Press.

———. 2010. "*Sant Tukaram* (1936)." In *The Cinema of India (24 Frames)*, edited by Lalitha Gopalan, 24–34. London: Wallflower.

Manto, Saadat Hasan. 1998. *Stars from Another Sky: The Bombay Film World of the 1940s*. Penguin.

Patil, S. K. (ed). 1951. *Report of the Film Enquiry Committee*. New Delhi: Government of India Press.

CHAPTER 13

American Women Screenwriters in the 1920s

GIULIANA MUSCIO

The credits of American silent cinema reveal a large number of screenplays written by women. Richard Corliss (1970) states that in the 1920s "the industry's leading scenarists were, by a large majority, women" (39). According to the AFI catalogs for the 1910s and 1920s, women screenwriters wrote at least one fourth of American silent films.[1] Some of them were very successful in their profession, performing crucial roles in the production process; and yet film history bears almost no trace of their work. American silent cinema employed a large number of women, from editors to stars, and their neglect in such a culturally significant phase of filmmaking erased a historical process, the impact of which is not limited to gender issues. If we compare the screenwriters' contribution with the analogous experience of women working in popular literature and theater in the United States between the end of the nineteenth century and the 1930s, we can argue that together, women writers performed a major function in the production of American popular culture.[2] For women screenwriters contributed to the development of cinema, the main mass medium of the time, in its very core—narrative construction—from its origins to the introduction of sound, when Hollywood completed the conquest of the world market.

Researching Women Scriptwriters

Researching screenwriters during this era is challenging. Information about the role of screenwriters in silent cinema has to be gleaned from a range of sources, including autobiographies, published interviews, contemporaneous film magazines, studies of specific studios, or general film histories, with their slim bibliographies for women screenwriters. The AFI catalogs allow a fairly accurate reconstruction of their filmographies but, most significantly, through the plot synopsis for each title they offer an approximate sense of a film's storyline.

Reconstructing the biographies of these women is not an easy task because many of the materials published in film magazines were studio materials, which are not necessarily correct with regard to dates or biographic data. In addition, such biographies as exist are often fragmentary because women's changes of studio or quitting work or following their husbands' careers went undocumented. The very evidence of their work—original scripts in progress—is almost impossible to find, because generally the scripts preserved in studio archives (such as the Fox collection at UCLA) are final drafts or "continuities" written after the film was finished. It is quite rare to find different drafts of a script, with notations and comments. Finally, since many wrote hundreds of films each, it would have been impossible to examine all the scripts by even a selection of writers.[3]

Writers' contracts could be useful in relation to gendered work practices, but one needs to compare documents across time and for different personalities, because clauses (about, for example, writing publicity materials) vary greatly, as do salaries and special provisions (such as being able to work at home). But to find legal files for most of these writers is rare. Nevertheless, Special Collections at USC, UCLA, Wisconsin, together with the Academy of Motion Picture Arts and Sciences in Los Angeles and the Billy Rose Division at the New York Public Library for the Performing Arts (just to mention a few precious institutions), have preserved important studio materials, including biographies, a few legal files, and contracts, in addition to press clippings. But one should be aware of the weak evidential value of some of this material, especially when it represents press releases.

Some of the major writers have received attention, thanks to researchers like Cari Beauchamp, but the work to be done is still daunting. The consolation is that some of the films these scriptwriters wrote have been restored or circulated in festivals, and this constitutes the best evidence of the value of their work. We can glimpse traces of their personalities through the recurrence of themes and situations, even in the complex artifacts of the studio system. Women scenarists of the 1920s deserving star billing in their category include: Clara Beranger, Ouida Bergere, Lenore Coffee, Beulah Marie Dix, Dorothy Farnum, Agnes Christine Johnston, Sonya Levien, Anita Loos, Josephine Lovett, Jeannie Macpherson, Frances Marion, June Mathis, Bess Meredyth, Jane Murfin, Olga Printzlau, Adela Rogers St. Johns, Gladys Unger, and Eve Unsell. Among them Anita Loos, who sold her first script to D. W. Griffith in 1912, wrote the experimental novel *Gentlemen*

Prefer Blondes, developed a comic persona for athletic Douglas Fairbanks, the "virtuous vamp" for Constance Talmadge, and, in the 1930s, the funny "gold-digger" for Jean Harlow (see Loos 1966; Beauchamp and Loos 2003). Frances Marion wrote for all the stars and particularly for Mary Pickford and Marie Dressler, made her husband Fred Thomson into a western hero, and won two Academy Awards (Beauchamp 1997). June Mathis discovered and launched Rodolfo Valentino, planned the production of *Ben Hur* (Fred Niblo, 1925) in Italy, and while remembered for cutting *Greed* (Eric von Stroheim, 1924), it is forgotten that it was she who approved its production (Slater 2002). Jeannie Macpherson wrote almost all of Cecil B. DeMille's films and masterminded their sadomasochist eroticism. Olga Printzlau and Clara Beranger wrote for William DeMille, himself a respected screenwriter (Muscio 2010).

The Scriptwriter's Working Context

Only a few of these women had a regular education, but all of them were good readers, of middle-class (or lower-middle-class) backgrounds. They started their careers writing short stories or stage plays; only the younger ones began writing directly for the movies. Formed by different circumstances, they represent a significant presence in the industry that calls for historical contextualization. Women's role in silent cinema is undoubtedly related to audience composition. Whether women represented 75 percent of filmgoers, as suggested by an article published by *Photoplay* in 1924, or less, historical sources agree that the audience of the 1920s was composed largely of women (see Studler 1996, 286). In late-nineteenth and early-twentieth-century WASP society, when men were busy working under the sign of Calvinist ethics, women played a key role in defining public/private spaces by minding the house and the family but also by exercising control over social institutions such as the school, social and religious life, and, most of all, leisure time (Douglas 1977). After World War I, the effects of industrialization, urbanization, and consumerism, the rise of a new wealthy elite, and mass immigration forced Victorian culture to adapt or give way to new sociocultural needs. The new medium of cinema provided the perfect answer. Social historians agree that modernization was centered on and targeted at women. And to this end, Hollywood utilized women's gender skills and talents.

Thus the significant presence of women screenwriters in American silent cinema can be explained on one hand by the historical context—that is, by women's entry into the public sphere, the wave of suffrage movements, and development of a consumption economy—and on the other hand by the mode of film production, which at that time entailed collaboration, flexible multitasking, and sensitivity to changing outlooks. Women writers entered the field when cinema, as a popular medium, was still considered a "low" practice. Representatives from high culture, such as theater and literature, were almost absent from the field (or unmotivated to join), while women were already established in sentimental literature, which offered a bridge into the cultural industries.

By the mid-1910s screenwriting had become specialized work, but its characteristics and functions have been ignored even within the history of the craft.[4] In American silent cinema, writers worked on a film throughout the entire production process, developing the story for a star or within a specific genre from the first draft to the finished product. The director entered the scene at a later stage, for the shooting—the only phase over which he or she had control. (As we know from a wealth of bitter anecdotes, few directors could participate in the editing.) In contrast, screenwriters continued working on a film after having completed the script: they often stayed on the set to write actors' lines to be lip-read or to adapt the script as shooting proceeded. "Titlists," who specialized in writing intertitles, participated in both scriptwriting and editing, because silent films could be easily modified by inserting new intertitles to solve narrative problems. "Continuity," the term often used in this era to define the script, points precisely to the coordinating work trusted to the screenwriter in the continuous management of the story, which, extending into editing, bridged pre- and postproduction. Within American silent cinema the screenwriter performed a more articulated and influential function than the director. This is not to argue that the film "author" was then the screenwriter (although sometimes this would be the case) but rather to identify the specificities of the production mode.

The tasks assigned to screenwriters implied their continuous presence in a work model based on the story-star relation and on close collaboration between producer and writer. Not only did writers attend the different phases of film production, but sometimes they held powerful positions within the studio hierarchy, similar to producers. (In fact, in the 1920s and 1930s several producers came from screenwriting, such as Darryl Zanuck at Warners or June Mathis at Metro.) In the case of Marion and Mathis, writing implied the task of star-making and included a say in casting or in picking directors. Studio contracts at times assigned scriptwriters the responsibility of writing publicity material for the launch of the film or the star.[5] This work was conducted, via the fan magazines, through film novelizations or other forms of promotion such as narrativized actor biographies, keeping the writer in constant contact with audiences. These contractual tasks reveal the strong interlacing of film story with advertising, optimizing the impact of narrative work and star system by making the screenwriter the hinge between film imaginary and cinema distribution. However, studios did not hire screenwriters on the basis of equal opportunities: male writers, specializing in action films, dominated Warners, while at MGM, given the large presence of female stars under contract, women writers were strongly represented.

Given their number and high profile in the craft, women screenwriters played an important role in developing the medium's core elements—the process of storytelling and its relation to the star—at the very moment when American cinema was consolidating its mode of narrative articulation. Their career profiles allow us to detect points of similarity, enabling a more general perspective on their contribution. Many of them worked with D. W. Griffith, Irving Thalberg, or Sam Goldwyn, all producers of quality films and sensitive to narrative issues. Most of them had a stage background (or, like Lenore Coffee, dreamed of acting); Jeannie Macpherson, Anita Loos, Frances Marion, and Josephine Lovett made their debuts as actresses. Thus they had a direct knowledge of acting, an ability to "feel" roles for the stars, and a familiarity with popular drama. All of them had gifts of flexibility, efficiency, and creativity—necessary assets in screenwriting. Even Anita Loos, who had become an established writer after *Gentlemen Prefer Blondes* and an active participant in New York's literary circles, always worked in film with professionalism and modesty, at the project's service. Starting in publicity was another experience some of them shared, as in the cases of Frances Marion and Lenore Coffee, thus developing notable communication skills. Several of them directed at least one film during their careers, but none of them opted to become a full time director: they preferred writing.

Women Scriptwriters and Modernizing Women

In addition to significantly contributing to film history, women screenwriters had a wider cultural influence, playing a crucial role in modernizing society, not only through the stories they wrote but also through their very presence in Hollywood—-a peculiar as well as visible job market. Fan magazines wrote about them, presenting their work and discussing their private lives in gossip columns, often illustrating the articles with photos as proof that they were not dangerous, bespectacled, intellectual, or masculinized ladies, but nice looking girls: they could represent a respectable career opportunity for women in the film industry, in contrast to film acting.[6] In the pages of fan magazines their story begins with a script sold when they were very young—the Hollywood myth of an initial "casual discovery," which, as for actresses, would open the door to success while concealing the hard work and stubborn dedication involved in their rise. This representational strategy is analogous to the portrayal of stars in the popular press, generating in either instance legends needing careful historiographic handling. When associated with their upper-middle-class backgrounds, such beginnings align these scriptwriters with their older Victorian literary colleagues. It should also be remarked that most were American born—young girls from a WASP background that might have kept them out of this lowbrow medium: instead, they became its key contributors.

Film magazines displayed Jeannie Macpherson in her pilot outfit; or humorous, coquettish Anita Loos with her dark hair bobbed; or nice, homely ladies like Agnes Christine Johnson, photographed with her typewriter and three kids. While independent from an economic viewpoint, they seemed to lead regular, married lives within a traditional family context. I say "seemed" because Frances Marion had four husbands, one of whom, George Hill, committed suicide, while Anita Loos's abusive husband, John Emerson, was confined to a mental hospital: their supposedly "happy married lives" were more media constructions than real. In fact, film magazines and studio materials conveyed a traditional image of their private lives: they were married, often working with their husbands, and in such close cooperation that it is difficult to identify their individual contributions, although in some instances it can be shown they were the leading personality within the couple. June Mathis married cameraman Silvano Balboni and made him into a Hollywood director; Anita Loos granted John Emerson credits that should have been hers; Sonya Levien refused to leave New York and move to Hollywood unless the studio signed her husband, too (Ceplair 1996). Despite this public presentation of a happy domestic/professional life, it is interesting to note that they did not use their married names in their credits. And today we remember *them*, not their husbands: they have entered film history as eternal "single girls." Feminist film historians have contributed to this reemergence of their names. In particular, Cari Beauchamp's work on Frances Marion and Anita Loos and their circle of friends has helped reconstruct this important aspect of American silent cinema.[7]

However, historiographic activity has also been stimulated by the very evidence of their work, by the scripts they wrote for silent stars or directors, in films which have reemerged at the Giornate del cinema muto in Pordenone (as in the case of homages to Rex Ingram, Frank Borzage, King Vidor, Monta Bell, et al.) or at Cinema ritrovato in Bologna, or in restorations of more- or less-famous silent titles. The variety of characters, ages, classes, and genres presented in these films, and their audacity or sensitivity in addressing social issues, including gender, further demand investigation of the story creators, with their exotic first names (Ouida, Beulah, Lorna).

The role these women played in American silent cinema entails interesting "feminist" implications, but we need to beware of applying twenty-first-century feminist thinking to writers of the 1920s: even the most innovative among them were not *ante litteram* "feminists." Although some of them held powerful posts within the industry, their work has not been recorded as an antagonistic presence inside the studio system or as threatening the patriarchal order that characterized silent Hollywood. The example of MGM, with its pyramidal structure, locating many women writers at the base and the paternalistic/authoritarian pair, Louis B. Mayer and Irving Thalberg, at the top, is illuminating. The women demonstrate a remarkably cooperative spirit and a special ability to work within fragmented processes, foregoing narcissistic ambition while playing an organic role within the system. At a time when division of labor in the industry was weak, their multitasking ability to do a little of everything, from writing to assisting with the costumes, made them precious, almost irreplaceable, in a mode of production still oscillating between family business and modern capitalism. But if their mutual solidarity often helped them cooperate in the same projects, they did not present a unified gendered front.

Their scripts, their worldview, their "official" biographies do not signal a "resistance culture," a "hidden voice," as feminists would say, but rather point to contradictions, revealing the tensions between gender, work, and society's expectations. In this way their work contributed to changes in social attitudes, mental outlooks, and popular imagery, creating, in just a decade, the culture of Modernity.

The cultural history of the 1920s emphasizes the fundamental role played by cinema in modernizing society and in articulating emerging images of women.[8] Historian Nancy Woloch (1994) writes: "The young woman growing up in the 1920s was more likely to be influenced by national culture, by the media and by her peers. Two particular influences, the campus and the movies, helped her to fuse the new morality with traditional roles." She proposes a list of new figures for women:

> the campus coed, now imbued more with hopes of marriage than with a sense of mission; the modern housewife, who adopted the role of companion and consumer; the new professional and businesswoman, who sought to integrate marriage and career; and the post-suffrage feminist, sometimes embroiled in battles over legal and constitutional change and sometimes preoccupied with the new ideal of economic independence. (402–3)

All these figures, coming often from the experiences of the women writing the stories, reached the screen not as a mechanical reflection but rather formed a representational chorus: they expressed experiences, desires, and concerns shared with the women in the audience. And, without ignoring social conditions, these films revealed that gender problems crossed class boundaries.

In the 1910s women scriptwriters wrote plots introducing the *new woman*, with her spirit of social engagement, expressing the tensions generated by industrialization and immigration, and even dealing with such controversial issues as abortion or white slavery. Mathis created an interesting series of active characters for Mabel Taliaferro, but also she proposed women of strong spiritual values such as Marguerite (Alice Terry) in *Four Horsemen of Apocalypse* (Rex Ingram, 1920), who gave up her love for Julio (Rudolph Valentino) in order to assist her blinded husband. Sonya Levien narrated stories of immigration in *Salome of the Tenements* (Sidney Olcott, 1925) and in the ethnic farce *Princess from Hoboken* (Allan Dale, 1927). Social transformations were often dealt with in comedies, which allowed an only apparently less violent shift from traditional attitudes.

Cinema "taught" women how to wear makeup, to dress up, to kiss: in a word—how to seduce. In the beginning of *What Price Hollywood* (George Cukor, 1932, written by Jane Murfin) a young waitress, poised in front of a mirror, copies a star's makeup from a fan magazine. Agnes Christine Johnston made fun of the emulation of film stardom in *The Patsy* (King Vidor, 1928), with Marion Davies imitating some famous silent stars. Anita Loos's comedies often dealt with fashion, proposed by the newly born consumption culture (see Lutes 1998; de Grazia and Furlough 1996; Peiss 1998). At the end of the 1920s the irreverent flapper was firmly established, thinking only of having fun—Joan Crawford, for example, in *Our Dancing Daughters* (Harry Beaumont, 1928) and *Our Modern Maidens* (Jack Conway, 1929), both written by Josephine Lovett—or Clara Bow, interpreting the "It" girl (in *It*, Clarence G. Badger, 1927), written by Elinor Glyn. Sensual and dynamic, the flapper moved the fight for equality away from politics onto the sentimental front. A modern version of the vamp, active in sports, the flapper is a media creature. Her bobbed (and often dyed) hair substituted the blond curls of the Victorian ingénues and the hats of the reformist *new woman*, who had appeared only intermittently in American silent cinema. In fact, according to historian Nancy Cott (1994), in the 1920s "the culture of modernity and urbanity absorbed the challenges of feminism and represented them in the form of the modern American woman" (90). However, Cott fails to note that this operation was not conducted only by a patriarchal elite but by a great number of women writers who were responsible for articulating this hegemonic vision.

Women screenwriters of American silent cinema represent an exceptional phenomenon from a sociocultural perspective because they were involved in the production of ideology within the then-prevailing mass medium. Popular literature in the 1920s, as well as women's magazines and cinema, played on the triumvirate constituting America's traditional femininity—marriage, sentimental life, and consumerism—articulating the complexities of women's economic and sexual emancipation, and offering ample space for diversification and double standards. For the middle class, these women scriptwriters allowed for the survival of Victorian values within modernization; to the turbulent lower strata they proposed social mobility and the culture of consumption. Within this cultural process they showed a special talent in depicting the complexity of family life and in creating a romantic imaginary around it, that is, *companionate marriage*. Together with their colleagues writing popular romantic literature, they gave marriage a new appeal, redefining this social institution that was threatened by women's possibilities of achieving economic independence. This was not the result of a gendered division of labor, for credits show that many sentimental pictures were written by men (as many action films and even westerns were written by women).[9] American films of the 1920s addressed women's emotional life and sexuality with an unprecedented sensitivity. We can mention *Miss Lulu Bett* (William DeMille, 1921), written by Clara Beranger, which depicted the drudgery of a spinster's life in her sister's house, or the silent reformulation of Anna Karenina with a happy ending devised in the name of profound family feeling in *Love*, by Frances Marion (Edmund Goulding, 1927), or the injection of romanticism into Valentino's sensuality by June Mathis, or the transgressive and yet sentimentally healthy flappers of so many comedy-dramas. Reading censors' detailed notes concerning flappers and gold diggers, it is evident that these female characters were perceived as more dangerous and destabilizing for the social order than gangsters (Jacobs 1995). Without sending female audiences back to a happiness made only of domesticity, smiling babies, or Victorian virginal love, the films of the 1920s depicted a family life made of companionship, equality, and satisfying sexuality—of companionate marriage. And yet, coinciding with women's entry into the job market and consequent economic autonomy, the erotic awakening and the desire for a gratifying sexual-sentimental life on the part of American women represents also an attack on middle-class standards and patriarchal authority—a powerful as well as dangerous cultural change activated by women through film.

Epilogue

The introduction of sound is conventionally used as a sad ending to this story, even though the actual role of this technological and cultural transition does not seem to have affected the craft of scriptwriting as much as it did the voice or linguistic competence of the actor. In the early 1930s Frances Marion won Academy Awards for the scripts of *The Big House* (George Hill, 1930) and *The Champ* (King Vidor, 1931) and signed pictures such as *Dinner at Eight* (George Cukor, 1933) and *Stella Dallas* (King Vidor, 1937); Jeannie Macpherson wrote for DeMille two bizarre talkies, very interesting in their use of sound: *Dynamite* (1929) and *Madam Satan* (1930); Josephine Lovett and Lenore Coffee continued writing, and Loos returned to Hollywood in the sound era, after her flirtation with New York theater. While these writers were as successful as before, in the talkies, it is evident that the filmographies of most women writers from the silent era did not continue into the 1930s. In some instances the new approach to screenwriting demanded by dialogue created difficulties for the older writers, who did not have either the desire or the will to learn new tricks; but even this explanation is weak because most of the women screenwriters of the first generation actually began their careers writing for the stage and were more than familiar with writing dialogue.

Arguably, the reason for the disappearance of women writers from film credits lies in cultural history. A generation, established earlier, could have felt uncomfortable in creating characters for Depression-era America. Flappers and gold diggers were discouraged by the Hays Code as undesirable figures. The Jazz Age seemed to have found its puritanical punishment in the crash of 1929: Hollywood confined sexually freer women in melodramas or in the elegant parlors of sophisticated comedy, and took a new look at working-class girls (Haralovich 1990). American 1930s movies seem more male oriented. The gender balance—and the balance among genres—was tilted toward male supremacy—if not on the screen, where female stars still prevailed, at least backstage, where women writers silently disappeared.

There were also structural problems with the tighter division of labor in the industry. The construction of writers' buildings (the screenwriters' offices within the studios) and the enforcement of increasingly rigid working schedules created difficulties for women writers, who were often used to working at home. Their specific capabilities, from teamwork to multitasking, did not help them to adjust to an overtly rigid and specialized mode of production. Studios were becoming complex industrial structures with rigid hierarchical organization, granting producers increasing powers, which induced a struggle for creative control evident in the unionization of Hollywood's creative crafts. Asked to become a producer, Lenore Coffee turned down the offer, while Frances Marion accepted the challenge but was not able to complete her projects.[10]

Marion, the "deacon" of this group of women writers, gave what I perceive as the most insightful account of this unrelenting erosion of the scriptwriter:

[But] we knew male writers were complaining about "the tyranny of the woman writer" supposedly prevalent at all studios then, and particularly at MGM. I'd always worked closely with directors and producers on my own scripts, and at their own request, often worked as writer on the set, making script changes during actual production. But it was apparent that if a writer wanted to maintain any control over what he wrote, he would have to become a writer-director, or a writer-producer. Writing a screenplay had become like writing on sand with the wind blowing (quoted in Bodeen 1969, 139).

Notes

1. Anthony Slide (2012) argues for a recount, stating that the correct figure for women screenwriters is "a little over twenty per cent" in the 1910s and "a little under twenty-five per cent" in the 1920s (114).

2. On women writers see Gilbert and Gubar (1979), Radway (1984), Dudden (1994), Raub (1994), Ammons (1992), and Armstrong (1987).

3. In addition, it is not often possible to photocopy an entire script, due to film rights restrictions.

4. On screenwriting for silent cinema, see Corliss (1970), McGilligan (1986), Stempel (1991), Fine (1985).

5. Some contracts are archived in Fox legal files at UCLA.

6. "Here Are Ladies! Stars seen on the screen in name only. Isn't it a shame their faces never get a chance?" (*Photoplay*, October 1920: 12). These are Jane Murfin, Frances Marion, Anita Loos, Ouida Bergere, and Clara Beranger.

7. See Beauchamp (1997), Acker (1991), Francke (1994), and McCreadie (1994).

8. On the 1920s see Susman (1984) and Dumenil (1995). On women's culture see Rabinovitz (1998), Peiss (1986), Wilson (1989), Evans (1989), Kerber, Kessler-Harris, and Sklar (1995), and Alpern et al. (1992).

9. Frances Marion, as Frank M. Clifton, wrote eleven westerns for her husband, Fred Thomson; Marion Fairfax invented the first canine star, Strongheart.

10. She wanted to make a western at Columbia, but the studio was in financial trouble, so the production was abandoned; when she tried to revamp Gloria Swanson's career, the project also failed. Nevertheless, she contributed to the unionization of screenwriters, becoming President of the first Board of the Screen Writer's Guild in 1933.

References

Acker, Ally. 1991. *Reel Women: Pioneers of the Cinema 1896 to the Present.* London: Batsford.

Alpern, Sara, Joyce Antler, Elisabeth Israels Perry, and Ingrid Winther Scobie, eds. 1992. *The Challenge of Feminist Biography: Writing the Lives of Modern American Women.* Urbana: University of Illinois Press.

Ammons, Elizabeth. 1992. *Conflicting Stories: American Women Writers at the Turn into the Twentieth Century.* New York: Oxford University Press.

Armstrong, Nancy. 1987. *Desire and Domestic Fiction: A Political History of the Novel.* New York: Oxford University Press.

Beauchamp, Cari. 1997. *Without Lying Down: Frances Marion and the Powerful Women of Early Hollywood.* New York: Scribner.

Beauchamp, Cari, and Mary Anita Loos. 2003. *Anita Loos Rediscovered.* Berkeley: University of California Press.

Bodeen, DeWitt. 1969. "Francis Marion." *Films in Review* 20 (2): 71–91.

Ceplair, Larry. 1996. *A Great Lady: A Life of the Screenwriter Sonya Levien.* Lanham, Md.: Scarecrow.

Corliss, Richard. 1970. *The Hollywood Screenwriters*. New York: Avon.

Cott, Nancy, 1994."The Modern Woman of the 1920s." In *A History of Women in the West*, edited by Francoise Thebaud, 76–91. Cambridge, Mass.: Belknap.

de Grazia, Victoria, and Ellen Furlough, eds. 1996. *The Sex of Things: Gender and Consumption in Historical Perspective*. Berkeley: University of California Press.

Douglas, Ann. 1977. *The Feminization of America*. New York: Anchor.

Dudden, Faye. 1994. *Women in the American Theatre: Actresses and Audiences, 1790–1870*. New Haven, Conn.: Yale University Press.

Dumenil, Lynn. 1995. *Modern Temper: American Culture and Society in the 1920s*. New York: Hill and Wang.

Evans, Sara M. 1989. *Born for Liberty: A History of Women in America*. New York: Free Press.

Fine, Richard. 1985. *Hollywood and the Profession of Authorship, 1928–1940*. Ann Arbor: UMI.

Francke, Lizzie. 1994. *Script Girls: Women Screenwriters in Hollywood*. London: BFI.

Gilbert, Sandra, and Susan Gubar. 1979. *The Madwoman in the Attic, The Woman Writer, and the Nineteenth-Century Literary Imagination*. New Haven, Conn.: Yale University Press.

Haralovich, Mary Beth. 1990. "The Proletarian Woman's Films of the 1930s: Contending with Censorship and Entertainment." *Screen* 31 (2): 172–87.

Jacobs, Lea. 1995. *The Wages of Sin: Censorship and the Fallen Woman Film, 1928–1942*. Berkeley: University of California Press.

Kerber, Linda, Alice Kessler-Harris, and Kathryn Kish Sklar. 1995. *U.S. History as Women's History*. Chapel Hill: University of North Carolina Press.

Leuchtenburg, William. 1958. *The Perils of Prosperity 1914–1932*. Chicago: University of Chicago Press.

Loos, Anita. 1966. *A Girl Like Us: An Autobiography*. New York: Viking.

———. 1974. *Kiss Hollywood Good-By*. New York: Viking.

Lutes, J. M. 1998. "Authoring *Gentlemen Prefer Blondes*: Mass-Market Beauty, Culture, and the Makeup of Writers." *Prospects* 25:431–60.

McCreadie, Marsha. 1994. *The Women Who Write the Movies*. New York: Birch Lane.

McGilligan, Pat. 1986. *Backstory*. Berkeley: University of California Press.

Muscio, Giuliana. 2010. "Clara, Ouida, Beulah, et al.: Women Screenwriters in American Silent Cinema." In *Reclaiming the Archive: Feminism and Film History*, edited by Vicki Callahan, 289–308. Detroit: Wayne State University Press.

Peiss, Kathy. 1986. *Cheap Amusements: Working Women and Leisure in the Turn-of-the-Century New York*. Philadelphia: Temple University Press.

———. 1998. *Hope in a Jar: The Making of America's Beauty Culture*. New York: Holt.

Rabinovitz, Lauren. 1998. *For the Love of Pleasure*. New Brunswick, N.J.: Rutgers University Press.

Radway, Janice. 1984. *Reading the Romance: Women, Patriarchy, and Popular Literature*. Chapel Hill: University of North Carolina Press.

Raub, Patricia. 1994. *Yesterday's Stories, Popular Women's Novels of the 1920s and 1930s*. Westport, Conn.: Greenwood.

Slater, Thomas J. 2002. "June Mathis: A Woman Who Spoke through Silents." In *American Silent Film: Discovering Marginalized Voices, edited by* Gregg Bachman and Thomas J. Slater, 201–16. Carbondale: Southern Illinois University Press.

Slide, Anthony. 2012. "Early Women Filmmakers: The Real Numbers." *Film History* 24 (1): 114–21.

Stamp, Shelley. 2000. *Movie-Struck Girls: Women and Motion Picture Culture after the Nickelodeon.* Princeton, N.J.: Princeton University Press.

Stempel, Tom. 1991. *FrameWork: A History of Screenwriting in the American Film.* New York: Ungar.

Studler, Gaylyn. 1996. "The Perils of Pleasure? Fan Magazines Discourse as Women's Commodified Culture in the 1920s." In *Silent Film,* edited by Richard Abel, 263–98. New Brunswick, N.J.: Rutgers University Press.

Susman, Warren. 1984. *Culture as History.* New York: Pantheon.

Wilson, Margaret Gibbons. 1989. *The American Woman in Transition.* Westport, Conn.: Greenwood.

Woloch, Nancy. 1994. *Women and the American Experience.* New York: McGraw-Hill.

CHAPTER 14

A Suitable Job for a Woman

Color and the Work of Natalie Kalmus

SARAH STREET

From cultural theorists linking the mystery of color with notions of femininity, fluidity, and nature, to scientists claiming women are genetically disposed to acute color perception, strong associations between women and color have been demonstrated throughout history. As John Gage observed, "Perhaps the most interesting area for feminists to explore is, indeed, the recurrent assumption that a feeling for colour is itself a peculiarly female province" (Gage 1999, 36). When color films were developed women made key contributions that further ingrained the idea that they were naturally predisposed to understand the color world both onscreen and off. In the silent era women worked as film colorists, operators of stenciling machines, and performers. When the first color films were screened, their display of the female form was a central trope in dance films such as *Annabelle Serpentine Dance* (no. 2, Edison, 1895), which featured American skirt dancer Annabelle Whitford performing in a billowing, diaphanous gown that appears to change color as she flaps her arms high like a restless creature with iridescent plumage. Advertising films aimed at women were typically fashion newsreels (Hanssen 2009), and elaborate marketing and merchandising campaigns for fiction films ensured female audiences were conscious of the impact of color selections. Film producers keenly exploited the gendered market potential of genres such as melodramas and musicals that were associated with obtrusive color display and popular with female audiences. That color was a "female province" was thus enshrined in color film production in silent and sound periods alike.

Color films were common in the silent era when applied methods of hand coloring, stenciling of prints, tinting, and toning produced beautiful images, many of which have not survived or are difficult to recreate through restoration (Yumibe 2012). The coming of sound cinema at the end of the 1920s was accompanied by a decline in applied-color films. Achieving color through alternate photographic methods was technically very difficult and expensive, so until the mid-1950s color films were outnumbered by black-and-white ones. While color was used for esoteric, experimental filmmaking, more typically it was part of the film industry's drive for profits through quality productions and commercial tie-ins with manufacturers. Products and fashions displayed onscreen could thus be found in department stores, and audiences were actively encouraged to link their shopping preferences with their favorite movies and stars.

No company was more aware of this than Technicolor, the brand name that dominated film color production worldwide from the mid-1930s through the 1950s. As well as technical ingenuity, the key to Technicolor's success was its monopolistic commercial strategy of leasing cameras, stock, and processing methods. The principle of controlling how color was deployed extended to insisting that producers consult the Color Advisory Service headed by Natalie Kalmus (1878–1965), the woman credited on many films for her expertise in color selection—advising directors, cinematographers, set designers, and costume designers on how best to work with Technicolor. This chapter will focus on her role as an ambassador for the company, considering her record and somewhat controversial legacy as a woman commanding an extremely important place in the history of color film. It will consider how as a public figure and advocate of color Kalmus wielded influence beyond film production, advising women to wear particular colors to go with their hair and mood. Being a color advisor was considered to be a very suitable job for a woman. As we shall see, this was grounded in notions about women and color that predated Kalmus's work for Technicolor. She was thus exemplary of a mode of employment created and perpetuated by gendered assumptions about color expertise. This led to opportunities as well as restrictions to operate within constraints when the extent of her influence was limited, and on occasion she experienced prejudice.

From the 1930s on, women's involvement in film production, apart from acting, was limited, far more so than during the silent era. In view of this, Natalie Kalmus's role was on the one hand remarkable, on the other consistent with the idea that women were particularly astute as far as color was concerned. The Technicolor Corporation used her expertise and public persona very much as a means of marketing its process, what the company stood for, and its ambitions to invade public consciousness beyond motion pictures. She was credited as "color consultant" on most Technicolor films from the late 1920s to 1949, a title that garnered respect. In the later years of her life Kalmus's reputation was, however, tainted by a court case and a publication that reviewed her achievements in a biased manner with regard to her personal life.

Kalmus became involved in Technicolor through her husband Herbert Kalmus, whom she had married in 1902. Herbert founded the company in 1915 with Daniel Comstock and W. Burton Westcott. The couple secretly divorced in 1921, but Natalie nevertheless worked reasonably amicably alongside Herbert during the key years of Technicolor's development until 1944, when relations between the couple began to break down. Herbert's affairs and his relationship with Eleanore King (whom he married in 1949) were the background to Natalie's filing a lawsuit in 1948, claiming that she was entitled to a financial settlement because their divorce in 1921 was invalid on the grounds that they had lived as man and wife subsequently (sharing a house in Bel Air, California, for which Herbert paid household expenses). The divorce was, however, declared to be legal, and Natalie was consequently not entitled to further financial support. Kalmus had been paying her alimony until 1945, and she also received a salary from the Technicolor Corporation, from which she retired in 1948.

For many years Kalmus's reputation as a professional woman was overshadowed by the sensational newspaper coverage of the court case and subsequent autobiography of Herbert Kalmus, *Mr. Technicolor*, published after his death and with commentary by Eleanore King Kalmus (Kalmus and Kalmus 1993). King made sure Natalie emerged as an important figure in Technicolor's history, but she was also depicted as an increasingly unstable and destructive figure in contrast with Herbert's technical brilliance and business acumen. It is against this controversial background that her career emerges as particularly significant. Together with Herbert, Natalie made a technical process a household name, with both personalities performing different but crucial showmanship functions for the company. One article described Herbert as the "Techni" and Natalie the "color" of Technicolor (Zeitlin 1939, 75). Returning to contemporary sources, and to Natalie Kalmus's papers, it is possible to reconstruct a sense of the multifaceted dimensions of her role that conventional film histories have tended to downplay. Although she was renowned for color expertise, the exclusion from most things "Techni" (unless convenient) does not quite equate with the role she actually performed or the knowledge she undoubtedly acquired about films and filming in Technicolor over many years. The tendency to demark her occupation as color consultant as strictly feminine is consistent with the gendering of her role to the extent that it ended up being easily belittled, subject to revision and reappropriation by those responsible for the technical, "masculine" aspects of filmmaking. A woman's instinct for color was deemed to be useful only up to a point.

Despite Kalmus's notoriety and the fact that she was the first person to be credited as color consultant on a motion picture, the employment of a woman in a position of authority over color direction was not unprecedented in other fields. In the 1920s a number of women were hired for their expertise in creating standards of color nomenclature and marketing color products. This occurred during a decade when the color choices available to consumers had multiplied with the advance of synthetic dyes, the onset of mass consumerism, and, particularly in the United States, a growing interest in exploiting color's suggestive power for commercial ends. One such expert was Margaret Hayden Rorke, an American actress and suffragette who in 1919 was appointed managing director of the Textile Color Card Association of the United States (TCCA). Formed in 1915, the TCCA aimed to report on and influence color trends, advising members by producing the Standard Color Card of America after extensive research with manufacturers (Blaszczyk 2012, 80). The job of standardizing colors for the textile industry and creating nomenclatures for colors that subsequently became fashionable was seen as a crucial part of modern advertising. Color's instability was harnessed by commercial acumen, and women, with their perceived acuity for color consciousness, were at the center of this operation.

Another woman who can be seen as a predecessor of Kalmus was Hazel H. Adler, a design consultant who formed an influential consultancy business deploying the Taylor System of Color Harmony in 1921. As well as advising clients such as the Ford Motor Company and the Kohler Company (a manufacturer of plumbing fixtures), Adler produced manuals on color and home furnishing. Adler "jazzed up color practice in the industrial arts with references to efficiency, psychology, and modern art" (Blaszczyk 2012, 144). Yet another example is Dorothy Nickerson, a U.S. color scientist who joined the Munsell Color Company in 1921 and went on to work for the Department of Agriculture in 1927, where she spent many years in a top, highly specialized position as a key scientist working on, among other things, colorimetry and standardization of light sources. While Nickerson was less typical in her role as a woman involved in color science ("Techni") rather than culture or psychology, she was nevertheless also a product of the world of opportunity created for women by color developments in the twentieth century.

The film industry was part of this phenomenon. *The Phantom of the Opera* (1925), for example—a film that used a number of applied-color methods (tinting; two-color Technicolor, and Handschiegl)—inspired the Textile Color Card Association to develop "Phantom Red," a new shade named by Margaret Hayden Rorke, that adorned numerous products including shoes, lipstick, bags, hats, slippers, and gowns. The trade press reported on how "Phantom Red Becomes the Rage" as commercial tie-ins accompanied the film's exhibition in the United States and beyond. Films were seen as generators of consumer desire, a trend that was accelerated by the development of Technicolor as a photographic process, as opposed to an applied-color technique. The significance of this was that a photographic process was better able to convey a mise-en-scène in which colors could be differentiated, showcasing objects, fashions, and décor with a precision that was difficult with techniques such as tinting, which bathed the entire screen in a single color. But the ground had been laid for Kalmus in the 1920s when a "color wave" surged across the arts, fueled by intertwined, intermedial cultures of color evident across cinema, fashion, industry, art, architecture, music, and theater (Street and Yumibe 2013).

It was within this context that Natalie Kalmus came to prominence within the Technicolor Corporation. She facilitated the branding of Technicolor as more than a motion-picture process; living life in Technicolor extended beyond the studio and outside the movie theater. Kalmus's public persona was constructed in the press and in radio interviews when she was asked about her work with Technicolor and for advice on the general importance of color in everyday life. Commentators were fascinated by her powerful—even exceptional—position, as when "Find the Woman," a 1941 radio broadcast introduced her thus: "A brilliant, beautiful woman whose knowledge of colors and their relation to moving images is helping to pave the way to an all-color screen. Petite, utterly feminine, she is, nevertheless, the supreme dictator of color technique in Hollywood ... and the world over. She schedules her day so she can supervise as many as six films in production or preparation at one time" (Kalmus papers, Radio, 1941). The admiration of her artistic ability, technical knowledge, and conscientiousness featured in other publicity. This journalistic discourse aimed to surprise the reader by foregrounding the (apparent) unusual combination of color knowledge and technical know-how.

Natalie Kalmus's influence was most prominent in the decade or so after the introduction of three-strip Technicolor in the mid-1930s, the process that became synonymous with film color for several decades, particularly in the United States and the United Kingdom. Technicolor's influence extended well beyond the screen to become an important aspect of the corporation's commercial drive. Kalmus was involved in complex commercial negotiations, facilitating tie-ins with department stores and discussions with studio heads. Tie-ins with consumer products worked extremely well with Kalmus's advocacy of color consciousness as a way of negotiating the modern world. "Color consciousness" was an established phrase suggesting that color's impact in art and life in general could be made apparent

FIGURE 14.1. Natalie Kalmus at work: Color Consultant, Technicolor (undated)

to all once they were made aware of it. But in an impressive advertising coup for Technicolor, Kalmus published a key essay titled "Color Consciousness" in a technical journal in 1935 that confirmed the currency of the phrase as central to debates about color film designs and practices. Crucially, the article established an approach that was grounded in notions of color harmony, strategic selection, and color accents and complements that drew loosely on art history, the drive toward color standardization in the 1920s, and shared affinities with Sergei Eisenstein's theoretical writings about color and meaning (Kalmus 1935 [in Dalle Vacche and Price 2006, 24–29]). Her insistence on nongarishness reaffirmed a code of taste around color that gravitated toward careful, artistic choices rather than nonnaturalistic "super-abundance." While Technicolor has tended to be associated with "brashness" in common parlance, it is important to note that the first principles upon which Kalmus's many designs were based and which informed the look of many Technicolor films were founded in notions of careful planning, restraint, and harmony.

While Kalmus often delegated responsibilities to other consultants, whom she trained, there is no doubt that she exercised a profound influence over how Technicolor was used for many years. Crucially, she developed guidelines, advocating a practice of color consciousness as inscribed in charts produced for each film. These principles were analogous to a musical score and associated color intensity with dominant moods or emotions. A chart was produced after reading a script; consultations would take place with producers and members of a studio's art and costume departments, and further adjustments would be made on the set and into postproduction. As the company explained, the function of the Color Advisory Service was to "offer suggestions where color enhances dramatic mood and story value. Under Mrs Kalmus's direction, Technicolor has tested literally thousands of fabrics and color combinations and this information is made available to producers" (*Technicolor News and Views* 1939, 3).

Kalmus's work was not devoid of controversy, however, and many reacted adversely to her recommendations. The company was bound to come up against such criticism since studios, particularly in Hollywood, were not used to having to conform to external directives for creative decisions, let alone by authority of a woman. As early as 1931 there were cases such as *Manhattan Parade*, a costume comedy set in Broadway, in which Warner Brothers ignored Technicolor's advice on costumes, threatening to create the wrong impression of how the process could typically be applied. Critical of the result, Technicolor resolved: "We must know and study the color relation between the sets, the furniture, the drapes and the costumes to obtain proper separation of values and harmony of colors. With due respect for the art director's architectural conception of a set, Technicolor's art department should be given the privilege of choosing the colors of the walls, decorations, wallpaper etc. The same thing applies to costumes" (Durenceau in Kalmus papers, 1931). Difficulties were also encountered when Fox Movietone resisted advice from Technicolor's experts on a series of fashion short films in 1939, resulting in their colors being in "bad taste" (Rackett in Kalmus papers, 1939). It thus became imperative for Technicolor's application to be controlled, even standardized, so that a sense of artistic and technical prowess could be seen to guide its application. This informed the commercial exploitation of the process at home and, as important, abroad. Kalmus was thus a key agent in Technicolor's quest to regulate the deployment of color, to reduce commercial risk by hallmarking the process with universally acknowledged quality standards guided by a feminine touch.

Natalie Kalmus was also involved at quite a detailed level in supervising Technicolor in British productions. Since Britain was the largest overseas market for American films and key links were being established between British and American companies, the British operation was very important for Technicolor. In the mid-1930s Natalie Kalmus spent time in the United Kingdom as color consultant. She prepared charts for significant films—including *The Divorce of Lady X* (1938), the first feature film in Technicolor produced by Alexander Korda's London Film Productions, the charts for which were photographed and sent to England in 1935. In an unusual record of how this actually worked, Kalmus advised in a long memo how the company should work with the photographs in anticipation of her arrival to supervise the production:

> I have shipped to you for Mr. [Vincent] Korda today a print in color of color charts which were photographed for his guidance in the use of our photographic process. Included with the print there is a set of the colored cards of which the charts were composed. Each one is numbered to correspond with its number on the chart, and the formula for mixing each color is written on the back of each card and on a separate list as well. By reconstructing the charts and comparing them with the projected print a general idea of the process of translation can be gained. (Kalmus papers, Kay Harrison folder, 1935)

The authoritative tone of such correspondence, as well as its particular details, confirms that Kalmus worked well with art directors, including Vincent Korda. The fact that Kalmus was able to bargain for a higher salary for working on some short films before she embarked on her second trip to Britain in 1937 can be taken as an indication of the increasing respect for her services. And when she crossed the Atlantic on the *Queen Mary* in February 1937, Kay Harrison, managing director of Technicolor Ltd., the British company established in 1935, arranged for her arrival to be celebrated by a brass band wearing red coats. This detail was rather more than a mere publicity stunt, since it welcomed her appropriately as an ambassador for Technicolor.

There are many examples, however, of cinematographers being less enthusiastic, claiming they knew better than Kalmus and taking the opportunity to belittle her expertise by questioning her technical competence; the tendency to excise her from all things "Techni" persisted. Criticisms were often inflected with personal remarks that would probably not have been the case had she been male. These involved her appearance, clothes, hats (reportedly gaudy and in bad taste), and assumed lack of technical expertise. *Sixty Glorious Years* (Herbert Wilcox, 1938), for example, attests to the contested nature of her work. While Kalmus's application of Technicolor in this British film earned high praise from Herbert Kalmus and Kay Harrison, camera assistant Freddie Young was extremely critical, asserting that Natalie did not possess adequate expertise (Young 1987). He found her presence an affront to his technical prowess, clearly thinking of her as an interfering woman from America. These nationalistic dimensions of responses to Kalmus's color control were bolstered by patriotic sentiment for the British film industry at a time when it was oppressed by Hollywood's export drive.

Natalie Kalmus nevertheless advised on many British films, working from 1941 with Joan Bridge, a British woman who had previously worked for rival company Dufaycolor in the 1930s. Bridge subsequently collaborated with Natalie Kalmus or was the sole Technicolor advisor on British Technicolor feature films and later worked with her partner Elizabeth Haffenden in film costume design. Joan Bridge is an intriguing figure in the British context because she held a similar job but did not provoke the same degrees of criticism leveled against Natalie Kalmus. Cinematographers such as Ossie Morris admired Bridge's skills but never accorded Kalmus with the same courtesy. A woman doing the job of color advisor was then not necessarily problematic on a film set, and so it is likely that criticisms of Kalmus were fueled by her personality and nationality, as well as by her gender. In spite of this, there is no doubt that the combination of Kalmus and Bridge assisted Technicolor in Britain, a record that has won begrudging recognition over the years.

Kalmus clearly played a crucial role in the public presentation and marketing of Technicolor. Despite the tenor of reactions against her expertise on the set, in wider parlance she was regarded as someone with artistic sensibilities and color expertise. This combination attracted a degree of curiosity that had partly to do with her gender. As one trade press commentator reported after interviewing her: "Mrs Kalmus I found a most delightful and enlightened character. . . . Indeed I'd like to see her in Technicolor herself for she's by no means a flat personality. It is clear that she has the technical side of the game at her fingertips and can be depended on not only to look after that angle but the creative color angle as well" (*Cinema* 1936, 1). This kind of reportage continued throughout Kalmus's career, and Technicolor clearly took advantage of her star value as an ambassador for the process who, as a woman, was in the fairly unusual position of heading up a complex and key operation in the company's development. It suited them to publicize her technical knowledge for this purpose, on one occasion putting her name on an article written by a male colleague in the company. Her growing reputation as a woman with exceptional intuition about color outweighed the tendency to downplay technical know-how as public curiosity grew about the role of color consultant.

Her work attracted widespread reports in fan magazines. She also gave radio interviews and was admired for her dedication and knowledge of Technicolor. As one commentator observed after meeting her: "Her vitality is incredible, almost electric in its force. You can feel it when you are anywhere near her. It's exhausting if you are not in tune with her" (Newman 1949, 148). Technicolor found it expedient to deploy Kalmus's color expertise on many occasions in their advertising, and in this she was tied to their general strategy of controlling every aspect of the process. Technicolor received fan mail, for example, that included letters from people whose viewing was immeasurably improved by an appreciation of Technicolor. Influencing audience preferences for color films was a key goal of the company, so these letters are evidence of how propagandizing color consciousness was a key marketing strategy and intimately related to the rhetoric deployed by Natalie Kalmus in interviews and on radio broadcasts.

The letters contain many enthusiastic comments from women and men, such as "I enjoy Technicolor movies enormously and hope the day will come when they are all made in Technicolor. In fact movies that I did not find quite so entertaining, I thought were worth while seeing just for the Technicolor." One correspondent declared that he was more interested in the quality of colors than anything else: "My mind, precisely trained in engineering, often brushes aside the dramatic influences of the picture to analyze the color play of the production. Undoubtedly, I reason, some massive intelligence is behind the combination of hue there" (Kalmus papers, Marshall Waller folder, 1943). Similarly enthusiastic comments were made by respondents to sociologist J. P. Mayer's surveys of cinema audiences in Britain, conducted in the 1940s and published in two books (1946, 1948). As a public figure and advocate of color, Kalmus's influence extended beyond film production to advising women to wear particular colors to go with their hair and mood; for example, a platinum blonde was urged to wear blues and somber colors rather than pink. Kalmus's public persona was thus widely disseminated. In hindsight, it is easy to see Technicolor dominating the color film market, although at the time the company did not take its success for granted and was keen to keep ahead of competitors.

The pervasiveness of Kalmus's public persona encouraged commercial links with department stores. Her dealings for example with J. H. Hugues, merchandise manager for A. Harris and Company of Dallas, Texas, in 1943–44, demonstrates how her views on color extended beyond Hollywood for this purpose (Kalmus papers, House of Westmore folder). Having read Kalmus's color consciousness article, Hughes sought her advice on how to tie in Technicolor with the colors of his incoming spring collections. She replied: "The word Technicolor is banned for use outside of the corporation, but it is permissible to use my name in your booklet." The collections were duly advertised as "Natalie Kalmus colors." On this basis, particular colors were selected and approved; she changed the description of one from "True Blue" to "Serene Blue," which further popularized her views on cool and warm colors. The costume display was erected in the store in February 1944, with coverage in *Vogue* and *Harper's Bazaar*. In gratitude for her cooperation, and after inquiring with Kalmus's secretary about a desirable gift, she received an alligator purse and perfume. Examples such as this make clear the extent or reach of Kalmus's role as an ambassador for the company in technical and aesthetic terms, and in this arena her gender was convenient. She was also consulted by makeup companies such as the House of Westmore and Max Factor, the latter having a special relationship with Technicolor as advisor to the company on makeup foundation. Tie-ins were also a feature of marketing Technicolor films in the United Kingdom. For example, reports on *The Divorce of Lady X* showed that color was indeed seen to be a notable feature by exhibitors, with one manager of a cinema in Nuneaton linking with a dyers and cleaners shop as well as with local decorators to show how Merle Oberon's gowns and the sets reproduced a range of colors that could be applied to everyday fashion and interior design (Street 2012, 69). In these ways Kalmus was instrumental in spreading Technicolor's reach, performing a vital function by propagandizing its values across the world.

The legacy of Natalie Kalmus is one tinged with personal controversy and mixed responses to her position as color expert. She nevertheless served as the ideological and symbolic lynchpin of Technicolor's reputation for color style and aesthetics during crucial decades of Hollywood's history. Although she occupied a key role in the company's development, beyond the credits on all those films less is known about what her job actually involved. Although there is a special collection of her papers at the Margaret Herrick Library, Los Angeles, this is relatively small and does not contain much evidence on the full extent of her business or technical activities relating to how color control worked in practice. Although many sought to marginalize her work ("color") by placing it in binary relation to Technicolor's serious business and technical operations (the "Techni"), as this chapter has demonstrated, these two areas could not be easily separated. In this context it was possible for Kalmus to obtain notoriety rare for women in motion pictures who were not performers. The women employed in roles as color consultants in other spheres helped pave the way for this position, their gendered expertise similarly allowing them to occupy roles that were unusual for their seniority and prestige. This explains the variety of responses to Natalie Kalmus throughout her career, as the idea of being a color expert as a suitable job for a woman became sustained and captured the public imagination.

References

Blaszczyk, Regina Lee. 2012. *The Color Revolution*. Cambridge, Mass.: MIT Press.

The Cinema. 1936. "Onlooker section," April 30, 1.

Gage, John. 1999. *Colour and Meaning: Art, Science and Symbolism*. London: Thames and Hudson.

Hanssen, Eirik Frisvold. 2009. "Symptoms of Desire: Color, Costume, and Commodities in Fashion Newsreels of the 1910s and 1920s." *Film History* 21 (2): 107–21.

Kalmus, Herbert T., and Eleanore Kalmus King. 1993. *Mr Technicolor*. Absecon, N.J.: Magic-Image Filmbooks.

Kalmus, Natalie. 1935. "Color Consciousness." *Journal of the Society of Motion Picture Engineers*. Reprinted in *Color: The Film Reader*, edited by Angela Dalle Vacche and Brian Price (2006), 24–39. London: Routledge.

———. 1939–1948. Special Collection, Margaret Herrick Library, Los Angeles: 1.f-9 Capt. Marshall Waller folder, April 22, 1943; 2-f.37 House of Westmore folder; 2.f-22 Radio

KNX-CBS, January 24, 1941; 1.f-11 Kay Harrison folder, September 24, 1935; 1-f.8, Andre Durenceau film, 1931; f.29, Color Control Dep., G. F. Rackett memo, October 19, 1939, 2.

Mayer, J. P. 1946. *Sociology of Film*. London: Faber.

Mayer, J. P. 1948. *British Cinemas and Their Audiences*. London: Dobson.

Newman, John K. 1949. "Profile of Natalie Kalmus." In *British Technicolor Films*, edited by John Huntley, 146–50. London: Robinson.

Street, Sarah. 2011. "Negotiating the Archives: The Natalie Kalmus Papers and the 'Branding' of Technicolor in Britain and the United States." *Moving Image* 11 (1): 1–24.

———. 2012. *Colour Films in Britain: The Negotiation of Innovation, 1900–55*. London: British Film Institute/Palgrave Macmillan.

Street, Sarah, and Joshua Yumibe. 2013. "The Temporalities of Intermediality: Colour in Cinema and the Arts of the 1920s." *Early Popular Visual Culture* 11 (2): 140–57.

Technicolor News and Views. 1939. Hollywood, Calif.: Technicolor.

Young, Freddie. 1987. BECTU (Broadcasting, Entertainment, Cinematograph and Theatre Union) interview no. 4.

Yumibe, Joshua. 2012. *Moving Color: Early Film, Mass Culture, Modernism*. New Brunswick, N.J.: Rutgers University Press.

Zeitlin, Ida. 1939. "Great Women of Motion Pictures: Natalie Kalmus." *Screenland* 38 (4): 64–65, 74–57.

CHAPTER 15

Cinema of Women

The Work of a Feminist Distributor

JULIA KNIGHT

In the 1980s, the UK women's distributor Cinema of Women (COW) released a string of feminist feature films, including: Leontine Sagan's *Maidens in Uniform* (Germany, 1931) in 1982; Marleen Gorris's *A Question of Silence* (Netherlands, 1982) in 1983; Margarethe von Trotta's *The Second Awakening of Christa Klages* (West Germany, 1979) and Lizzie Borden's *Born in Flames* (USA, 1983), both in 1984; Heiny Srour's *Leila and the Wolves* (UK/Lebanon, 1984) and Sheila McLaughlin and Lynne Tillman's *Committed* (USA, 1983), both in 1985; and Pat Murphy's *Anne Devlin* (Ireland, 1984) in 1986. The most visible and accessible evidence of COW's role in releasing these films lies in the reviews and editorial features they managed to gain in the national press and various magazines. Searching through the British Film Institute's library holdings can quickly give you access to, for instance, the highly critical and mostly damning response from male film critics to *A Question of Silence*, a story of feminist solidarity in the face of sexism experienced by three women in their personal and working lives.

However, while gaining media coverage plays a crucial role in releasing films, it is only one aspect of a distributor's work. Examining a distributor's records not only reveals a much fuller picture of the distributor's role but also provides important insights into a range of issues that come into play in getting films from their makers to their potential audiences. The records may include distribution contracts, funding applications to help with print acquisition costs, promotion and advertising budgets, correspondence, minutes or notes of meetings, press releases, publicity material such as flyers and posters, copies of reviews, booking forms, box office returns, invoices, annual accounts, cash flows, and royalty statements.

Studying COW's records helps us understand what the usually invisible work of a distributor entails and—in the context of "doing women's film history"—the particular challenges that faced a women's distributor of feminist feature films, and consequently their makers, in the 1980s.

Cinema of Women was set up in 1979 by a collective of six women—Mandy Rose, Fern Presant, Audrey Summerhill, Caroline Spry, Melanie Chail, and Maggie Sellers (COW 1979)—who had been "shocked by the limited availability of good films made by women" (COW 1983b). They were keen to get feminist films into first-run cinemas and onto television, but they felt also that women filmmakers should be able to exercise some control over where and how their films were exhibited. They began on a voluntary basis, with virtually no resources, working from one of the collective member's homes. Initially COW acquired a range of shorts and documentaries that found receptive audiences for screenings held by the growing number of women's groups and initiatives coming out of the women's movement. Within two years, that business had grown sufficiently to enable them to rent a small office and employ a part-time worker, Jane Root. A little later they succeeded in getting revenue funding from the Greater London Council (GLC), which gave them a degree of financial stability and enabled them to start undertaking cinema releases as well. With the demise of the GLC, responsibility for their revenue funding passed to the British Film Institute (BFI), but by the end of the 1980s the BFI was faced with funding cuts and had to rationalize its portfolio of funded clients. COW was one of the casualties and had to close down in 1991, while the United Kingdom's other women's distributor, Circles, survived and was relaunched as Cinenova (see Knight and Thomas 2011, 187–207). Fortunately, some of COW's records were saved and have been preserved by Cinenova.

Although partial and not a complete record of more than a decade of activity, this material does include filmmaker and film files for a significant number of the films COW distributed. Some files, however, are more extensive than others—the files for *A Question of Silence, Leila and the Wolves,* and *Anne Devlin,* for instance, run to several folders and contain correspondence, box office returns, publicity information, contracts, budgets, reviews, and so on, while those for *Born in Flames* and *Committed* contain only a thin batch of documents. Nevertheless, browsing through these files starts to reveal some interesting stories (all documents referenced in this chapter are available online—see references for details).

Box Office Returns

Looking at COW's files for *A Question of Silence* and *Leila and the Wolves* reveals, for example, that both films opened at central London cinemas, but while the former ran for four weeks at its two opening cinemas and then transferred to a third for an additional eight weeks, the latter ran for only three weeks at a single cinema. This information comes from a combination of documents, but primarily press releases, copies of adverts, box office figures, and COW's correspondence with the exhibitors. Writing in 1985, Jane Root (1986, 213–23) described the experience of distributing *A Question of Silence*, relating how "by the end of the first week the audience figures were so low it looked in danger of sinking without trace" and detailing COW's grass-roots marketing campaign to build audiences. Box office returns, which list the daily audience numbers and ticket sales for each week of a film's run, clearly evidence the effect of that campaign and shed light on the different opening theatrical exhibition histories of these two films.

A *Question of Silence* opened at Screen on the Green in Islington and the Paris Pullman in Kensington (see figure 15.1), both of which specialized in European cinema and American cult films. The box office returns show audience figures at the Green of 1,171 in the first week, rising to 1,453 in the second and 1,802 in the third; and at the Pullman of 412 in the first week, rising to 449 in the second and 641 in the third. Although figures then fell slightly in the fourth week at both venues—to 1,599 at the Green and to 629 at the Pullman—the film clearly enjoyed growing audience figures for a sustained period and was continuing to produce relatively good box office returns. *Leila and the Wolves*—an exploration of the recent history of Palestine and Lebanon through the eyes of a female Lebanese student— opened at the Gate Notting Hill, known for showing art cinema and foreign-language films. In contrast to *A Question of Silence*, the box office returns for *Leila and the Wolves* show audience figures falling off from the outset, with 910 in the first week, 704 in the second, and 678 in the third. Hence, from a straightforward business point of view, it is

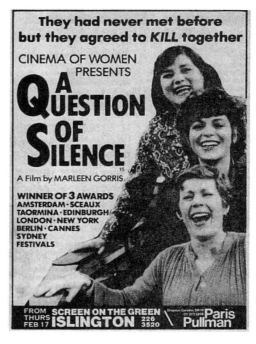

FIGURE 15.1. Poster for *A Question of Silence* at Screen on the Green, Islington and Paris Pullman, London (Courtesy of Cinenova)

hardly surprising that *Leila and the Wolves* disappeared from cinemas relatively quickly, while *A Question of Silence* was able to secure a follow-on run.

Correspondence and Notes

However, richer sources of information are a distributor's correspondence and records of communication with both filmmakers and exhibitors, together with file notes of meetings and negotiations. Here we see the challenges that COW faced in trying to get feminist feature films into cinemas. In the case of *Leila and the Wolves*, for instance, a file note of meetings held in August and September 1984 reports that, having viewed the film in June, COW was "interested but not committed" and took until late September to decide to take it on (COW 1984a). Notes from a subsequent meeting in December suggest that their reservations stemmed partly from the fact that the film had "too little background of history of Lebanon to be clear to a British Audience" (COW 1984d). This is an interesting contrast to COW's experience with *A Question of Silence*, which—according to Root (1986)—with its clear "central theme of unspoken female solidarity" (214) had a ready appeal for a young, middle-class feminist audience. The nature of *Leila*'s content meant that in order to build audiences for the film, COW might have to provide pre-screening contextual information for audiences, which would involve additional work and expense.

Furthermore, notes from a telephone conversation between a COW worker and *Leila*'s director, Heiny Srour, on December 12, 1984 (COW 1984b), followed up by a letter from COW on December 14 (McNulty 1984b), state that Srour had already shown the film to several central London exhibitors and received no interest in opening the film. These two documents suggest that at least part of the reason for the exhibitors' lack of interest was the fact that the film was being distributed on the nontheatrical format of 16mm. In itself this was not necessarily an insurmountable problem: other correspondence shows that COW had already distributed *Born in Flames* on 16mm, managing to persuade the Screen on the Green (where *A Question of Silence* had opened) to install the necessary projection equipment (Ashbrook 1983). However, COW's notes from the December 12 telephone conversation with Srour record that COW had tried the Screen on the Green for *Leila* and met with a negative response—although no reason is given.

In the face of these challenges, according to a December 14 letter to Srour and notes made of a phone call with one of the uninterested exhibitors four days later, COW was starting to explore the possibility of releasing the film via four-walling—a process whereby a distributor rents a cinema exclusively for their own use (COW 1984e). COW's record of the phone conversation notes that the cost of four-walling was usually based on a cinema's running costs plus 10 percent of the box office. While they were advised that this avenue was not particularly risky financially for the distributor, they were also told that "a cinema would only be interested if there is nothing available for them to open" (COW 1984c).

Nevertheless, as already noted above, COW did eventually succeed in securing an opening cinema in central London for the film (see figure 15.2). While there is no documentation detailing how they managed to achieve this, a letter to the exhibitor, Cinegate, reveals that the film had to meet minimum audience numbers. In January 1985 COW wrote to Cinegate, confirming their agreement:

LEILA will remain at the Gate, Notting Hill for 4 weeks provided that it does not fall below your minimum running costs which need a weekly attendance of 1200. If during the first week, attendance is below this, but not below 1000 and it appears that word of mouth recommendation will increase attendance, then you will consider retaining it.

After 4 weeks (or longer if it is doing well) the film will be transferred to The Gate, Bloomsbury where it will run for an unspecified period provided your costs are being covered. In the event of the film falling below the required figures at The Gate Notting Hill it will transfer to The Bloomsbury before four weeks. (McNulty 1985a)

FIGURE 15.2. COW advertisement for *Leila and the Wolves* at the Gate, Notting Hill, London (Courtesy of Cinenova)

Given that *Leila* failed to achieve the fall-back weekly attendance figure of 1,000, it is encouraging that Cinegate retained it at the opening cinema for three weeks. But this also explains why the opening run was shorter than that enjoyed by *A Question of Silence*, and, because the box office figures quickly fell well below the minimum requirement, it is not surprising that *Leila* did not transfer for a follow-on run.

Finding Recurring Issues

Delving deeper into COW's files, it fairly quickly becomes apparent that, despite their string of cinema releases, securing an opening venue and/or a sustained run was in fact not an uncommon problem. For instance, while the records for the release of *Committed*—an experimental exploration of the turbulent life of Holly-wood actress Frances Farmer—are sparse, the press releases and the promotional flyers that have been kept show that COW was only able to secure a two-week opening run for the film.

However, the records for Pat Murphy's *Anne Devlin*—set in Ireland during the Republican uprisings of 1798 and based on Devlin's prison journals—are more extensive. In particular they contain a string of correspondence with the filmmaker and the media that documents the film's difficult journey to its opening. A very detailed letter from COW to Murphy, written in August 1985, explains that their preference for opening *Anne Devlin* was, once again, Screen on the Green—or possibly its more prestigious sister venue, Screen on the Hill in Belsize Park—and that they have been negotiating with Mainline, the company that ran the Screen cinemas, to secure a venue and dates (McNulty 1985b). But COW observed:

> [I]n negotiating with the cinema owners/programmers we are in competition with what they consider to be more commercial, or "less difficult" films than the ones we distribute, in terms of choice of cinema and length of run. With *Anne Devlin* we have had the basic problem that we are having to convince Mainline that the film is more commercial than they choose to think it is. . . . Because of the reservations Mainline have about *Anne Devlin's* commercial potential they only wanted to offer us two weeks. . . . What is likely to happen is that they will offer us a two weeks guaranteed run with an extension if the film does well. If that is what they offer we will try and negotiate for a follow-on run at [the Screen on] Baker Street. (McNulty 1985b, 1)

In the end COW failed to convince Mainline that the film was commercially viable enough to open at either the Screen on the Green or the Screen on the Hill. A press release and letter to *Living* magazine in the *Anne Devlin* files both announce that in fact the film would open at, rather than transfer to, the Baker Street Screen cinema at the end of January 1986 (Ashbrook 1985b). However, a letter written to

Observer magazine in February 1986 explains that in fact the Baker Street opening failed to materialize as well: "We were originally planning to open at the Screen on Baker St., but due to the extraordinary success of *Letter to Brezhnev*, which looks set to sit on there for months to come, we've had to change our plans. The film is now opening at the Everyman Cinema, Hampstead" (Ashbrook 1986b).

However, in contrast to the first-run Baker Street Screen, the Hampstead Everyman was a repertory cinema. Although it did occasionally open new films, it was better known for its varied mix of Hollywood, European, independent, and cult film revivals. With the opening finally confirmed, COW wrote the following day to the *Irish Post* as part of the process of trying to secure press coverage for the film's release. The letter is interesting for the light it sheds on Mainline's reservations about *Anne Devlin's* commercial potential. COW confirmed that:

> *ANNE DEVLIN* will be opening at the Everyman Cinema, Hampstead on the 14th March, where it will run until at least the end of the month. Within London it will then transfer to other independent cinemas. . . . However, at this stage none of these follow-on venues can be confirmed, since this is dependent upon how successful the opening run is. . . . Since this is the first feature film to be entirely cast, crewed and financed from Ireland we have found a certain amount of hesitation in this country from cinemas who want to wait and see how well it does before they commit themselves. It is, thus, extremely important that the opening is successful as this will show that Irish films are commercially viable over here. (McNulty 1986a)[1]

While the precise nature of the problems varied from one film to the next, and in several cases the documentation is incomplete, a picture starts to emerge from the records of the *ongoing* struggle COW faced in order to get feminist feature films into cinemas and keep them there. Indeed, one file contained a draft for a possible promotional flyer in which COW asserted: "To anyone who has seen *Born in Flames* or *[A] Question of Silence* it might seem obvious that they can be watched in warm comfortable cinemas by large audiences. To us, at Cinema of Women it is a major achievement" (COW 1983a, 1).

Talking Money

COW's files also contain financial information in the form of budgets, funding applications, invoices, box office returns, royalty statements, and so on. Looking through this material where it exists demonstrates that the relatively short cinema runs COW was able to secure produced relatively low levels of revenue—which usually yielded very little income for the filmmaker after COW's recovery of release costs (such as sums paid for advertising, press screenings, promotional materials, certification costs, freight charges, and the like). But again it is frequently in the correspondence where we can learn more about the financial side of feminist distribution. What becomes apparent is that many filmmakers ran up debts in the course of making their films and hence were often desperate for any monies COW could get for them. Lynne Tillman, for instance, wrote to COW the year after the UK release of *Committed*, saying: "We still have an $1,100 debt to be paid off, and monies from you would help" (Tillman 1986, 2). A more urgent plea came from Pat Murphy in 1987: "I am writing in a state of urgency to ask you for the second installment of the Channel 4 licensing fee for *Anne Devlin* . . . the previous payment went to the Film Board. This next sum is to come to me at Aeon Films. And it is badly, urgently needed" (Murphy 1987).

When Channel 4 was set up in 1982, it included an Independent Film and Video department with a remit to promote experimentation and innovation. Murphy was among a number of women (and indeed other independent) filmmakers who benefited from both the broadcast opportunities and additional source of income that this department was able to offer. The TV sale for *Anne Devlin* is well documented in the files via a series of letters between Pat Murphy, Channel 4, and COW during the period November 1985 to January 1987. The story that unfolds across that correspondence is that in 1982 Murphy had sold the rights to Channel 4 for one screening of her earlier film *Maeve* (co-directed with John Davies, UK/Ireland 1981)—about a twenty-year-old woman returning to her native Belfast—for £17,500—and took that as a benchmark. Since she regarded *Anne Devlin* to have been "a much more successful film in terms of theatrical impact and critical acclaim," she instructed COW to ask for a £50,000 fee for the rights to three transmissions (Murphy 1986). Channel 4 responded by offering only £15,000, asserting that the fee paid for *Maeve* was "indicative of occasional inconsistency and paying over the going rate in the early days of the Channel" (Stoneman 1986). Other information in COW's files certainly indicates that generally Channel 4 did not pay high amounts for broadcast rights. For instance, COW had previously sold the TV rights for Cristina Perincioli's *The Power of Men Is the Patience of Women* (West Germany, 1978) to the channel for a licence fee of only £5,000 (Pattinson 1988).[2] Although Murphy was understandably keen to maximise the fee for the broadcast rights, she eventually reduced her price to £20,000 (Ashbrook 1985a), while Channel 4 increased its offer to £17,500—initially still for three transmissions (Sharma 1985) but revising it subsequently to only two transmissions since "we have not repeated any feature more than once in the past" (Stoneman 1986).

While Murphy made it clear in one letter that £17,500 was "still not enough" (Murphy 1986), she was eventually persuaded to accept the offer, since if she did not, she risked missing the proposed transmission slot of spring 1987. Channel 4 wrote to her in December 1986, explaining that if the film was not screened in this slot, "we would have to postpone acquisition for some time as the next relevant scheduling place would be a fiction season planned for Spring 1988" (Stoneman 1986). The outcome was obviously not to Murphy's liking, but because she had debts to pay off, she had little choice but to accept Channel 4's offer. At the same time, the negotiations show that when COW was able to get the TV rights—and that was not always the case—making the sale to television, like getting feminist feature films into cinemas, was not always straightforward.

Identifying Other Issues

Despite the challenges that COW had to deal with on a continuing basis, it is evident that filmmakers placed their films with COW because they wanted to support a feminist film distributor. In one letter Pat Murphy emphasizes, "I do support your work, and feel that that goodwill has been expressed in the terms of our distribution agreement" (Murphy 1985a, 1). Another example can be found in a series of letters and accompanying documents in the file for *Born in Flames*—a futuristic look at women's continuing oppression after a peaceful socialist revolution (figure 15.3)—which evidence that its director Lizzie Borden had offers from both COW and The Other Cinema (TOC) to distribute the film in the United Kingdom. The documentation shows that in April 1983 Borden decided to sign a contract with TOC, a small independent distributor known for its catalog of left-wing political films, but changed her mind in July and wrote to TOC asking them to release her from the contract so she could go with COW. She explains in the letter that her decision is due to "all the attacks on feminism and the regressive atmosphere in general of the past few years" and states, "Because of the content of BORN IN FLAMES I feel that it must be allied to a specifically feminist network" (Borden 1983).

At the same time, however, COW's records show that their performance and the level of service the distributor offered did not always meet filmmakers' expectations. On August 12, 1985, for instance, Pat Murphy (1985a) wrote to COW complaining of numerous postponements to the release date for *Anne Devlin*, saying that possible opening dates had been suggested for November 1984, April 1985, and September 1985. There are also letters from several filmmakers or their representatives complaining about a lack of communication on COW's part. In January 1986 Lynne Tillman wrote, "Sheila [McLaughlin] and I haven't heard from you in a long time, so we'd appreciate your writing us to say how *Committed* is do-

FIGURE 15.3. Poster for *Born in Flames*, a futuristic look at women's oppression, followed by *The Big Chill* at Screen on the Green, which specialised in European cinema and American cult films (Courtesy of Cinenova)

ing (where it's been screened, etc.)" (Tillman 1986, 1). In another instance, Playpont Film, the UK sales agent for *A Question of Silence*, wrote to COW requesting an activity report for the film: "This is part of the contract and if we do not have a report by 15th July we shall serve you notice of the breach and demand cancellation of the contract" (Playpont 1983). Indeed, browsing through COW's correspondence for various films, it becomes quickly apparent that it was not unusual for COW to take two to three months to reply to letters, and on one occasion American filmmaker Michelle Parkerson had to wait five months for a response (Wallace 1985).

These comments tend to suggest that COW was remiss in fulfilling its obligations and role as a distributor. Murphy implies this in the August 1985 letter, wherein she complains about the postponement of the release date. A copy of the returns for *Anne Devlin*'s release in Ireland that she sent to COW shows the film had enjoyed good audiences over a five-week run in Dublin a few months earlier (Murphy 1985b, 2). Although the subject matter may have easily attracted its Irish audience, in her August letter Murphy nevertheless notes, "The success of the Dublin run was the result of a tremendous amount of concerted effort between myself and the Irish distributors" (1985a, 2). However, what emerges from other correspondence is the highly limited nature of COW's resources. As if in response to Murphy's implied criticism, COW worker Eileen McNulty explains their staffing situation to her on two separate occasions. On the first, in a letter to

Murphy dated August 21, 1985, McNulty observes she is "the only person in the office this week" (1985b, 1), while in a second letter sent in June 1986 she notes, "I am on leave for three months, now (much needed, I assure you). If you need to contact us or want any information during that time you could contact Sue (a new full-time worker), Jenny (now part-time) or Vida (a temporary worker replacing me for two days a week)" (McNulty 1986b).

Other correspondence with Murphy fleshes out further the picture of COW's resources and the degree to which the distributor was frequently overstretched. As already noted, COW had been able to access revenue funding from the Greater London Council (GLC) to help subsidise their operating costs. However, in February 1986 COW wrote to the filmmaker explaining that in the middle of preparing for the March release of *Anne Devlin* at the Hampstead Everyman:

> We are also having enormous problems with our GLC funding at the moment, which is wasting enormous amounts of time—we are in danger of losing our revenue funding for the *current* year due to admin problems at the GLC, and are having to continually lobby the politicians there. It won't effect the launch of 'Anne Devlin,' but it makes things much more pressurised here. (Ashbrook 1986a)

While the filmmaker correspondence does not tell the full story of grant aid dependency and the shifting arts funding landscape that led to COW's demise, other documents highlight the major problem it created for COW. Notes from a telephone conversation with the director of *Leila and the Wolves* record that Srour was threatening to withdraw the film from COW if the organization did not put sufficient effort and resources into opening it. COW's response is telling: "I said COW couldn't invest beyond a certain point because we just don't have the money" (COW 1984c, 1).

As noted above, the original collective of six women set up COW to increase the availability of "good films made by women." Examining COW's records reveals not only the enormous and ongoing challenges they faced in getting feminist feature films to wider audiences via cinema releases and TV sales but also the fact that they secured that exposure on very limited resources. Without COW, it is likely that a significant number of those films may never have been released in the United Kingdom. Hence, making it possible for wider audiences to see these films means that COW played a crucial role in expanding the diversity of film culture in the United Kingdom. Moreover, in the context of "doing women's film history," it also means COW made women's contribution to cinema far more visible in the United Kingdom and thereby helped nurture the careers of the women directors they championed.

Acknowledgments

All the documents referenced above are available online via the Film and Video Distribution Database (FVDD) at http://fv-distribution-database.ac.uk. The database is an AHRC funded project that explores the histories of key distributors and promoters of British artists' and independent film and video, namely: the London Film-makers' Co-op, The Other Cinema, LVA/London Electronic Arts, Cinema of Women, Circles, Film and Video Umbrella, Albany Video Distribution, Cinenova, and Lux. The FVDD makes available documents from the organizations (and their funders) and makes the material searchable via narrative chronologies. It is an ongoing project with further documents being added on a regular basis.

The FVDD and the research that underpins this chapter resulted from two AHRC-funded research projects examining independent moving-image distribution in the United Kingdom from the 1970s through 2000, led by Julia Knight, with co-investigator Geoffrey Nowell-Smith and research fellow Peter Thomas.

Notes

This chapter includes a substantially revised version of some material previously published in Albert Moran and Karina Aveyard, eds., *Watching Films: New Perspectives on Movie-Going, Exhibition and Reception* (Intellect, 2013).

1. Unfortunately there are no box office returns in the COW files from the film's run at the Hampstead Everyman, although there are returns from screenings at some regional cinemas and arts centers.

2. To add to the problems, Channel 4 could be very slow in paying up. It took three years, for instance, for COW and Perincioli to receive payment from the Channel for the TV rights to *The Power of Men* (see Perincioli 1982, and McNulty 1984a).

References

URLs for PDFs of documents referenced in this chapter are given below. But to further explore the history of women's film and video distribution in the United Kingdom, go to the Film and Video Distribution Database at http://fv-distribution-database.ac.uk.

Ashbrook, P. (COW). 1983. Letter to Ian Christie (BFI), October 27 (http://fv-distribution-database.ac.uk/PDFs/Ashbrook831027.pdf).

———. 1985a. Letter to Poonam Sharma (Channel 4), November 7 (http://fv-distribution-database.ac.uk/PDFs/Ashbrook851107.pdf).

———. 1985b. Letter to Elizabeth Atkinson (*Living* magazine), November 13 (http://fv-distribution-database.ac.uk/PDFs/Ashbrook851113.pdf).

———. 1986a. Letter to Pat Murphy, February 6 (http://fv-distribution-database.ac.uk/PDFs/Ashbrook860206.pdf).

————. 1986b. Letter to Lesley Thornton (*Observer* magazine), February 17 (http://fv-distribution-database.ac.uk/PDFs/Ashbrook860217.pdf).

Borden, L. 1983. Letter to Tony Kirkhope (The Other Cinema), July 24 (http://fv-distribution-database.ac.uk/PDFs/Borden830724.pdf).

COW. 1979. COW: Cinema of Women Films. Meeting July 26 (http://fv-distribution-database.ac.uk/PDFs/COW790726.pdf).

————. 1983a. Draft press release for *Born in Flames*, undated/September? (http://fv-distribution-database.ac.uk/PDFs/COW8309.pdf).

————. 1983b. *Born in Flames* press release, undated/October? (http://fv-distribution-database.ac.uk/PDFs/COW8310.pdf).

————. 1984a. *Leila and the Wolves*, June–October (http://fv-distribution-database.ac.uk/PDFs/COW-Leila8410.pdf).

————. 1984b. Telephone conversation with Heiny, December 12 (http://fv-distribution-database.ac.uk/PDFs/COW-Srour841212.pdf).

————. 1984c. Phone call to Heiny, December 16 (http://fv-distribution-database.ac.uk/PDFs/COW-Srour841216.pdf).

————. 1984d. Notes on IBT discussion, December 17 (http://fv-distribution-database.ac.uk/PDFs/COW-IBT841217.pdf).

————. 1984e. Phone call with Andy Engels, December 18 (http://fv-distribution-database.ac.uk/PDFs/COW-Engels841218.pdf).

————. 1985. *Anne Devlin* press release, undated/December? (http://fv-distribution-database.ac.uk/PDFs/COW8512.pdf).

Knight, J., and P. Thomas. 2011. *Reaching Audiences: Distribution and Promotion of Alternative Moving Image*. Bristol/Chicago: Intellect.

McNulty, E. (COW). 1984a. Letter to Cristina Perincioli, September 29 (http://fv-distribution-database.ac.uk/PDFs/McNulty840929.pdf).

————. 1984b. Letter to Heiny Srour, December 14 (http://fv-distribution-database.ac.uk/PDFs/McNulty841214.pdf).

————. 1985a. Letter to David Stone (Cinegate), January 31 (http://fv-distribution-database.ac.uk/PDFs/McNulty850131.pdf).

————. 1985b. Letter to Pat Murphy, August 21 (http://fv-distribution-database.ac.uk/PDFs/McNulty850821.pdf).

————. 1986a. Letter to Brenda MacLua (*Irish Post*), February 18 (http://fv-distribution-database.ac.uk/PDFs/McNulty860218.pdf).

————. 1986b. Letter to Pat Murphy, June 27 (http://fv-distribution-database.ac.uk/PDFs/McNulty860627.pdf).

————. 1987. Letter to Pat Murphy, January 21 (http://fv-distribution-database.ac.uk/PDFs/McNulty870121.pdf).

Murphy, P. 1985a. Letter to COW, August 12 (http://fv-distribution-database.ac.uk/PDFs/Murphy850812.pdf).

————. 1985b. Letter to COW, September 4 (http://fv-distribution-database.ac.uk/PDFs/Murphy850904.pdf).

————. 1986. Letter to Rod Stoneman (Channel 4), December 1 (http://fv-distribution
-database.ac.uk/PDFs/Murphy861201.pdf).

————. 1987. Letter to Eileen McNulty (COW), August 30 (http://fv-distribution
-database.ac.uk/PDFs/Murphy870830.pdf).

Pattinson, G. (Channel 4). 1988. Letter to Jenny Wallace (COW), July 7 (http://fv-distribution
-database.ac.uk/PDFs/Pattinson880707.pdf).

Perincioli, C. 1982. Letter to COW, November 26 (http://fv-distribution-database.ac.uk/
PDFs/Perincioli821126.pdf).

Playpont Films Ltd. 1983. Letter to COW, July 8 (http://fv-distribution-database.ac.uk/
PDFs/Playpont830708.pdf).

Root, J. 1986. "Distributing 'A Question of Silence'—A Cautionary Tale," in *Films for Women*,
edited by C. Brunsdon. London: BFI.

Sharma, P. (Channel 4). 1985. Letter to Penny Ashbrook (COW), November 28 (http://
fv-distribution-database.ac.uk/PDFs/Sharma851128.pdf).

Stoneman, R. (Channel 4). 1986. Letter to Pat Murphy, December 22 (http://fv-distribution
-database.ac.uk/PDFs/Stoneman861222.pdf).

Tillman, L. 1986. Letter to COW, January 7 (http://fv-distribution-database.ac.uk/PDFs/
Tillman860107.pdf).

Wallace, J. (COW). 1985. Letter to Michelle Parkerson, June 18 (http://fv-distribution-database
.ac.uk/PDFs/Wallace850618.pdf).

CHAPTER 16

"Our Place"

Women at the Cinema
in Rural Australia

KARINA AVEYARD

The field of women's film history has opened up new and more nuanced ways of understanding the role of film and cinema as a force in women's lives. This chapter focuses on women as cinema audiences. It centers specifically on the experiences of a modern-day group of women who patronize and actively support the First Avenue Cinema, a 1950s single-screen film theater located in the coastal town of Sawtell on the mid-north coast of New South Wales, Australia (population 18,900,[1] ABS 2013). This case study seeks to examine the practices of a "social audience"— what Annette Kuhn (2002) terms "the flesh and blood human beings who go to cinemas to see films" (4). Grounded in the pluralistic and multidisciplinary field of "new cinema history" (Maltby, Biltereyst, and Meers 2011), the chapter examines cinema-going as an act of sociocultural participation.

I begin by briefly looking at the geographic and economic contours of Sawtell, including its range of public venues and spaces and their availability (both practically and socially) to local women. This leads into a more detailed examination of the town's First Avenue Cinema, which caters to a core audience of mature female filmgoers (ages thirty-five and older). The chapter looks at how the cinema positions itself as a social space that local women want to inhabit, and how and why these women use it. The focus then narrows to examine the efforts and activism of a particular group of local residents (almost all women) who rallied together in 2009 in an effort to help save and support the cinema when it was under threat of permanent closure. This unique period of uncertainty at the cinema and the response among its patrons offer a window into the everyday significance of film-going for rural women—something that, as we will see, is connected to a desire to maintain cultural access but is also bound up in broader issues to do with marking out and preserving social spaces and affirming identity.

My research in Sawtell was conducted between 2009 and 2011 as part of a larger three-year study of contemporary rural cinema-going and exhibition. As I have discussed at length elsewhere,[2] this was a multimethod project that incorporated elements of ethnography (observing cinemas and their wider environments), narrative analysis (interviews and written surveys), and social anthropology (immersion and extended participation, centered on understanding social relationships rather than societies as a whole [Beattie 2006, 149]). The anthropological component of the study was carried out in Sawtell, where I lived over the two-year period. During this time I was a regular patron of the local film theater, the First Avenue Cinema, and made numerous friends and acquaintances there. I worked also as a volunteer and executive committee member for a local film support group known as Friends of the Sawtell Cinema (FOSC), which ran monthly screening events and raised funds to assist with the operational costs of the cinema. As a committee member, I was an active participant in the group's activities and decisions but deliberately avoided taking on senior roles (such as president or liaison with the cinema manager) in order not to overtly influence the organization. While FOSC was not established as an exclusively female organization or with the advancement of gender-based issues particularly in mind, its day-to-day management was composed almost entirely of women, and this had a noticeable influence on the framing of the group's agenda. By looking at the activities of this group through the lens of women's issues, it is possible to understand more clearly the motivations and actions of its members.

Sawtell—Geographic and Social Contexts

The town of Sawtell is located on the east coast of Australia. It is part of the mid-north coast region of New South Wales, roughly halfway between the capital cities of Brisbane and Sydney, approximately five hundred kilometers north and south, respectively. Sawtell is a picturesque village featuring an attractive main street close to a long stretch of beach with fine white sand. Not surprisingly, the town is a very popular tourist destination, with the season running from around October to April and peaking over the long summer school holidays in December and January. Like many coastal areas, Sawtell is also favored by retirees, particularly those from major cities looking for a peaceful life in a warm climate. The influx of these new residents over the past few decades has brought significant numbers of relatively affluent and educated people to the area. They represent an often-stark contrast to many of younger and longer-term residents who live on low incomes and struggle to find regular employment.

While Sawtell is a reasonably modest settlement, it is situated only fifteen to twenty minutes' drive from the much larger town of Coffs Harbour, which has a population of around fifty thousand (ABS 2013). The proximity to Coffs Harbour provides additional employment opportunities and access to a range of services and facilities that are not available locally. Coffs Harbour also has a five-screen multiplex cinema operated by one of Australia's largest exhibition chains, Birch Carroll and Coyle (part of the Greater Union group). This cinema has many of the same features as metropolitan-based multiplexes, including a well-stocked candy bar, 3D options, online ticketing, and immediate access to latest-release films.

The economic divide that runs through the Sawtell community has a noticeable effect on its social scene, which is often delineated along economic but also gender lines. In terms of places to "go out," there are several options. The local pub, the Sawtell Hotel, serves drinks and meals. The main hotel bar tends to be a very masculine environment and attracts a significant number of men from manual-based occupations and industries. Some women drink there, although they tend to be relatively young (under age thirty). The pub also has a restaurant where local women from a wider range of age groups socialize, although it tends to be a venue for special occasions or for a Friday or Saturday night out with family rather than somewhere they would go on a weekly basis. The second major social space in the town is just across the road—the RSL (Returned and Services League of Australia) Club, also a licensed premise. It serves cheaper drinks and food, which are subsidized by gambling—mostly poker machines and to a lesser extent bingo. With lower prices and an older demographic that tends to be attracted to its gaming, it is very much an over-fifty set that frequents the club. Providing a third option are several cafés and a couple of restaurants on the main street, although these tend to be sustained by tourism rather than local business. The restaurants, in particular, are expensive compared with the Hotel and RSL Club, although during the day the cafes are popular with local women, especially retirees and those with babies and young children.

Away from these venues, the other important social hubs center around sport in several forms, principally surf lifesaving (based around the local beach and involving a season of home and away competitions), football, and cricket. Here women often play support roles—as mothers, spouses, friends—rather than actually participating in the sporting activities. Once their children are grown, many older women gravitate toward social groups centered on activities such as charities, baking, reading, and arts and crafts. Traditionally, groups like the Country

Women's Association (CWA) have been the center of these kinds of pursuits but have a reputation for being socially and politically conservative. The Tennis Club is also quite popular among retired women, with social matches played on weekdays. Several of the members of the FOSC group were already acquainted through the Tennis Club, and its rustic, weatherboard clubhouse was used as the venue for most of our committee meetings.

The First Avenue Cinema

The First Avenue Cinema falls somewhere in the middle of this wider range of public spaces. Located in a prime position on the main street, the theater was established as a simple timber-and-corrugated-iron building in 1929. It was purchased by Alan and Doris Brissett in 1942 and has remained in the family's ownership ever since, most recently managed by their grandson Col Brissett. In 1955 the cinema was severely damaged by a mini-cyclone and was rebuilt in its present triple-brick configuration, reopening in 1957. The building is of a fairly simple design but has some attractive art deco–style glass and other decorative plaster features. Lending it a rustic character are features such as outdoor toilets (located down a laneway at the back of the cinema) and the cinema's original seats, which are small and many have worn-out springs. The 35mm projector and sound systems are also quite dated, and from the seats toward the rear of the auditorium you hear the whir of the film going around in the bio box. The cinema is listed with the National Trust in Australia, which places some limitations on the improvements that can be made, but its aesthetic style also reflects the relatively low profit margins of the business and the lack of funds for capital improvements.

The First Avenue Cinema caters principally to two audience groups—children younger than age fourteen and their families, and women aged thirty-five and older (although they are mostly fifty-five-plus). Children tend to dominate during school holiday periods; the older female audience provides the regular, stable base that sustains the cinema during the rest of the year. While men, of course, attend the cinema as well, they tend to be accompanying partners or wives, and it is women who are seen by the cinema's manager as the key influence over decisions about attendance (Brissett interview, July 31, 2009). The film program reflects the preferences and needs of these two groups. Children's films saturate the schedule during school holidays—with popular titles including the *Ice Age* series, *Alvin and the Chipmunks: Chipwrecked* (Mitchell 2011), *The Muppets* (Bobbin 2011), *The Princess and the Frog* (Clements and Musker 2009), and *Up* (Docter and Peterson 2009). During the remainder of the year the program is organized largely around older audiences—with films like *Young Victoria* (Vallée 2009), *The Best Exotic Marigold*

FIGURE 16.1. First Avenue Cinema, Sawtell, New South Wales, February 2011
(Photo © Aveyard)

Hotel (Madden 2011), *Julie and Julia* (Ephron 2009), *Harry Brown* (Barber 2009), and *Red* (Schwentke 2010). The cinema also screens some foreign language—and what might be termed art-house—films, particularly titles that have won awards at international festivals, such as the Japanese film *Departures* (Takita 2008), and accessible or light-hearted stories, such as the French title *Micmacs* (Jeunet 2009). The cinema runs two self-programmed, week-long international film festivals each year, which generally feature a mix of Australian and foreign films.

The Brissetts have strategically positioned their cinema as an art-house or specialist theater and actively target their core mature-audience demographic. When the Birch Carroll and Coyle cinema opened in nearby Coffs Harbour, Col Brissett explained that it became apparent very quickly that they had to differentiate or go under: "There was no point in us trying to compete with Birch Carroll and Coyle. That's where the teenagers want to go, they want their McDonald's and that whole experience. The young kids are their audience. Here we have created a different type of audience" (Brissett interview, July 31, 2009). Another key distinguishing feature of the cinema is its lower ticket prices, which are typically around 25 percent less than those charged at the multiplex in Coffs Harbour. This greater affordability plays a key role in attracting local families as well as older patrons.

Women Audiences at the First Avenue Cinema

Interviews and surveys conducted with Sawtell women (from their mid- to late thirties and older, but predominantly fifties and older) suggest the First Avenue Cinema is seen as a relatively unique public space within the context of the village. It is distinct from the unappealing heavy drinking and gambling atmospheres of Sawtell Hotel and RSL Club, and it is viewed as more sophisticated and less senior-citizen oriented than knitting and baking at the CWA or one of the other local art-craft groups. The cinema is a space that women consider to be broadly accessible, and it is often described in terms such as "welcoming," "friendly," and "relaxed." For those not born or raised in Sawtell, the presence of the cinema was often cited as a key reason they were attracted to settle in the town—something they saw as contributing positively to the liveliness of its social and cultural scene.

The different ways local women articulated why the First Avenue Cinema is important to them can be summarized under five main headings—films, affordability, sense of belonging, safety, and nostalgia. These categories traverse a wide range of sociocultural factors that can only be touched on briefly here. However, by focusing on that breadth, the analysis illustrates the complex and interconnected nature of the issues that frame women's participation in cinema at Sawtell. It also establishes the context for the formation of the FOSC group, discussed later in this chapter. This broader view enables us to understand more clearly what was at stake for local women when the cinema was under threat of closure in 2009 and what galvanized them to try to save it.

Turning first to the issues of price and programming, the First Avenue Cinema, as mentioned above, maintains lower ticket prices than the nearby multiplex. It offers particularly generous seniors' (sixty and older) discounts and also sells a seniors' five-film ticket, which brings the price of attending a film down to around A$7–8. There are many widowed or single women in Sawtell who live on limited incomes, and this financial aspect of the cinema's accessibility was rated as particularly important. They reported that going out helped them to feel happier and stay in touch with local friends, while the lower cost meant going to the cinema was something they could do regularly. Complimenting this is a film program tailored quite specifically to their demographic. The women interviewed indicated they regarded the films screened at Sawtell as more "interesting" and "thought provoking" than the regional multiplex, which most considered to be a more mindless, youth-orientated experience that they did not relate to. Most of the films at the First Avenue Cinema featured actors older women could recognize and followed storylines and subjects that they perceived as "interesting for our age group."

The cinema was rated very highly for its friendly atmosphere and for the opportunities this facilitates for interaction that patrons felt was personal and where they felt socially at ease. All respondents spoke positively about this—either in terms of the staff or others that they knew or met at the cinema, as the following two quotes illustrate:

> We are a community at Sawtell [cinema]. People are friendly and a lot of us know each other anyway so going to a film is a good chance to catch up, especially with people you might not have seen for a while.
> (Sawtell resident, female, 56–65 years)

> I live locally and I like the friendly atmosphere there [First Avenue Cinema]. I usually have a bit of a chat with the owner as I buy my ticket and I often see other people I know there . . . it's quite different to going to a cinema in a big city like Melbourne where I used to live.
> (Sawtell resident, female, mid-40s)

Connected with the perceived friendly environment was a sense of confidence about personal safety. The cinema provides local women with access to a social space that is convenient, low risk to get to, and secure once they arrive. Older women spoke frequently of their aversion to traveling longer distances, especially at night, and indicated that having a venue close by was very important in terms of maintaining a social life. As one patron explained:

> I don't like driving to Coffs at night. The area around the cinema there can get a bit rough with all the young people there. Sawtell [cinema] is good because you can park nearby, sometimes directly out front, and there are more older people like myself there. (Sawtell resident, female, 65+ years)

Other women were more direct in linking the venue to their social opportunities, with one local lady in her mid-sixties declaring that if the Sawtell film theater closed, she would be forced to stop going to the cinema altogether.

As a fixture in the town of Sawtell for more than eighty years, the First Avenue Cinema also evokes feelings of nostalgia among long-term residents of the town who can recall earlier experiences there as well as newcomers for whom it conjures up memories of a past cinema-going age spent in different places and often associated with their youth. For locals there is sometimes a particular sense of continuity in the longevity of the venue that evokes a nostalgic element that is more connected to place and family than to cinematic experience per se. As one life-long resident of Sawtell explained:

> I have been going to the [Sawtell] cinema for a long time. My husband and I went there on dates before we got married and my kids went there too. Now

my grandkids are the ones going along. I've a lot of memories there and I think that it is a real asset to the town that it is still going much like it always has after all this time.

(Sawtell resident, female, early 70s)

The issues that frame cinema-going for numerous women in Sawtell indicate that the cinema is important both for the films it shows and for the social opportunities it provides. With regard to the latter, it is evident that this is not just about interacting with people but also linked to the accessibility of public spaces and the sense of satisfaction and empowerment that flows from that. For older women in Sawtell, cinema-going can be seen as part of everyday life, but for most it was not something they did every day or even every week. Crucially, however, it was considered to be a very important part of a fixed social landscape that women relied on to be there when they wanted to access it. The threat of the cinema's closure brought this dependability very sharply into focus and underpinned what was quite a rapid community response to the risk that the venue might be lost.

The Flood and the Friends

Sawtell is in a semi-tropical area of Australia and has a high average annual rainfall. In March 2009 there were several days of very heavy rain that flooded large parts of the town including the main street. The bottom section of the cinema ended up underwater, which destroyed the screen and its curtains, an organ, and the first fifteen rows of seats. The cinema was closed, and uncertainty hung over its repair and reopening. The manager, Col Brissett, is a well-known local figure, and he spoke openly about his family's concerns over whether their insurance would cover the cost of the necessary restoration and whether in fact it was worth doing the work at all, given the economically marginal and often stressful nature of running the business. This news alarmed some sections of the local community, particularly older women, who were among the cinema's most regular patrons.

In the end, the cinema was repaired, and it reopened in May 2009 after being closed for eight weeks. This happy outcome was attributable almost entirely to a generous insurance settlement received by the cinema's owners. Nevertheless, two patrons, both local women in their sixties, remained convinced of the need to get Sawtell residents to use the cinema more regularly. During the closure and in the period immediately after the cinema's reopening, they called on local friends and acquaintances to back a film support group. They began collecting memberships, charging A$50 each, despite the fact that at this stage no formal organization had been set up. Encouraged by the positive response and feeling confident there was wider community interest, these two women organized a meeting at the cinema a month or so after it reopened; between thirty and thirty-five people attended. This gathering elected a committee of eight (including myself) and established an official organization.

The immediate objectives of the group were to increase audience numbers and to raise the cinema's profile in order to ensure its continued viability. In practical terms this centered on providing and promoting what were viewed as "value-added experiences" in the form of special screening events (discussed below) and raising money to help with the cost of operating the venue. One of the early ideas was to work toward amassing funds for a digital projector, thereby helping to ensure the cinema's longer-term sustainability. However, the high cost of the equipment relative to the size and capacity of the group meant this never became a tangible goal.

The Brissett family appreciated the group's efforts and any financial help the group might be able to provide; however, it was not always an easy relationship. It was slightly unusual in the sense that FOSC was a community-led organization supporting a commercial business rather than a charity or volunteer group, as might be more typical. There was consequently a more complex boundary between what was perceived by the cinema as kindly support and that which seemed like unwelcome advice regarding its day-to-day affairs. This line, per se, was perceived by the Brissetts to have been overstepped on a number of occasions, and it gave rise to tensions, which came to a head in early 2010 with a breakdown in communications between some of the FOSC committee members and the cinema's management. The committee as a whole was deeply concerned about the situation and sought a positive solution. It deputized two members to broker a reconciliation, the successful outcome of which included some executive members removing themselves from roles that brought them into direct contact with the cinema manager.

The women who assembled around the FOSC enterprise and its executive committee came from a variety of backgrounds—some were close friends, others were connected through local organizations such as walking clubs, the tennis club, or an art group. Most were people already active in the community via volunteer organizations, and most were retired, meaning they had the time to devote to the group. Some were long-term residents, many of whom had been homemakers most of their lives and wanted simply to do something straightforward and practical to help keep the local cinema going. Other participants were relatively new residents or "incomers," having come from larger cities where they had had a diverse range of life experiences, including overseas travel, senior jobs and careers, and busy social lives. Perhaps it is no surprise, then, that their vision for the FOSC group was often a little more ambitious, with regular discussions about contributing to the expansion of film culture more broadly—for example, funding a film festival or organizing events and bus trips to other cinemas in the region. Although on occasions these differing approaches became a point of tension, they never came to be the source of serious discontent within the group, since lack of funds and the time absorbed by organizing FOSC's core monthly screening events meant there were limited resources to actively pursue the larger visions.

Within three months of its official launch the group had nearly one hundred members. The membership fees had raised nearly A\$5,000 toward cinema support activities. These included funding a series of television adverts over the summer holiday period for two consecutive years (2009–10 and 2010–11), something the cinema had been unable to afford to do for some time. At the center of the group's activities were special once-monthly screening events that were themed around a new film opening at the cinema. These events raised additional funds, although this was not their primary purpose. The aim was instead to draw people to the cinema with a view toward encouraging them to attend more often. Attendance at these special screenings suggests that the events were at least partly successful in that aim. Most events attracted audiences of seventy people or more, and many drew crowds in excess of one hundred. While not necessarily large by metropolitan standards, audiences of only ten to twenty for off-peak screenings were not uncommon. Priced slightly higher than normal screenings, the cost of the ticket was designed to provide valuable income for the cinema and cover the accompanying catering and entertainment expenses, with any surplus banked for future FOSC use.

These FOSC's screening events were designed as an expanded evening out. They always involved the serving of food and drinks (organized by the group) before the film, with the attendant opportunity to socialize and chat; also, there was often a guest speaker, live music, and/or a dressing-up theme. In terms of organizing the event, an appointed FOSC member would communicate with the cinema about upcoming releases, and the committee as a whole would decide which film (selected from three to four options provided by the cinema) to feature at that month's special event and then agree on the nature of the accompanying entertainment. The cinema manager was always consulted in advance about the plans. Examples of successful events organized by FOSC include a special screening of the internationally acclaimed Aboriginal film *Samson and Delilah* (Thornton 2009), which was attended by several local Aboriginal residents—an elder who gave the "welcome to country" (an acknowledgement of the traditional custodians of the land), an actor who spoke about his career, and a musician who performed on the didgeridoo. Despite the film's difficult subject matter, this event attracted an almost full house at the cinema. Successful dressing-up events included *The King's Speech* (Hooper 2010, see poster in figure 16.2) and a 1960s-theme evening for *A Single Man* (Ford 2009), which also included a retro buffet featuring foods such as cheese cubes, deviled eggs, and Devils on Horseback. For many FOSC members, the majority of whom were women, these screenings fulfilled a dual purpose: they could feel as if they were actively contributing to the sustainability of their beloved local cinema and could, at the same time, enjoy the company of friends and acquaintances in surroundings that were both convenient and familiar.

Conclusion

Cinemas are spaces that have long been associated with women—as far back (and probably further) than Iris Barry's assertion in 1926 that "one thing never to be lost sight of in considering

FIGURE 16.2. Poster for *The King's Speech* screening

the cinema is that it exists for the purpose of pleasing women." While Barry was concerned largely with the content of the films themselves, later scholars such as Jackie Stacey (1994) have shown these attractions rarely operate in isolation from wider sociocultural practices. Annette Kuhn's (2002, 2011) work with audiences from the 1930s complicates these notions by suggesting the social act of "going to the pictures" is of far greater consequence in memory than the cultural activity of seeing films. As this chapter has sought to demonstrate, all three of these areas of concern are relevant, and indeed crucial, to understanding the scope and motivations for cinematic engagement by women at the First Avenue Cinema in Sawtell. Here we see cinema-going as connected not just with cultural consumption, social interaction, nostalgia, and preservation, but also with the claiming and ownership of public spaces. And indeed, it is the latter, perhaps more than any other single factor, that can be understood as motivating the members of the FOSC group and its supporters.

Epilogue

Sadly, the efforts of the First Avenue Cinema's owners and of the FOSC group and its supporters were not sufficient to save the theater in the long term. While the cinema continued to operate for several years after reopening in May 2009, it was put up for sale in mid-2012 and closed its doors in January 2013. The Brissett family cited the prohibitive cost of converting to digital projection as a key factor in their decision. At the time of this writing, the cinema remains closed but is still for sale, and local investors have formed a consortium to attempt to buy and redevelop the theater into a more modern cinema complex.

Acknowledgments

This research was supported by a Linkage Grant from the Australian Research Council and industry partners the National Film and Sound Archive and Screen Australia.

Notes

1. Includes Sawtell village (population 3,500) and substantial suburban surrounding areas.
2. Aveyard, Karina. 2012. "Observation, Mediation and Intervention: An Account of Methodological Fusion in the Study of Rural Cinema Audiences in Australia." *Participations: Journal of Audience and Reception Studies* 9 (2). Available at http://www.participations.org/Volume%209/Issue%202/35%20Aveyard.pdf.

References

Australian Bureau of Statistics. 2013. "2011 Census QuickStats." Available at http://www.abs.gov.au/websitedbs/censushome.nsf/home/quickstats?opendocument&navpos=220 (accessed July 15, 2013).

Barry, Iris. (1926) 2006. "The Public's Pleasure." In *Red Velvet Seat: Women's Writings on the First Fifty Years of Cinema*, edited by Antonia Lant with Ingrid Perez, 128–34. London: Verso.

Beattie, John H. M. 2006. "Understanding and Explanation in Social Anthropology." In *Anthropology in Theory: Issues in Epistemology*, edited by Henrietta L. Moore and Todd Sanders, 148–58. Malden: Blackwell. Reprinted from *British Journal of Sociology* 10 (1) (1959): 45–56, 57–60.

Kuhn, Annette. 2002. *An Everyday Magic: Cinema and Cultural Memory*. London: Tauris.

———. 2011. "What to Do with Cinema Memory?" In Maltby, Biltereyst, and Meers, *Explorations in New Cinema History*, 85–97.

Maltby, Richard, Daniel Biltereyst, and Philippe Meers, eds. 2011. *Explorations in New Cinema History: Approaches and Case Studies*. Oxford: Blackwell.

Stacey, Jackie. 1994. *Star Gazing: Hollywood Cinema and Female Spectatorship*. London: Routledge.

CHAPTER 17

Barbara Willis Sweete

Queen of HD Transmissions

KAY ARMATAGE

On November 19, 2011, within five minutes after the curtain went up on Phillip Glass's *Satyagraha*, the fourth presentation in the Metropolitan Opera's sixth season of live, high-definition (HD) transmissions, I whispered to my Met HD pals in the movie theater, "I'm calling it now: I'm betting this is directed by Barbara Willis Sweete." I can't remember the shot that tipped me off, as I have only seen the transmission once, but I was certain. As the euphorically beautiful opera proceeded, with its surreal sets, giant puppets, wonderful singing, and ravishing score, the visual style of the HD transmission seemed to rhyme at every moment with both the action and the music. In one scene, for example, as long ribbons of shipping tape traversed the stage from both sides, eventually creating a shimmering transparent wall, the shots panned or tracked laterally, following a character pulling the tape from one side, then reversing direction as another character was met coming from the other wing. The visual language of the live transmission was choreographed to the tempo of the music, the action of the characters, the staging of the scenes, and the narrative and historical gestures of the libretto. As the credits rolled at the end of the transmission, I was pleased to find that I was right and that I had been able to discern the distinctive elements of Barbara Willis Sweete's direction.

One of the two principal directors of the Metropolitan Opera Live in HD transmissions, Sweete has a varied media background. She co-founded Rhombus Media, a production company that has become an international force in cultural television and "quality" films, such as *Thirty-Two Short Films about Glenn Gould*

(1993), which Sweete produced. She has directed a range of cultural documentaries, including works on dance, Yo-Yo Ma, and avant-garde music. She is also well versed in television drama, having produced *Slings and Arrows* (a television series loosely based on the Shakespeare theater at Stratford, Ontario) and directed adaptations from theater to television, including, most recently, *Billy Bishop Goes to War* (2011). Peter Gelb, the Metropolitan Opera General Manager, was already acquainted with Sweete from his time at Sony Classical Records, and he invited her to direct Met HD transmissions in its second season (2007–08). She has now directed sixteen of the sixty-two transmissions over seven seasons, about 25 percent of the broadcasts.

Sweete's work in the intermedial territory of live HD transmissions is of interest to this volume for a number of reasons. First, she is the lone woman in this enormous new enterprise, working with an all-male film crew. Second, as a woman from Toronto, her work is seen regularly by larger numbers of people around the world than any other Canadian filmmaker, except for directors of blockbusters such as James Cameron and Ivan Reitman. Third, Sweete is operating on a global stage that is highly publicized but in which her role as director is all but completely unacknowledged. The (Met-provided) handouts available at the cinema, which detail stage director and designer as well as the conductor and performers, overlook HD transmission technical personnel; the Met press releases for the HD transmissions list production director and designer and choreographer, costume and lighting designer, and occasionally even assistant or associate directors but similarly omit the HD personnel; full credits are given at the end of the transmissions, but they whiz by on the roll and are not searchable on the Met Web site.[1] Sweete is by no means singled out for such egregious neglect, yet in this invisibility she epitomizes the historical profile of the woman director, who, overlooked, forgotten, even erased, must constantly be re-authored by the woman scholar, as Giuliana Bruno (1992) argued long ago.

But more important, Sweete has registered considerable attention in the opera blogs; the comments are sometimes highly critical, but they are indications that people are paying attention to her work and that—like it or not—she is doing something distinctive. The material constraints of the live HD transmission tend to limit HD directorial control, since the production and staging belong to the theatrical director. Yet many cinema-savvy attendees are beginning to discern recognizably different visual modus operandi among the principal HD directors. Gary Halvorson, who directs the majority of the productions has, for instance, delivered a conventionally realist transparency over the first six seasons, following the central characters, cutting on action and with the music. Barbara Willis Sweete, who directs these HD transmissions less frequently, brings to them a carefully calibrated practice that attends not only to music, staging, and performance but also to visual narrativity and what she calls visual architecture. This chapter explores how that practice engages with the intermedial nature of the live HD broadcast of opera. It will then go on to argue that Sweete's practice places her at the center of this new cultural form—one we can term an intermedial hybrid—which can be viewed as currently in its "transitional" period, much as cinema "transitioned" in the 1910s.

Sweete's Visual Practice

I observed the exacting creative process that Sweete undertakes over the nearly ten-day run-up to the live transmission of *Lucia di Lammermoor* (March 19, 2011). A rough camera taping is made of the production's final lighting and dress rehearsal, from which Sweete makes notes on the staging and blocking, actions of the performers, orchestral score, tempi and timing. She then scripts every shot for coverage of the action by the live transmission's (usually) ten cameras. Some are fixed, such as the full-proscenium wide shot from the rear of the house; there is a robotic camera that can track, pan, and zoom from the floor level at the front of the stage, and two—from side tiers—operated from long jib-arms that function effectively as cranes. Others are handheld for backstage documentaries and between-acts interviews.

Next, Sweete, the assistant director, and cinematographers go over every shot—on average nine hundred to one thousand—each detailed in their individualized scripts with cues to track, zoom, tilt, reverse directions, and so on. "Scratch taping"—often lasting until midnight—takes place on the Wednesday before the Saturday afternoon transmission. Following a 9:30 Thursday morning meeting with Peter Gelb and Production Director Mary Zimmerman, Sweete works with her assistant director and musical assistant to re-script many sequences. During an all-day meeting on Friday they go through the edited scratch taping and the new script with the cinematographers. On Saturday the live transmission goes out to fifteen hundred screens in forty-six countries. The ten cameras feed to monitors in a truck outside Lincoln Center, where the director and editor work simultaneously from multiple screens.

This highly pressurized process works to render into cinematic language a medium—live operatic performance—that is essentially noncinematic. As a result certain constraints are at play at all times. Crucially, no camera appears onstage to disrupt the pleasure of the in-house audience, though they are visible in the house. Thus, special set-ups, such as close-ups of the contents of the locket in *Simon Boccanegra* (2010–11), are almost impossible. And yet sometimes the impossible

246

is achieved: the crew in the truck applauded for the close-up sequence of the ex-change of rings in *Lucia di Lammermoor* (March 19, 2011), for which the robotic camera was in place at the exact moment and the performers "cheated" their ges-tures in consideration of the camera angle. An additional constraint is that, even though a variety of angles are possible, all the cameras of the HD transmissions face the stage.[2] Without cameras in direct relation to the characters as they move about the stage, the classic cinematic device of the shot-reverse-shot also pres-ents an enormous challenge. All of these production constraints are additionally complicated by the stage blocking, which is looser than the tight marks to be hit in film production, and exacerbated further by the improvisational performance style of the more expressive singers, such as Anna Netrebko and Nathalie Dessay.

In the face of such taxing technical and material restrictions, inordinately pres-surized production conditions, and indeed, as will become evident, enormous professional risk, Sweete has carved out a very particular approach to the visual text. In her second commission as director of a live HD transmission, Sweete was assigned *Tristan and Isolde* (2007). Well versed in classical music, she knew Wagner, of course. His ability, especially in *Tristan*, to spin out and develop long intertwining musical phrases that resist musical closure or cadencing, which in turn create long expanses of uninterrupted musical flow, is unique. Faced with long expanses of slow-moving musical drama, and especially when the drama involves only two or three characters onstage, what is the director of an HD transmission to do?[3] Sweete addressed the problem by proposing the use of a split-screen format: rather than editing within a musical phrase, which would be antithetical to the musical aesthetic, a multiple-image screen could offer visual interest and several views without interrupting the musical flow by cutting from one camera to another. Gelb agreed. When the transmission went out, four or five images (and occasionally more) occupied the screen, with some dominating the center while others offered alternate views, melding and transmogrifying from one to another in slow glissandos that matched the pace of the musical and narrative developments.

As a film scholar with a taste for the avant-garde, I was mesmerized. The stark, minimalist setting, with a specially woven one-piece white fabric backdrop (sixty meters wide) and sparse gestural furnishings, was rendered with jewel-like preci-sion in the multiple images that carved the vast space into comprehensible zones, each—I thought—with its particular affective motif. The complex relationships among the images on the screen provided a parallel visual architecture that rhymed with the deeply imbricated relationships among the characters. The HD transmis-sion of the close-to-five-hour performance mounted a capacious visuality that matched the music and libretto in a synaesthetic plenitude.

Apparently, many of the spectators who attended the live transmission were not as entranced as I was. Sweete said that the response in the blogosphere was tantamount to a fatwa.[4] Among many vituperative commentators was *Yappa Ding Ding* blogger Ruth Haworth (2009):

> At its worst, the effect was reminiscent of Hollywood Squares, and brought on the giggles. (And believe me, no-one should giggle during Wagner.) At its best it was annoying and distracting. . . . A woman I was talking to during the intermission said the worst part of it for her was that she wanted a theater-like experience, and the framing effects made the opera feel more like a movie. I think she has a good point. But for me, the biggest problem was the distraction. You can try frilly high-tech special effects on a car race or a music video, but for god's sake, not Wagner.

After this assault (and many more like it), Sweete concluded that the language of classic narrative cinema was the way to go.

There could not be a more exacting example of the cinematic requirements of classic narratology and of the ingenious methods of overcoming them than the live transmission of *Orfeo ed Euridice* (2008–9), which Sweete directed. In Gluck's opera, as in the myth, the narrative devolves upon the look. If Orfeo is to retrieve Euridice from Hades, he is prohibited from looking at her until they return to Olympus. Ignorant of the prohibition, to which Orfeo has been sworn to silence, Euridice seeks a sign of Orfeo's love and does everything she can to entice him to look at her as they exit the netherworld. Of course Orfeo succumbs to desire and thereby trips the lever of tragedy. The most appropriate formal convention for rendering this narrative is the shot-reverse-shot that is so characteristic of classic narrative cinema. Sweete used the convention to the limited degree possible, straining with long lenses for close-ups (as the convention requires) with over-the-shoulder shots from the gib-arm cameras in opposite balconies.

A corollary of classic narrative cinema in the context of the Met HD productions is that a closed diegetic world is maintained within the acts: no cuts to conductor, musicians, audience reaction, or behind the scenes.[5] The key here is that the formal conventions, such as shot-reverse-shot, are those practiced regularly in scripted and unscripted television as well as classic narrative cinema and have come to be seen as "natural" and thus, for many an untrained eye, rendered "invisible." Yet even while operating within classic narrative conventions, Sweete has continued to make a distinctive intervention in a world where recognition of the HD director has been suppressed, and she has done so through use of visual narrativity and visual architecture.

Visual Narrativity and Visual Architecture

In the setting of a live theatrical performance, to achieve cinematic visual narrativity requires specific strategies. To give an example: in the plot of *Simon Boccanegra*, disguise plays a significant part and, as in Shakespeare, the convention in opera is that once in disguise, the character is unrecognizable. For the audience in the opera house, all the action is visible—to greater or lesser degrees according to the price point of your seat. Thus, if a character assumes a disguise, even one so flimsy as just donning a hood, the narrative will be comprehensible to the audience (many of whom know the plot already anyway). In the HD transmission, however, we see only what the cameras have caught, which can be limited by many factors. Therefore, to achieve the dis-recognition required by the narrative of the other characters, the HD audience must see the donning of the disguise in the opera's prologue when Fiesco pulls his hood up (signifying unrecognizability), so that later when he doffs his hood, Simon Boccanegra can exclaim "Fiesco!" without appearing to be an idiot. While the live theater audience tends to keep their eyes on the central characters even in a busy courtroom set, for the HD audience these actions might easily be overlooked in a full-proscenium wide shot. Thus, for narrative comprehensibility in the HD transmissions, both actions should happen on camera, preferably in mid-shots or close-ups. For another example, in *Lucia di Lammermoor*, in order to instill the sense of fear and dread that underwrites the complex musical motifs and presages the narrative tragedy, it is crucial that the HD audience see Lucia pick up the knife (with which she will later murder her husband) and slip it up her sleeve. For these significant narrative actions to be visible to the HD audience, there has to be a camera in place, in the right shot scale (close-up, mid-shot, wide-shot, and so on) and in focus—not always easy if the singer improvises on the stage blocking or the gesture, since the cinematographers may then not know where and when that action is happening.

In *Simon Boccanegra* Act 3, there is a similar plot exigency, when Fiesco exits the council chamber and then peeks back in. For the narrative to make sense visually, the audience in the movie theater has to know what the characters in the libretto and the audience in the house know. So we need to see that peek through the door, which lasts only a second, and we need to see it in close-up to make sure that we recognize the character. On a large stage, with many characters moving in and out, it is possible for the HD cameras to miss a great deal—signifying gestures, crucial entrances and exits—or render spatial relationships confusing.

That is why scripting is so important and also why Sweete has found ways to make sure that a camera will be in place with the appropriate shot scale to catch

FIGURE 17.1. Fiesco peeks through the door, *Simon Boccanegra* (2010)
(Reproduced by permission of The Metropolitan Opera)

these significant plot points. Many productions are tightly blocked, but when improvisational performers such as Dessay or Netrebko are the stars, alternative measures may be necessary. As she has absolutely no contact with the theater director, conductor, or performers, Sweete is often able to broker the camera needs through the very cooperative stage manager, who may intervene with other performers. In *Lucia di Lammermoor* (2011), for example, Ludovic Tezier, who played Lucia's cruel brother, was willing to keep his hand on Dessay's shoulder until she was seated in the proper place to reveal a crucial narrative element. In these ways, Sweete creates a comprehensible cinematic narrative that actualizes the stage and libretto narrative.

What Sweete calls visual architecture is an intermedial equivalent to the musical architecture. Here the cinematic responds to the emotion in the music and drama through particular kinds of camera movement, shot scale, and mise-en-scène. On a simple level, this can mean that when the music soars, so does the camera. Sweete has used the two jib-arm cameras in the side balconies particularly effectively in such tropes. Although their only possible movement is to boom up or down, with the addition of simultaneous zooming these cameras can create the impression of soaring or swooping that aligns the visual architecture with the music. In the third act of *Simon Boccanegra*, for example, the repeated stately and slow forward-soaring movement of gib-arm cameras on either side of the stage formally underlines the gravitas of the concluding narrative movement of the libretto while limning the grandeur of the Doge's court at the same time.

Eventually, Fiesco and Boccanegra reconcile and sing together in an intimate, flowing duet while lounging in a close embrace on the floor. This is a moment that Sweete blocked using only one camera—the robotic unit that sits at floor level at the edge of the stage, which moves only laterally but has the capacity to tilt and zoom. The choreography of the shot involved seventeen cues in a continuous three-minute shot that flowed with the music, back and forth and side to side, in as intimate a connection to the characters as they are to each other. All the moves were timed to the music, as is the case for all the shots in the production, for—as Sweete says—the cinematographers have very good metronomes in their heads.[6]

Another example from *Simon Boccanegra* (2010–11) deploys a well-understood trope of classic narrative cinema. In the final act, the eponymous hero (performed by Plàcido Domingo) dies by degrees, repeatedly collapsing and rising to his feet to sing again (it's opera!). In the HD transmission, as Boccanegra is on his feet for the last time, the shot is a medium portrait in which Domingo is centered in the frame, heroically dominating the HD image as well as the narrative, the court, the music, and our empathic emotions. With the last fall to his death, there is a cut to a high overhead shot in which the formerly powerful Doge now lies small and weak in death, a mere mortal—a conventional trope, but sublimely effective.

In *Lucia di Lammermoor* (2011), the priest descends the great third-act staircase, his movement a metaphor for the narrative and musical descent into tragedy that he recites—Lucia has murdered her husband and is descending into madness—and which the score underlines with his bass aria that dips into the deepest notes in the opera. In Sweete's rendering, the camera booms down following the priest's physical movement, the spiral arc of the staircase, and the narrative trajectory, producing a visual metaphor that rhymes with all the other elements of the piece.[7] The passage from *Satyagraha* discussed at the start of this chapter is another wonderful example, as the rhythms and repetitions of Philip Glass's score are rendered visible in the production design and blocking, and the movement of the cameras and editing respond in kind.

These are the marks of Sweete's distinctive practice: the rhythmic tracking and panning, swooping and soaring shots that are carefully choreographed, and editing that blends the gestures of the performers (cutting on action) with the rhythms of the music. At such glorious moments, the sensations are escalated as all elements of the score, setting, character movement, and narrative emotion come together with the choreography of the cameras and tempo of the editing.

The Transitional Era in HD Transmissions

In the liminal space that the HD transmissions occupy—simulating the experience of the opera as aficionados know it in the opera house, yet on the large screen in the multiplex at much lower prices—the sticking point for many in the movie theater audience seems to be the close-up. Here is a typical comment from a reviewer:

> Presenting the production via a set of cameras basically turns the opera into a movie, which fundamentally changes how the opera is supposed to be seen. As my companion observed, the unnatural, high-definition close-ups are un-flattering to the costumes and scenery, which are not meant to be seen under high-tech scrutiny. (Stoff 2009)

In a similar vein, an anonymous WTJU radio commentator (2009) blogged:

> At a massive house like the Met in particular, HD compresses the sense of dis-tance that is an integral part of the opera experience. Instead, the direction of the Met's HD broadcasts is much more intimate, with almost claustrophobic obsession with close-ups of the principals. . . . Especially in a production as large-scaled as Zeffirelli's *Turandot* at the Met, the intimacy of the obsessive close-ups is jarring.

Another commentator objected to the close-ups because "singers tend to sweat, and a giant screen filled with a close-up of their face is not always a pleasant image. There is also much too much camera movement, zooming in, panning, pulling back, changing cameras. It is all very distracting" (Haworth 2009).

Linnea Leonard Kickasola (2009) offers a somewhat more balanced view: "Visually, the close-ups available in the filmed opera are both a strength and weak-ness of the HD transmission. The incredible details and precision of Han Feng's gorgeous costume design [in *Madama Butterfly*, 2008–09] were seen much bet-ter on the movie screen than they could be from most seats in the opera house." Nevertheless, she argues:

> Some directors have chosen to focus on close-up details to the detriment of the overall effect of the theatrical elements. Shots of individual instruments play-ing in the orchestra, numerous cuts to dancers' feet or reaction shots from the chorus may all be interesting filmic elements available to the camera director, but they ultimately detract from the power of the theatrical experience, which is the sum of many parts working at once.

In opposition to those who hold these more doctrinaire views, I would argue that the live HD transmission is a transitional cultural object, caught between recording apparatuses and live performance, neither an (impossible) replication of the experience of being in the opera house nor a perfect filmic treatment in the vein of Bergman or Zeffirelli, who filmed operas on a sound stage shot by shot and, in the case of Zeffirelli, with the singing lip-synched to a perfect recording. In the Met transmissions, with the addition of the preedited credit sequence and the live address to the HD audience by an opera luminary, backstage documentary ("Maestro to the pit please") and intermission divertissements, we are in a new terrain—a regime of intermedial musical and theatrical performance, costume and setting, linear narrative, and cinematic rendering.

The historical moment we are experiencing recalls the history of the development of cinematic language and culture.[8] In the early years of cinema, a form of tableau was held over from theater (Gaudreault 1983, 322). Equivalent to the full proscenium view, it employed static long shots, more-or-less proscenium staging, full figures in the frame, and depth of focus. These conventions were first breached in what is known today as the "transitional" period of early cinema (1907–13), in which the tableau began to be displaced by camera movement, a variety of camera angles, more frequent editing, and variations in shot scale.

Just as we are experiencing today in the cybersphere regarding the Met HD transmissions, film-trade discourse in the 1910s responded with howls of outrage and confusion. The close-up was a particularly contested terrain, as anything that presented figures larger than life size was seen as grotesque. Commentators also expressed fear that close-ups would block backgrounds, causing reduced depth and the loss of figure placement in the setting. One commentator wrote, echoing the responses above: "Nowhere does the well-known adage, 'Distance lends enchantment to the view,' apply with such force as to dramatic performances. Distance is an absolute requisite to any kind of idealistic illusion" (quoted in Keil 2002, 165).

In the silent period of film production, the debate came down to the issue of verisimilitude. On one side was the belief that close-ups represented a direct affront to cinema's realization of vraisemblance by destroying the illusion of "the natural" (Keil 2002, 165). As the tendency prevailed, however, some writers in industry publications advanced the view that the use of closer views would increase the spectator's involvement, inspire a new mode of nonhistrionic performance, and improve narrative clarity at critical moments. In a startling analogy with opera, one critic wrote, "When we would see more clearly what emotions the features of the heroine express or what is in the locket she takes from her bosom we have no need to pick up our opera glasses. The [film-maker] has foreseen our desire and suddenly the detail is enlarged for us until it fills the canvas" (quoted in Keil 2002, 166).

By the end of the transitional period, the early tableau was replaced by standard framing of actors just below the knee and a shot scale that occasionally approximated the medium shot. With the emergence of the great era of silent cinema, usually associated with the work of D. W. Griffith, Carl Dreyer, and others, the close-up was abundantly deployed in the construction of the star system, classic narratology, verisimilar rather than histrionic performance techniques, temporality as a regulating mechanism, and modes of spectatorial identification.

This, I believe, is the moment we are currently experiencing in the intermedial live operatic transmission. Certainly HD transmission directors have to account for the exigencies of the operatic body: the need to clear the nasal passages, for example, as well as sweat and spit. At the same time, it is now well known that the presence of cameras and their capacity for close-ups have brought about enormous changes in opera production: makeup and wigs (hiding places for mics) are much more naturalistic, costumes are more fully detailed (for example, the multilayered and intricately worked outfits for Caliban's mother in *The Enchanted Island*, 2012), and acting styles are under pressure, as more naturalistic performances are lauded (just watch Anna Netrebko "listening" as her lover sings to her in the Gary Halberston directed HD transmission of *Lucia di Lammermoor* [2008–9]) while stiff or histrionic performances are denigrated.

Of course there are objections to such changes. Yet, while bloggers still complain about title sequences and close-ups, they simultaneously—if contradictorily—enjoy enhanced access to the stars, narrative continuity, and (whether consciously or not) the filmic mechanisms of verisimilitude and identification. And so we see in the HD broadcasts the emergence of new forms, as the limitations of camera placement are exacting their own reworkings of visual grammar and technological evocations of affect and sensation. It is for these reasons that I would suggest we are presently in the "transitional" period of HD broadcasts of theatrical and musical events.

Rather than excoriating the cinematic as intrusive or manipulative, deploring the experience as different from attending a performance in the opera house—what W. Anthony Sheppard calls "presence envy"—I think we will come to see these broadcasts as a truly intermedial hybrid that, as Marcia Citron puts it, "is a carefully crafted construction that is distinct from the performance it is recording" (2000, 66). With her carefully calibrated practice, I would argue that Barbara Willis Sweete is clearly at the center of this new intermedial formation, as were women in the first years of cinema.

Notes

This chapter is a substantially revised version of material previously published in *University of Toronto Quarterly* 81, no. 4 (Fall 2012).

1. Only limited credits are available on the International Movie Database (IMDb), the most relied-upon source of technical information on film and television. Full crew listings are not available.

2. From time to time, a camera may be placed in the wings for a special shot, as in the "god's eye view" shot inserted as a trope in *Iphigénie en Tauride* (2010–11), directed by Sweete.

3. Thanks to Caryl Clark for elucidating this for me. Private email correspondence, October 30, 2011.

4. Personal interview, 2009.

5. For some, the breach of the closed diegetic world is desirable. Caryl Clark, for example, is interested in seeing beyond the stage: "Especially when instruments are used soloistically 'within' an aria, or when their special timbral effects are being used by the composer to underscore a specific theatrical event unfolding on stage, then the manner in which an orchestral player is rendering that effect becomes important in the visual mise-en-scène, I would argue—although I must confess this is far from standard thinking." Private email correspondence, October 30, 2011.

6. This robotic camera, by the way, is controlled from a station beneath the stage; the operator doesn't even have a full visual of the proscenium.

7. Halvorson also directed an earlier version of *Lucia*, starring Anna Netrebko. This version has not been available for detailed comparison.

8. I am indebted to Charlie Keil for this suggestion, made when I described to him the responses of opera specialists to the HD transmissions.

References

Anonymous. 2009. "The Metropolitan Opera in HD." *WTJU Classical Comments*, November 25. Available at http://wtjuclassical.blogspot.ca/2009/11/metropolitan-opera-in-hd.html (accessed January 18, 2014).

Bruno, Guiliana. 1992. *Street Walking on a Ruined Map: Cultural Theory and the City Films of Elvira Notari*. Princeton, N.J.: Princeton University Press.

Citron, Marcia. 2000. *Opera on Screen*. New Haven, Conn.: Yale University Press.

Gaudreault, André. 1983. "Temporality and Narrativity in Early Cinema, 1985–1908." In *Film Before Griffith*, edited by John L. Fell. Oakland: University of California Press.

Haworth, Ruth. 2009. "Is Barbara Willis Sweete Destroying the Met?" *Yappa Ding Ding*, January 18. Available at http://yappadingding.blogspot.com/2009/01/is-barbara-willis-sweete-destroying-met.html (accessed January 16, 2014).

Keil, Charlie. 2002. *Early American Cinema in Transition: Story, Style, and Filmmaking, 1907–1913*. Madison: University of Wisconsin Press.

Kickasola, Linnea Leonard. 2009. "Performance Review: Madama Butterfly." *Cardus*, April 3. Available at http://www.cardus.ca/comment/article/945/13/04/09 (accessed January 16, 2014).

Stoff, Matthew. 2009. "A Night at the Opera: Cinemark in Lufkin Offers Live Met Opera Performances." *Daily Sentinel*, March 28. Available at http://www.dailysentinel.com/featr/content/features/stories/2009/03/28/leisure_met_opera_032909.html (accessed June 2012).

Contributors

KAY ARMATAGE is professor emerita at the Institutes of Cinema Studies and Women and Gender Studies, University of Toronto. As well as writing academic and popular articles on women filmmakers and Canadian cinema, she is the author of *The Girl From God's Country: Nell Shipman and the Silent Cinema* (2003), co-editor of *Gendering the Nation: Canadian Women's Cinema* (1999), and editor of *Equity and How to Get It* (1999). She was part of the group that founded Women's Studies at the University of Toronto and one of the first to teach Cinema Studies in its founding stages, taking many administrative roles in both programs. In addition to academic work, she directed documentary and experimental narrative films from 1975 to 1987 and worked as an international programmer for Toronto International Film Festival from 1983 to 2004.

EYLEM ATAKAV is senior lecturer in Film and Television Studies at the University of East Anglia, UK, where she teaches courses on women and film; women, Islam, and media; and Middle Eastern media. She is the author of *Women and Turkish Cinema: Gender Politics, Cultural Identity and Representation* (2012) and editor of *Directory of World Cinema: Turkey* (2013). Her academic interests include Middle Eastern film and television, representation of "honour" crimes in the media, and women's cinema. She writes frequently on issues around gender and culture for the *Huffington Post* (UK) and for her co-authored blog on women's cinema, *Auteuse Theories.*

KARINA AVEYARD is lecturer in the School of Film, Television, and Media Studies at the University of East Anglia, UK. Her recent publications include *The Lure of the Big Screen: Cinema in Rural Australia and the United Kingdom* (2015) and the edited collection *Watching Films: New Perspectives on Movie-Going, Exhibition and Reception* (2013). Her research interests include cinema exhibition, film consumption practices, and rural media.

CANAN BALAN is assistant professor at Istanbul Şehir University in the department of Cinema and Television. Balan earned her PhD in Film Studies at the University of St. Andrews with a project on early cinema in Istanbul. After publishing articles related to this topic, she is currently working on her first monograph.

CÉCILE CHICH is a London-based independent researcher who has been following acclaimed media artists Klonaris/Thomadaki since 1986. She was their assistant for Rencontres internationales art cinéma/vidéo/ordinateur (Paris), has edited a book on their *Cinéma corporel* (L'Harmattan, Paris, 2006), and presented their work in several conferences in both France and the United Kingdom. In London she was associated with both the LFMC and LUX. She is interested in women's experimental cinema, feminist and queer aesthetics, interactions between art and politics, and issues of spectatorship and historiography.

MONICA DALL'ASTA is associate professor of Film and Television Studies at the University of Bologna, Italy. She is the author of *Trame spezzate: Archeologia del film seriale* (Limina Award as Best Italian Book in Film Studies in 2009). She is co-editor, with Jane Gaines and Radha Vatsal, of the *Women Film Pioneers Project* database. In 2008 she edited a new Italian translation of Alice Guy's memoires (*Memorie di una pioniera del cinema*) and the first collection on women filmmaking in Italian silent cinema, *Non solo dive*. Her latest work is a collection on Guy Debord's films (with Marco Grosoli, *Consumato dal fuoco: Il cinema di Guy Debord*, 2012).

ELIZA ANNA DELVEROUDI retired from the University of Crete, Greece, as professor in the history of Greek cinema and theater. She has published widely (in Greek, English, and French) on film and theater history, film press and criticism, silent cinema, stardom in Greek cinema, and young people in Greek film comedy. For the past ten years she has been working on a major project mapping the work of women filmmakers in Greece from the 1950s to the present. She is also working on a project titled "Child-on-screen" at the University of Athens.

JANE M. GAINES, professor emerita of Duke University, is now professor of Film at Columbia University. She has published two award-winning books, *Contested Culture: The Image, the Voice, and the Law* (1991) and *Fire and Desire: Mixed Race Movies in the Silent Era* (2001). She is currently completing *Pink-Slipped: What Happened to Women in the Silent Film Industry?* She is co-editor with Monica Dall'Asta and Radha Vatsal of the *Women Film Pioneers Project* database.

CHRISTINE GLEDHILL is visiting professor in Cinema Studies at the University of Sunderland, UK. She has written on feminist film criticism, on melodrama and cinema, and on British cinema, publishing in 2003 *Reframing British Cinema, 1918–1928: Between Restraint and Passion*. She has published on early stardom and the film actress and recently on British scriptwriter Lydia Hayward. With Julia Knight she coordinated the establishment of the Arts and Humanities Research Council–funded Women's Film and Television History Network–UK/Ireland and co-organized the first of the Doing Women's Film History conferences, held at University of Sunderland in April 2011.

JULIA KNIGHT is professor of Moving Image at the University of Sunderland, UK, and co-editor of *Convergence: The International Journal of Research into New Media Technologies*. Before entering academia she was co-manager of Albany Video Distribution and subsequently a member of the management committee of Cinenova, the surviving women's film and video distributor in the United Kingdom. Her recent AHRC-funded research has addressed artists' and independent moving-image distribution in the United Kingdom, which resulted in *Reaching Audiences: Distribution and Promotion of Alternative Moving Image* (2011) and the Film and Video Distribution Database (http://fv-distribution-database.ac.uk), which makes available a selection of primary research material, both co-authored with Peter Thomas.

MICHELE LEIGH is assistant professor of Cinema History at Southern Illinois University, Carbondale. She is currently the co-president of Women in Film History International. She specializes in female representation and female industrial practice in Russian cinema prior to the Revolution. She is also interested in questions of gender construction in contemporary adult animation and science fiction television programming. Some of her favorite courses to teach are: Protocinematic Media Production, Gender in Film/TV, History/Theory of Animation, Women in Silent Cinema, and Historical Research Methods. She has articles in *American Cinematographer* and essays in several collected works.

NEEPA MAJUMDAR is associate professor of English and Film Studies at the University of Pittsburgh and the author of *Wanted Cultured Ladies Only! Female Stardom and*

Cinema in India, 1930s to 1950s (2009). Her essays have appeared in *Canadian Journal of Film Studies, South Asian Popular Culture,* and *Post Script,* as well as collections such as *Global Neorealism: The Transnational History of a Film Style* (2012), *The Continuum Companion to Sound in Film and Visual Media* (2011), *Film Analysis: A Norton Reader* (2005), and *Soundtrack Available: Essays on Film and Popular Music* (2001).

LUKE MCKERNAN is lead curator, News and Moving Image, at the British Library. He is a film historian with a particular interest in early cinema. His publications include *Topical Budget: The Great British News Film* (1992), *Who's Who of Victorian Cinema* (1996, co-edited with Stephen Herbert), and *Charles Urban: Pioneering the Non-Fiction Film in Britain and America, 1897–1925* (2013). His websites include http://thebioscope. net, http://victorian-cinema.net and http://picturegoing.com.

DEBASHREE MUKHERJEE earned her doctorate in the Department of Cinema Studies at New York University (2015), and is now Assistant Professor in the Department of Middle Eastern, South Asia, and African Studies (MESAAS) at Columbia University. Her dissertation tracks cultures of work and material practice in the late colonial Bombay film industry (1930s–1940s). She has published with journals such as *BioScope: South Asian Screen Studies, Seminar, MARG, Art Papers,* and *Wide Screen,* and has contributed essays to the edited collections *No Limits: Media Studies from India* (2013) and *Women Screenwriters: An International Guide* (forthcoming 2015).

GIULIANA MUSCIO is retired as professor in Film History at the University of Padova, Italy. She has taught and published on both sides of the Atlantic. Published works include *Hollywood's New Deal* (1996) and *Naples/New York/ Hollywood* (forthcoming). She was a founding participant of "Women and the Silent Screen" Congress at Utrecht, 2000. Currently she is writing a book on women screenwriters in American silent cinema.

KATARZYNA PASZKIEWICZ is a postdoctoral researcher at the Centre Dona i Literatura, University of Barcelona, Spain. She has recently completed her doctoral thesis on the intersection of film genre, authorship, and gender in contemporary women's filmmaking. Her research focuses on women's cinema, popular culture, feminist film theory, and Spanish cinema. She is also interested in the issues of spectatorship and the turn to affect in cultural theory. Her work in the area of cinema and gender studies has been published in international journals and edited volumes, and she is currently co-editing a collection of essays on women making genre films.

ELIZABETH RAMÍREZ SOTO is a FONDECYT postdoctoral researcher at the Institute of Philosophy at the University of Valparaíso, Chile, and an associate fellow of the Department of Film and Television Studies at the University of Warwick, UK. She is currently investigating the contesting images of the nation in Chilean films produced in partnership with European television channels. She is also co-editing a book on Chilean women filmmakers in exile. Her essays have appeared in *Rethinking History: The Journal of Theory and Practice, Aisthesis,* and *Journal of Latin American Cultural Studies: Travesia,* among others.

RASHMI SAWHNEY is associate professor of Cinema Studies at the School of Arts and Aesthetics, Jawaharlal Nehru University, Delhi. She has previously taught at Trinity College, Dublin, and the Centre for Transcultural Research and Media Practice, Dublin, and led the Arts Practice and Curatorship programs at India Foundation for the Arts, Bangalore. She has published in the journals *Studies in South Asian Film and Media, Deep Focus, Film Studies, Interventions, Moving Wor/ds* and contributed to the edited volumes *South Asian Media Cultures: Audiences, Reception, Contexts; Studies in Irish Cinema: National Cinemas and World Cinemas;* and *Indigeneity: Culture and Representation.* She also writes for the Indian newspaper *Daily News and Analysis.*

SARAH STREET is professor of Film at the University of Bristol, UK. She has published several books including *British National Cinema* (1997; 2nd ed. 2009), *Transatlantic Crossings: British Feature Films in the USA* (2002), *Black Narcissus* (2005), and (co-authored with Tim Bergfelder and Sue Harris) *Film Architecture and the Transnational Imagination: Set Design in 1930s European Cinema* (2007). Her latest publications are on color film, including *Colour Films in Britain: The Negotiation of Innovation, 1900–55* (2012), which won the BAFTSS 2014 Best Monograph Prize, and two co-edited collections (with Simon Brown and Liz Watkins), *Color and the Moving Image: History, Theory, Aesthetics, Archive* (2012) and *British Colour Cinema: Practices and Theories* (2013).

KIMBERLY TOMADJOGLOU is an independent curator and preservationist who has worked for the Library of Congress Packard Center for Audio Visual Conservation (Washington, D.C., and Virginia). She was preservation director for the exhibition "Alice Guy Blaché: Cinema Pioneer," held at the Whitney Museum of American Art, New York (2009–2010), and also curated the program "Alice Guy, A Pioneer of Cinema" for the 2011 "Recovered and Restored" festival held in Bologna, Italy. Among her restorations are *La Venganza de Pancho Villa* (ca. 1930), a compilation film on the life and times of rebel Francisco "Pancho" Villa, composed of Mexican and American newsreel and fictional footage. She is currently working on a study of Mexican itinerant exhibitors Felix and Edmundo Padilla of El Paso, Texas, and is editor for a series of scholarly essays dedicated to silent Mexican cinema culture.

Index

COW. *See* Cinema of Women

credit(s): disappeared, hidden, ignored, omitted, or scattered, 2, 4, 39, 43, 44, 45–46, 49, 70, 72, 202, 245, 253; International Movie Database (IMDB), 79, 86, 255n1; Kalmus, 207, 208, 209, 216; 1920s American scriptwriters, 193, 198, 201; shared, 100. *See also* McKernan

critical-historical approach, 16; elements separated by time, 18; in feminist film historiography, 21; multiple contemporaneities, 162. *See also* Delveroudi; (the) past

cultural: centers, 66; cultural-historical translation, 155; identity, 121–22; industries, 1910s, 196; intercultural histories, 8; labor of stardom, 192; memories, 148; translation, 153

culture, mass/popular: "culture," 169, 170, 174; drama, 197; entertainment, 76; genre films, 132; imagery, 199; literature, 45, 46, 193, 200, 201; "mass culture," 168, 169, 170, 171, 174, 176; of modernity, 199, 200; specifically female, 104–5; Westernization, 60. *See also* Paszkiewicz

Curse of the Quon Gwon, The. See Wong

Cycle of the Unheimlich, The, 115, 119–23, **120**. *See also* Chich; Klonaris and Thomadaki

D'Agostino, Annette, M., 83

Dall'Asta, Monica, 16; "beautiful failures," 19, 22. *See also* Dall'Asta, Monica and Jane M. Gaines

Dall'Asta, Monica and Jane M. Gaines, 2, 3, 5, 6, 7, 9, 13–25; Giallanella, 19–22; "history" and history's history, 13–17, 22–23, 23n1, 23n10; supposed absence of women, 14, 15, 21, 23n6

Delveroudi, Eliza Anna, 66–77; "imagined community," 4, 75; 1920s Greece film culture, 10, 66; Skaravaiou, research sources, 4, 8, 67–69; women's film writing in the 1920s, 67. *See also* Barry; Skaravaiou

"*desexilio,*" 141; documentaries, 141–42

digital: arts event, France, 124n2; film, 124, 162; Klonaris and Thomadaki, 110, 124; projection, 240, 243; rights issues, 9; sharing research, 11; technologies and film history, 11, 23; works, 23. *See also* McKernan

director (the): in the American silent cinema, 196; directors, 15, 72, 188; dominance of, 11, 16, 113; limited control of HD transmissions, 245, 247; and stars' salaries (India), 188; of "woman's cinema," 163n2. *See also* Aguiló; authorship; Bigelow; Borden; Carmona; Giallanella; Gorris; Guy (Blaché); Karanth; Klonaris and Thomadaki; Mehta, Vijaya; Murphy; Rossi; Sen; Soray; Srour

disnarrativity (*dysnarrativité*), 113

distribution, 2, 7, 9–10, 11; and the critic, 72, 73; early cinema, transnational approach, 97, 102; Klonaris and Thomadaki, 111, 113, 125n4; lack of, 21; and the screenwriter, early American, 196; SP-ARK and *Orlando,* 11; struggles to find, 10. *See also* Cinema of Women

Doane, Mary Ann, Patricia Mellencamp, and Linda Williams, 15–16

documentary film(s), 10; backstage (HD transmissions of opera), 246, 253; Cinema of Women, 219; "*desexilio*" 141–42; on Guy, 95, 23n11; Hollows, 176n2; innovative approach (Latin American), 140; Klonaris and Thomadaki, 112; 1980s Indian women's, 157; practice, 2; style in *The Hurt Locker,* 172. *See also* "homecoming films"

documentation, absences in, 43, 181, 222, 224; Skaravaiou's, 71

documents: absence of, 4, 5; accumulating, 18; Cinema of Women, 219, 220, 229; comparison of, 194; and "facts," 3; as "historical objects," 6, 8, 17; official, 88; personal, 4; Russia, 43; 35mm film, 17. *See also* evidence; facts; online resources

doing women's film history, xi, 2, 11; Aveyard, 233; Dall'Asta and Gaines, 23; Hershman-Leeson, 103–4; Klonaris and Thomadaki, 112–13; Knight, 219, 228; Majumdar, 182, 185; McKernan, 78–92; polymorphous historical frameworks, 168–69; Skaravaiou, Iris, 10, 67; Tomadjoglou, 95–99; women's film writings of the 1920s, 67. *See also* women's film history

Doing Women's Film History conference, xi, xiii, 1, 13

domestic (the): Apte, 187, 191; comedy (Guy), 9, 105; footage, 149; landscape genres, 170;

WOMEN AND FILM HISTORY INTERNATIONAL

The University of Illinois Press
is a founding member of the
Association of American University Presses.

———————————————————————

Composed in 10.75/13 Arno Pro
with Univers display
by Jim Proefrock
at the University of Illinois Press
Manufactured by Sheridan Books, Inc.

University of Illinois Press
1325 South Oak Street
Champaign, IL 61820-6903
www.press.uillinois.edu